HOW TO INVEST IN REAL ESTATE

PRAISE FOR
How to Invest in Real Estate

"To put it simply: This book is going to change lives; a lot of lives!"
— **Matt Aitchison**, 7-figure real estate investor
and host of *The Millionaire Mindcast Podcast*

"I've dabbled in real estate before, but I never fully understood what I was doing. What Joshua and Brandon have compiled is essentially the ultimate treasure map in understanding every facet of investing in real estate. From getting your own personal financial house in order to finding and exiting deals, you will find yourself referencing this book over and over again in your journey."
— **Jim Wang**, Founder of WalletHacks.com

"I think this should be required reading for anyone considering real estate investing, and for that matter, anyone joining BiggerPockets."
— **Ben Leybovich**, real estate investor
and Founder of JustAskBenWhy.com

"This book will give you the context and direction you need to get your investing business off the ground and will allow you to kickstart the process of real estate freedom and profits."
— **J Scott**, Author of *The Book on Flipping Houses*, *The Book on Estimating Rehab Costs*, and *The Book on Negotiating Real Estate*

HOW TO
INVEST IN
REAL ESTATE

the ULTIMATE
BEGINNER'S GUIDE *to*
GETTING STARTED

JOSHUA DORKIN AND BRANDON TURNER

BiggerPockets®
PUBLISHING

How to Invest in Real Estate
Joshua Dorkin and Brandon Turner

Published by BiggerPockets Publishing LLC, Denver, CO
Copyright © 2018 by Joshua Dorkin and Brandon Turner
All Rights Reserved.

Publisher's Cataloging-in-Publication Data
Names: Dorkin, Joshua, author. | Turner, Brandon Richard, author.

Title: How to invest in real estate : the ultimate beginner's guide to getting started / by Joshua Dorkin and Brandon Turner.

Description: Includes bibliographical references. | Denver, CO: BiggerPockets Publishing, 2018.

Identifiers: ISBN 978-0-9975847-0-7 (pbk.) | 978-1-947200-05-0 | LCCN 2018940497

Subjects: LCSH Real estate investment--United States | Personal finance. | BUSINESS & ECONOMICS / Real Estate / General

Classification: LCC HD1382.5 .D67 2018 | DDC 332.63/24--dc23

Published in the United States of America
MBP 10 9 8

Printed in Canada

Dedication

This book is dedicated to the more than 1 million members
of The BiggerPockets Community.

Together, we proved that success in real estate investing doesn't need
to be at the *expense* of one another, but *through* one another.

Thank you.

—Joshua Dorkin and Brandon Turner

Table of Contents

CHAPTER THREE
Getting Your Ducks in a Row

CHAPTER FOUR
Real Estate Investment Niches

CHAPTER EIGHT
Real Estate Exit Strategies

CHAPTER NINE
How to Work (FAR) Less and Get (WAY) More Done

Acknowledgments

About the Authors

INTRODUCTION
The Elephant In The Room

The hot afternoon sun was naked in the blue sky—not a cloud to be seen—when the three travelers stepped out of the jungle and into the clearing.

But among the three, not a bit of light was observed ... because all three travelers were blind from birth.

As they walked through the clearing, they bumped into—quite literally—a large object blocking their path. Unsure of the nature of the obstacle in their way, the three blind travelers attempted to determine just what blocked their path by explaining, in turn, what the object felt like to them.

"It's long and flexible, like a snake!" said the first traveler.

"Long and flexible? Are you crazy?!" the second traveler declared. "It feels more like a wall—unmoving, but smooth and soft!"

"What are you two babbling about!?" the third traveler exclaimed. "This is like a tree trunk that has fallen over! I can wrap my arms all around it!"

The travelers argued back and forth for several minutes until, finally, the great big *elephant* stood up from its nap and walked away, leaving the three blind travelers to forever wonder what had been in their path.

Like the obstacle in this story, there is an enormous elephant lying directly in the path ahead of you, and this elephant is called "real estate."

And like the blind travelers, we all walk through life with limited vision, trying to make sense of the world around us. At some point, we bumped into the idea of real estate investing and began to feel around. But that's when the confusion set in, because the real estate we saw and felt was very different from what others were seeing.

The world of real estate is so large that most only see a small part of the great beast. To one person, it means one thing, and to the next, something entirely different. Real estate "experts" argue with each other about what real estate investing truly is, and what it is not.

Rental properties. House flipping. Vacation rentals. Commercial. Direct mail marketing. SEO. Door knocking. Wholesaling.

Yes, these terms are all aspects of real estate, yet they differ as much as an elephant's trunk from its body. All are important, but to truly understand the animal at hand, one needs to turn on the light and see the big picture.

And that's the goal of this book! It's time to see the big picture, and help you get to where you are going.

How Do I Get Started with Real Estate?

Over the many years that we've been serving real estate investors at BiggerPockets.com, perhaps the most commonly asked question is simply, how do I get started in real estate investing?

Sorry, we can't tell you that.

We know, that's probably a disappointing answer, but remember: Real estate is a gigantic beast with numerous ways to get started. Instead, we can help you develop your own path.

As the largest, most-trafficked real estate investing website on the planet, BiggerPockets has been helping people develop their own path for more than 12 years. Millions come to BiggerPockets every month to ask questions, get answers, read content, interact with others, analyze real estate deals, and in many other ways improve their business. So we know a thing or two about helping people on their journey.

And the one consistent thing we've seen is that there is no "one right path." While some might lead you to believe that there is a simple real estate path that works for everyone, that simply isn't the case. Just take a listen to some of the interviews we've done on the podcast. No two stories are the same. Every journey is unique—and that's a really good thing because it's a beast that can be ridden differently based on your personality, your location, and your financial state. There is absolutely no reason why you can't build wealth through real estate, because there are so many options that exist.

We've written this book to help simplify the process of figuring out how *you* can get started by seeing the whole picture. Unlike other books we've published at BiggerPockets, this book is not going into the weeds on the specifics of one type of real estate. Instead, this book will give you a broad-stroke overview of the entire industry, that way, you can best decide how to begin your own path to financial freedom through real estate investments.

Why Real Estate Investing?

To get filthy rich!

We're kidding ... sort of.

Yes, people invest in real estate because they want to build wealth. In fact, we believe that real estate investing is the best investment on the planet for helping the average person build wealth and passive income. But it's more than that, isn't it? As discussed earlier, real estate is diverse enough to allow anyone—regardless of personality, financial position, or location—to invest. It can be done with a lot of money or with very little. It can be done on a large scale or a small scale. It can make someone a billionaire or simply provide a few thousand dollars in extra spending money each month. It's plentiful. It's beautiful (or can be). It's relatable. It's outsource-able. And it's fun.

There are many different places you can stick your money other than under your pillow, like stocks, bonds, savings, mutual funds, CDs, currencies, cryptocurrencies, commodities, and more. We're not knocking any of these investments—many people have become rich off of investing in them. But there is something special about real estate, isn't there?

Perhaps more than anything else, real estate is attractive because it leads people closer to financial independence—the ability to live life on one's own terms, rather than simply earning enough to pay bills and survive. Real estate can offer investors an incredible life now, and an incredible life later.

Throughout this book, you'll see this pattern emerge over and over and over. You'll find dozens of real-life stories of investors just like you who are achieving success through various real estate strategies. These stories are meant not only to encourage you on your journey but also to give you a smorgasbord of ideas to choose from as you embark on your own real estate journey. Take what you want and leave what you don't. That's the beauty of real estate! Each of the investor stories was taken from interviews we've conducted on the *BiggerPockets Podcast*. Dig in, learn, grow.

CHAD CARSON

BiggerPockets Podcast ▪ Episodes 84, 141, and 293

Like many young adults leaving college today, Chad wasn't sure what he wanted to do for a career. Being a pre-med biology major, his original plan was to go to medical school, but after graduating he wasn't completely sold on the idea. He decided to try his hand at real estate investing first. Chad learned about real estate investing from his father and mentors, including a former college professor. Chad partnered with a college buddy, and with financial help from the professor, they started flipping houses.

Chad's business slowly began to take off, and he and his partner began to do more and more deals. Chad recalled going to a seminar and hearing someone talk about doing 50 properties a year, so he and his partner set a goal to do just that.

Along the way, though, Chad and his partner came to the realization that the more properties you have, the more work, time, and energy it costs. Chad learned from Tim Ferriss's book *The 4-Hour Workweek* that you have to build in measurement tools for more than just money; you also have to quantify time and mobility. You have to think, *How much time will it cost me to reach my goals? How much mobility do I need?* Every time you make a business decision, buy a property, or hire someone, you have to ask yourself these questions.

After the chaos of closing on 47 properties in one year, Chad decided to slow things down a bit.

"We had an 'aha moment' where we put the brakes on to think about what we were doing here," Chad says. "What kind of business model do we want to have? We wanted to think about, 'What is the objective here?

What are we measuring our success by?' When we looked at our goals in the short run and long run, we realized we could do it without being huge. It was fortunate that we realized it at that point because we saw that we could slow things down, and we've been adjusting our strategy ever since."

Chad and his partner switched gears and focused on "being a big fish in a small pond." "We focus solely on real estate investing," Chad says. "We've been able to make enough money, keeping it nice and simple, working out of our house, just doing it ourselves. ... I can keep a manageable number. Keep it small. And that's been really important for us lifestyle-wise. I want to grow and make more money, but I am not really interested in being the 'take over the whole territory' business and 'have the most sales in the whole area' or 'the biggest flips' or 'manage the most properties.' I just want to do enough to meet my goals, and it's moving me forward toward where I want to get to personally. As long as I'm doing that, I can avoid getting so big that it takes all my energy and time. And I'm able to travel more and be with my kids more."

Chad currently focuses on three or four flips and three or four rentals a year. He says this strategy pays the bills, increases his long-term wealth, and, more importantly, gives him more freedom to play pickup basketball with his business partner for a couple of hours in the middle of the workday, walk through the neighborhood with his kids in the evenings, and go on extended vacations with his wife. Chad and his family even lived in Ecuador, South America, for a year, experiencing a new culture, learning a new language, and finding a new way of life.

ARIANNE LEMIRE
BiggerPockets Podcast ■ Episode 233

Arianne was born in the Philippines, moved with her family to New Zealand at age 14, and made her way to the United States at age 23 after marrying her husband. Early into her career as a speech language pathologist, a major realization came to her: She could not easily get more than a week or two of vacation time each year. This was a major problem for her because she wanted to be able to visit her family in New Zealand every year and, for such a long and expensive trip, a mere week each year would not suffice. So she did what most people do when confronted with a problem—she decided to search out an answer on Google. What she found on that search was BiggerPockets and the world of real estate investing and financial independence. She found example after example of others who were living in financial freedom through real estate—people able to leave their careers, invest full-time, and enjoy the life that comes along with that independence.

Arianne obtained her real estate license, and in 2015 through an auction website, she and her husband purchased a house in their area for $50,000. They paid for the house using cash they had saved for many years, and after a small rehab, they refinanced the property. In 2016 they repeated the process with a similar home, this one for $72,000. While their original plan was to buy and hold enough houses to live off of the cash flow, Arianne soon realized that this process would take too long for her to achieve her goal of having the freedom to visit her family regularly in New Zealand. She switched tactics and began to focus on flipping and wholesaling houses to generate cash faster.

Their first flip was primarily just a quick cosmetic upgrade—a tactic Arianne recommends for first-time investors because there is less risk, less work, and fewer things that can go wrong. After the success with their first flip, the couple decided to take on a more difficult project that required a lot more rehab. To help with this job, they hired a general contractor who was recommended by a peer, but it soon became apparent that they had hired the wrong man for the job. His work was sloppy and, in the end, he caused more harm than good. This experience ended up costing Arianne an extra $10,000 in repairs and two additional months of construction. Due to these setbacks, Arianne ended up breaking even on the deal, but she learned a lot from the experience, and the couple kept going. "It comes down to how strong is your 'why'? There's always going to be something in your way," she wisely reasons.

Since they started investing, Arianne and her husband have completed more than 15 flips and 35 wholesale deals. Their current goals include building a team and completing 20 flips and 40–60 wholesale deals, and acquiring 100-plus rental units. Thanks to their success through real estate investing, Arianne is able to visit her family in New Zealand anytime she wants, and her "why" continues to push her forward, through the ups and downs.

Who Are "We"?

Okay, so far in this book you've seen the word *we* quite often.

So ... who are *we*?

We would be Josh Dorkin and Brandon Turner.

This book is not about us, so we're not going to spend a lot of time talking about us. If you want to hear more about our stories, you can find them on episodes 100 and 92 of the *BiggerPockets Podcast*. But to give you a brief background:

Josh Dorkin began investing in real estate while living in Los Angeles in the early 2000s. After buying some multifamily properties in the Midwest, Josh soon realized that real estate investing was a lot harder than the "Get Rich Quick" gurus on TV made it out be. When he began looking for help online, he quickly found those same gurus charging tens of thousands of dollars for their help. Instead, Josh decided to buck the system and build a simple website where he could ask questions and get encouragement from other investors, and BiggerPockets was born. Soon it became apparent that this little community wasn't going to stay little for long. The site grew, helping millions in the process. Since the inception of BiggerPockets, more than 67 million individuals from nearly every corner of the globe have visited the website to learn, grow, and network.

Brandon Turner began investing in real estate because of John Grisham. Yes, the author of bestselling legal thrillers like *The Firm*, *The Rainmaker*, and *A Time to Kill*. Brandon had been set on going to law school when he realized the lawyer life of 9-to-5 drudgery (or more likely "9-to-9 hell") he'd have to put up with for 50 years in order to find financial freedom was not what he wanted. In his quest for answers, he stumbled across BiggerPockets in its infancy, and quickly became part of the community, using the site and its resources to purchase nearly 100 units and find true financial freedom.

In 2012, the two of us got together and started the *BiggerPockets Podcast*, a weekly interview-style audio (and eventually video) show that rapidly became the No. 1 real estate podcast in the world and, to date, has more than 300 episodes and a total of 50 million-plus downloads.

From here on out in this book, we'll just say "we," unless we decide to tell a story that only applies to one of us, in which case we'll say "I" and make it clear who "I" is.

What to Expect in This Book

This book has nine chapters, each focusing on a specific part of your investing journey. If you can master these, you increase your chance of building wealth through real estate and minimize the risk of failure or loss. Therefore, our goal is to get you from "brand-new to real estate" to "I know what I'm doing!" by the time you get through this book.

Specifically, this book will walk you through the following:

Chapter One: Nine Questions Every Real Estate Beginner Wants Answered

Before you go investing all this time into reading a book on real estate investing, let's get some of the "big questions" out of the way. For example: Do you need money to invest? If so, how much? What if you live in an expensive market? What if you have a full-time job? Do you need an LLC? These questions, and more, are addressed in Chapter One.

Chapter Two: Boring Financial Stuff ... That Just Might Save Your Life!

Just as a home is built upon a solid foundation, your real estate investments *must* be built upon a solid foundation: your personal finances. In this chapter, you are going to learn how to quickly get a snapshot of your personal finances, how to create a Financial Spending Plan, more than a dozen ways to save extra money, starting *right now*, and even 18 powerful and unique ways to make more income, from either a job or side hustles.

Chapter Three: Getting Your Ducks in a Row

Before you buy a single property, there are a few key decisions you need to make. Will you bring in a partner or go it alone? Do you have all the members of your team figured out? Do you need some kind of corporation? What about paying for mentors? These, and many other decisions and important topics, will be covered in Chapter Three to make sure you are fully prepared to start on your path.

Chapter Four: Real Estate Investment Niches

What's the best kind of real estate to invest in? Large, small, residential, commercial, land? In Chapter Four, we break down all the different property types to help you make sense of where you should place your focus.

Chapter Five: Real Estate Investment Strategies

There are a number of different strategies and angles from which to approach the business of real estate investing. The more you focus on one specific strategy, and the better and more knowledgeable you become at that strategy, the more money you'll make. This will be the focus of Chapter Five, as we dive deeper into looking at the various strategies you can profit from in your real estate journey.

Chapter Six: 27 Ways to Find Incredible Real Estate Deals

Regardless of which aspect of real estate investing you choose to focus on, great deals can be tough to find. That's why Chapter Six will dive deep into 27 different methods you can use to find deals in any real estate market.

Chapter Seven: 12 Ways to Finance Your Real Estate Deals

Paying for your investment is much different than paying for a loaf of bread—and the method used can often mean the difference between success and failure in a real estate investment. Chapter Seven will dive into the various financing tools you can use throughout your investing career, no matter how much money you currently have to put into a deal.

Chapter Eight: Real Estate Exit Strategies

How you plan on exiting your real estate investments is just as important as the way you enter them. Whether you sell, rent, or exchange your property, it is vital to have a clear understanding of your exit strategy options for any investment deal from the beginning in order to minimize your risk. This chapter will discuss these exit options in detail to help you plot your investing course.

Chapter Nine: How to Work (FAR) Less and Get (WAY) More Done

Real estate investing takes time, so in this final chapter, we explore several key strategies that you can use to fit your new journey into your existing life. You'll learn the power of killing "dead space" in accomplishing your goals, and how giving your money away can, scientifically, make you more successful.

Are You Ready to Begin?

As you work your way through this book, remember that it is not designed to go into the weeds on the various aspects. This book's goal is simple: to give you the big and broad view of how real estate investing works and to give you the basic tools to get past the all-important question of how to get started. As you read along, make note of any questions or highlights, and then come back to BiggerPockets.com and search the site or ask questions on our forums to learn more.

Finally, if you are not a member already, please take a moment right now to sign up for a free account on BiggerPockets.com. Seriously. Like … right now. We'll wait.

And with that, we invite you to start this journey toward real estate investing success. We'll be with you every step of the way. It is perfectly natural to be intimidated, but our goal at BiggerPockets is to help you overcome your fears and your countless questions by providing as much information as possible to help you make the best decisions for your own needs.

If you are ready to begin your journey, turn to Chapter One now.

CHAPTER ONE
Nine Questions Every Real Estate Beginner Wants Answered

"Ask better questions."

That was the answer given by Tim Ferriss on episode 254 of the *BiggerPockets Podcast* when asked, "What makes someone successful in any of life's ventures?" As the author of four *New York Times* bestselling books, including *The 4-Hour Workweek* and *Tools of Titans*, Tim knows a thing or two about success. As Tim says, "Great questions lead to great answers."

If the most complex question you ask in life is "How do I pay my rent this month?" you'll likely get an answer and solve the question. But when you increase the depth or intensity of your questions, you'll find the depths of your answers, and your life, increase as well.

Additionally, questions have a powerful way of opening doors, allowing one to continue moving through their journey rather than giving up. As taught in, perhaps, the most popular finance book of all time, *Rich Dad, Poor Dad* by Robert Kiyosaki, the right questions put your mind to work, rather than simply shutting it down with a statement like "it can't be done."

For example, many people simply argue, "I can't invest in real estate because I have no money." But asking the right question—like "*How* can I invest in real estate even though I have no money?"—opens doors, expands one's world, and ultimately leads to an answer that can change a life forever.

It's for this reason that we decided to begin this book addressing the most common questions new real estate investors have. Rather than forcing you to read through the entire book while wondering about these issues, let's just clear them from your mind once and for all and address them.

The following pages include answers to the nine questions below, which have come up again and again on the BiggerPockets Forums and on the live weekly BiggerPockets webinar.

- Can I invest in real estate if I have a full-time job?
- Do I need to pay some guru in order to be successful?
- Can I invest in real estate if I have no money?
- Can I invest in real estate with bad credit?
- Is real estate investing a way to get rich quick?
- What if my market is too expensive?
- Do I need some kind of LLC to invest?
- Should I wait to invest until the market changes?
- Do I need to have a real estate license?

Let's jump in.

1. Can I Invest in Real Estate if I Have a Full-Time Job?

Yes.

There are hundreds of ways to make money in real estate, as you'll see throughout this book. Some of these techniques or strategies might require 40 hours a week, while others might only require 40 hours per decade. The amount of time it takes to grow your real estate business largely depends on your investing strategy, your personality, your skills, your knowledge, and your timeline.

Furthermore, remember the story of the tortoise and the hare? The hare continually sprinted through the race, while the tortoise took the slow-and-steady approach. While many investors have "sprinted" toward their investment goals, success is most often found by consistent action, not "big action."

Consider two types of people who try to lose weight. The first person sets a goal and heads to the gym for a three-hour run on the treadmill. A few weeks later they go back to the gym and use the free weights for a few hours. Then a month later they go back and try the elliptical machine. The second person, however, sets the goal and goes to the gym five days a week, but just works out for 30 minutes every single day, while also watching calorie intake. After three months, which person would you assume lost more weight? As any personal trainer will tell you: The second person will win almost every time. Why? Because consistency in action is far more important than sporadic big action.

So what does this have to do with investing in real estate while working full time? Simple: Even if you can only spare a few minutes each day, but you are consistent with it, you can invest in real estate. Most real estate tasks don't require hours and hours of work. For example, analyzing a real estate deal might take ten minutes (especially if you are using the BiggerPockets Property Analysis Tools at www.Bigger Pockets.com/analysis). If you simply analyzed one deal a day, but did it consistently for three months, that's nearly 100 properties analyzed! If you purchased just 1 percent of those properties, you could end up buying a deal every three months!

So, yes, you can invest in real estate while working a full-time job. In fact, it might even be beneficial. First, by holding on to your day job, you do not need to live off of any of the cash flow or profits you make from your investments—that's what your 9-to-5 job is for! By reinvesting all the profits from your investments, you can fully realize the incredible benefit of exponential growth.

Additionally, it's much easier to get long-term bank financing, thanks to the steady income from work, which can also help increase and stabilize your wealth-building.

Real estate can be highly profitable—both as a career and as a side hustle while working a "normal" job. However, the choice is yours as to which path you take. Don't simply decide to quit your job and become a full-time investor because you read about other investors who have been successful doing it that way.

You've probably heard the age-old high school guidance counselor question: "If you suddenly had $1 million and didn't have to work anymore, what would you do?" Your answer, it is said, is the career field you should be in. Would you invest in real estate? If your dream path would be to open up a shelter for abused animals or to move to Aruba and train tourists to surf, you probably should not be a full-time real estate investor, or you should make sure that your investing lines up with that vision and can get you there.

That's not to say that you shouldn't invest in real estate—you just maybe shouldn't go full time. You don't need to make real estate your career in order to build wealth in real estate. If you love your job, you don't need to quit to invest in real estate. In fact, you can achieve the same or better results as a full-time real estate investor by investing on the side.

That said, life is too short to be stuck in a job you hate. Choose a career that makes you excited to wake up in the morning, energized throughout the day, and content when you fall asleep at night. If that desire leads you to full-time real estate investing, welcome to the club! Just make sure you are not simply building a career, but building a future.

MICHAEL "SWANNY" SWAN
BiggerPockets Podcast ▪ Episode 238

Michael "Swanny" Swan was happily working as a teacher in San Diego when he heard a terrifying rumor: Potential budget cuts might reduce his salary by $12,000 in the coming year. If this rumor turned out to be true, it would be a devastating blow to his already meek earnings. He and his family were barely getting by as it was, so the thought that he was powerless over this potential financial tragedy rocked him to the core. Right then and there he decided that he needed to be fully in charge of his financial future.

After looking into different investing strategies, Michael settled on real estate after he talked with an old high school buddy who was a real estate broker. The broker helped him find a one-bedroom, one-bathroom condo in his area for $135,000, and it cash-flowed $335 per month after all the expenses. Michael was hooked! He had an extra $335 per month coming in with very little work. "If this worked so well for one, why not do ten?" he reasoned.

Michael started taking money out of his IRA to invest in condos. He quickly learned that three-bedroom condos did not cost much more than one- or two-bedroom ones, but they cash-flowed $500–$600 a month. Despite still working 60 hours a week as a teacher, Michael soon owned and managed ten condos and had zero money left in his IRA. But he was perfectly okay with that, because not only did these properties cash-flow well, they were also appreciating in value at an incredible rate. This created a unique "problem" for him, though: He suddenly had $1.6 million in equity and wasn't sure what to do with it!

Since he frequently encouraged his students to look to books for answers to their problems, he took his own advice and researched what to do with all this equity. It was then that he learned about the wonders of the 1031 exchange (discussed at length in Chapter Eight). If he sold his properties and purchased another at a similar or greater value, he could delay paying taxes on that property.

Michael sold one of his properties and made a $140,000 profit after it was all said and done. After talking with a coworker whose family owned and managed properties in the Cleveland, Ohio, area, he decided to use his profits to invest there as well. He purchased a duplex in a suburb of Cleveland and hired his coworker's family to manage it. This cash-flowed better than his condos in San Diego, so he began to sell off all his condos and purchase properties in Ohio. He soon found a 15-unit apartment building in a suburb of Cleveland for $595,000. At the time it was cash-flowing for $15,000 per year, but he knew it had the potential to cash-flow for $30,000 with a little work. Later, he purchased a 24-unit apartment that was cash-flowing for $24,000 per year.

Today Michael owns eight apartment complexes and four single-family homes for a total of 122 front doors—and counting. He is also beginning to take on investors as he continues to get more deal flow. Despite the fact that he has more than $2.5 million in equity net worth, and earns more than $160,000 in annual income, he continues to work full time as a teacher. Michael loves teaching—especially now that he is free from the worries of a change to his teaching salary.

- - - - - - ———————————————————————————————————— - - - - - -

2. Do I Need to Pay Some Guru in Order to Be Successful?

Absolutely not.

Countless investors have become successful without the help of the "guru crowd." The goal of many of these individuals is to sell you on the dream of fast riches, fancy cars, easy money, and so on—and many gurus prey on people who desperately want to make money; they often use very slick and dangerous (for you) techniques to sell you on their very expensive courses, boot camps, mentoring, training, etc.

Keep in mind that there are many in our industry who benefit from the marketing of these gurus. Most websites focused on the investment niche affiliate with them, making large referral fees—often on the order of 50 percent—in return for marketing their wares. Additionally, a large percentage of real estate clubs derive their revenues from splitting the money from products and events sold by gurus who "teach" at those events.

Remember, real estate gurus are in the business of marketing and selling you on the dream. Through this book, and the thousands of articles and millions of discussions available on BiggerPockets, you can absolutely learn everything that you would pay thousands of dollars to a guru for, and you can do so for free.

Now, that's not to say coaching or training doesn't have a place in the industry or in your future. Even Serena Williams, arguably one of the best tennis players in the world, has a coach. Coaches or mentors can be incredibly helpful in answering questions, allowing you to break through mental barriers, holding you accountable to action steps, or working alongside you on a deal. Some of these individuals are very knowledgeable, and there are plenty of stories of individuals who have paid money to a coach or a mentor and found incredible success. Maybe the "hand-holding" is just what you need. But caveat emptor ("let the buyer beware"): Do your homework on the educator (searching BiggerPockets is a great way to do this), and don't get caught up in the hype or promise of "secrets." There aren't any secrets.

The point we're making is this: Before throwing money at someone else to make you successful, understand that success comes from within first. In today's world, real estate information has been democratized. That is to say, the information you need is out there, ripe for the taking. You don't need to pay $20,000 to some national guru (that you'll likely never even meet) to tell you how to find real estate deals, how to get funding, or how to structure your business. We'll cover all that within this book, and you can find hundreds of online resources that discuss these topics on BiggerPockets.

3. Can I Invest in Real Estate if I Have No Money?

The simple answer is yes, it is possible to invest in real estate if you don't have any money at all.

However, there is money involved in every real estate transaction.

The issue, therefore, is not that you're investing with "no money," but rather that you're investing with "none of your own money." Investing in real estate without using any of your own money requires using Other People's Money (OPM). Learning to strategically invest in real estate without any of your own money is one of the most complex but important tools you can develop in your real estate investing career.

The key to investing in real estate without any money of your own is simple: Bring something to the table. If you lack money, there are other things you can bring to the table in a transaction—if structured correctly—including education, time, connections, confidence, intelligence, and creativity. By reading this book, you are already taking steps toward building your strengths in those areas.

Many investors use little or none of their own money when investing in real estate by applying one of several methods that include:

- Partners
- Lease option strategies
- FHA 3.5 percent down payment loans
- USDA or VA no-down payment loans
- Home equity loans or lines of credit
- Seller financing
- Private/hard money
- Wholesaling

We will look at each of these areas in more depth later in this guide. We want you to recognize that investing in real estate without income is possible but may not be as easy as the gurus would have you believe.

ANSON YOUNG

BiggerPockets Podcast ▪ Episodes 34, 96, and 235

Anson Young was moving to Phoenix, Arizona, with his wife but had no job waiting for him there. On the road, he read *Rich Dad, Poor Dad* by Robert Kiyosaki and decided he wanted to invest in real estate as a way to generate real income and long-term wealth. He decided he wanted to try his hand at house flipping. Not knowing much about the business, he wisely began to work simple, low-paying jobs for investors to learn everything he could. While he found the work to be less than fulfilling, he did learn a lot about analyzing properties, finding deals, and networking.

Soon he felt ready to buy his own properties, but there was just one problem—Anson didn't have money to flip a house. He partnered with a friend who had money and was looking for a deal. They joined together, purchased a property for $80,000, and after putting $14,000 into fixing it up, sold the home for $144,000 and split the profits. Anson looks back at that deal as an amazing learning experience, a stepping-stone he needed on his journey. Without a lot of spare cash to use, Anson used his skill and his free time to find incredible deals and, rather than flip them himself, began to wholesale those deals to other investors. However, as he built up capital, he began to add some flips into the mix, improving his skills on managing contractors and earning more and more income.

One of Anson's "superpowers" has been his ability to find deals even in competitive markets, using a variety of creative strategies. One of his favorite methods, which he began using early on, is simply knocking on doors of people who are significantly late on their mortgage payments and in danger of losing their homes. If no one is home, he tapes a simple message to the door. According to Anson, "It's easy to ignore a generic mailer, but hard to ignore a person standing at your door. Since most other wholesalers and flippers are not out there knocking on doors, you tend to stand out."

To this day, Anson has completed more than 100 wholesale deals and 75 house flips. He is always seeking to expand his business and to adapt to the market as it changes, but credits his continual success to the systems he consistently works at improving, doing the hard things every day that his competition isn't willing to do. According to Anson, "You're either consistent or you're nonexistent."

4. Can I Invest in Real Estate with Bad Credit?

According to Credit.com,[1] nearly 68 million Americans, one in three, have a credit score of less than 601. That's a huge number of individuals who are unable to obtain a traditional mortgage, because most banks require a score of at least 580 to get a loan. This makes real estate investing a difficult task for many.

So, can you invest in real estate with bad credit? Well, we have good news, and we have bad news: The good news is yes, you can invest with bad credit, using the same techniques that we touched on briefly a few moments ago in regard to investing with no money. The bad news is you probably shouldn't invest in real estate if you have bad credit, depending on the reason for your poor credit score.

Bad credit can happen for a variety of reasons. Perhaps medical bills caused the issue, or maybe identity theft was the culprit. Maybe a person lost their job and had to miss some payments. The economic recession that started in 2007 led millions of Americans into financial difficulties, destroying credit scores in the process.

But sometimes bad credit is caused by good old-fashioned stupidity and ignorance. A credit card here, a credit account there. Vacations, new clothes, and other "need-it-now" luxuries have caused thousands of people to lose their good credit score and wind up in a rough spot. Refusing to live on a budget, buying nonessentials because of desire, or simply refusing to see reality for what it is can lead to missed payments and a poor credit score.

This takes us to the big question: Is your bad credit a symptom of a greater problem? We ask this because most of the time, it is. It's a symptom of greed, selfishness, impatience, and other terrible money habits. Think of it this way: If everyone's credit score was suddenly boosted to 800, and 100 percent of their debts were wiped out, what would happen? Within three years, you would likely find the same people with the same low credit scores and high debt—because the credit score is merely a number that represents your financial ability to manage your money. A low credit score is just a symptom of a greater problem.

Do some deep reflection and look at your life. Have you found the solution to ending your bad credit? Answer that question honestly, and until you can 100 percent say yes, don't invest in real estate. To help you

---

[1] http://blog.credit.com/2016/02/how-many-americans-have-bad-credit-136868/

answer that question, ask yourself these three things:

- When is the last time you put something other than food on a credit card because you didn't have enough money to pay for it?
- If your credit is poor, when is the last time you read a book on credit repair? If you haven't made any attempts to improve it, are you really past it?
- What does your written budget look like? (What? You don't have one? Uh-oh...)

Real estate investing will not solve your bad money habits, and anyone who says otherwise is trying to sell you something. Get your credit problems under control, and *then* invest in real estate.

5. Is Real Estate Investing a Way to Get Rich Quick?

No doubt one of the largest draws to real estate investing is the image of investors driving fancy cars, living in large homes, and being all-around "rich." While many real estate investors do build significant wealth over their career, real estate investing is not a get-rich-quick scheme. Yes, there are some who make a lot of money in a short time; however, these situations are generally the exception, not the rule.

Investing in real estate takes planning, patience, and persistence. Don't expect to make millions of dollars in your first year. Instead, plan on creating a business through real estate that will grow steadily year after year to enable you to meet your financial goals—and, hopefully, your dreams. No matter what you might hear otherwise, being successful in real estate requires hard work, just like it does in any other field. It is also important to know that there are no shortcuts to being successful in real estate. There are no products or tools that will do the work for you, either. You must learn the fundamentals and then apply them. Of course, our goal here is to help you with that.

At the same time, we believe real estate is one of the fastest ways to generate real wealth in today's world. Many financial experts' only advice is to set aside 10 percent of your paycheck into a 401(k) or IRA and wait patiently for 40 years so you can retire with a moderate income when you are too old to truly enjoy it. No thanks. Real estate, when done correctly, gives you the ability to supercharge your growth because of the power of leverage (the ability to use other people's money to get higher returns) and the ability to hustle. Of course, this isn't to say that real estate should be the only investment one makes, as its important to have a well-rounded financial plan. But we still believe real estate to be the best!

For example, if you were to start with $10,000 and save $200 per month, after five years you will have a bit more than $22,000, depending on the interest you earned during those five years. However, if you took that same $10,000 and used it to successfully flip a house, you could turn that $10,000 into $40,000 in less than six months. Could you turn that $40,000 into $70,000 in another six months of house flipping? Work your deals right, and you definitely can. Or maybe you'll simply put the money into a rental property and, if you get the right deal, begin earning a passive return significantly higher than other investments.

So yes, real estate investing can make you wealthy, and it can make you wealthy faster than any other investment out there, if you are willing to work toward it. And that's the key: work. Unlike that 401(k) or IRA or stock account, real estate investing is going to require some more work from you. You need to learn what a good deal is. You need to learn how to find those deals. You need to learn how to fund those deals. You need to learn how to manage those deals. But that's what this book is all about: helping you learn the fundamentals so you can build wealth faster than you ever thought possible.

BRIAN BURKE
BiggerPockets Podcast ▪ Episodes 3, 76, and 152

Brian Burke grew up in California and was just 20 years old when he decided that he wanted to be a real estate investor, coming to that conclusion after deciding he would help a family member out by buying a property and renting it back to them. He got the deal with no money down, thanks to a combination of seller financing and a traditional bank loan. Although he made no money from the deal, Brian did learn a few important lessons.

After failing the test to be an air traffic controller, Brian went into law enforcement. He worked mostly evenings and weekends, which freed up his days to learn about real estate. Eventually he decided to try his hand at flipping houses. Being that these were the days before the internet was mainstream, Brian learned to code and wrote his own computer software to compile information from various sources, giving him a competitive advantage in his market. Using this software, he had access to everything he needed to know to make quick and accurate decisions when bidding on a piece of property.

Brian funded his first flip with his credit card and, because of excessive costs, he ended up making only $1,500 when it was all said and done. Despite making less than $1 per hour for his time, he didn't give up and decided to figure out better ways to find, finance, and rehab properties. He then had several successful deals and decided that he was ready to quit his job as a police officer and work as a real estate investor full time. Brian walked into his job one day, informed his coworkers that he was quitting, and invited them to attend his presentation on real estate. At the end of his presentation, he raised $500,000 from 28 "investors." With that capital, Brian started buying 15–20 houses per year. He ended up giving his colleagues a 20 percent return on their investment, and of those 28, almost all are continuing to invest with him today.

When the crash happened in 2008, Brian saw a huge potential to purchase and flip foreclosed houses at rock-bottom prices. He knew that in order to truly expand his business, though, he would need a partner. So he teamed up with the CEO of one of the biggest home-building companies in the area who also saw the market crashing and wanted to scale back his home-building company to flip houses instead. Together they purchased and rehabbed houses in a production-line fashion. Within six months of teaming up, they were buying, fixing, and selling more than 100 homes per year, and continued at that pace for almost five years. Recognizing that the market had bottomed after the crash, Brian and his team also bought $15 million worth of homes in the Bay Area in Northern California, rented them out, and sold them a few years later for nearly $35 million.

Brian's business has done 700-plus deals totaling nearly $300 million in real estate. His favorite deals are multifamily properties larger than 200 units. As the business has grown, so has its need to raise capital for investments. "About one-third of my time right now is building capital," Brian states. Today, Brian and his company spend their time focusing on larger multifamily properties across the United States, utilizing the "syndication model" to fund his deals. He currently owns nearly 2,000 apartment units in six states: California, Arizona, Texas, Georgia, Florida, and New York.

6. What if My Market Is Too Expensive?

You should probably give up and head back to the TV.

I'm kidding, of course!

In many parts of the world, the real estate market is insanely expensive. In Denver, where I (this is Josh) live, the average price of a single-family home has more than doubled in the past seven years, climbing from a low of approximately \$208,000 to a high of \$416,000.[2] It's absolutely nuts, yet each year prices continue to increase. However, people are making a killing in Denver real estate; they just aren't doing it in the same way that I want to. You see, different markets allow for different types of investments to prosper. Denver (or any expensive city) might not be conducive to cash-flowing rental properties, but many house flippers, pop toppers (adding a second story to a single-story home to increase value), and developers are raking in the cash right now.

This example of Denver illustrates an important point: If your market is incredibly expensive, you have four real options:

1. Don't invest, but simply wait on the sidelines for the market to change. I don't recommend this one, but it's a possibility.
2. Look harder. Oftentimes, the market might be overheated, but good deals can be found for those willing to look harder for those deals. Luckily, we'll look at 27 unique strategies for finding real estate deals in Chapter Six.
3. Change your strategy to something that your expensive market does allow (like flipping or development).
4. Invest someplace else. This might mean driving 60 minutes outside the expensive city to find deals in smaller, more rural markets, or it might mean building a team at a distance and investing 2,000 miles away.

---

2 www.zillow.com/denver-co/home-values/

Only you can determine the best path to take, but if you are considering investing at a distance, it's vital that you do your homework. As mentioned in the introduction, when I (Josh) first began investing in real estate, I lived in Los Angeles but bought properties in the Midwest. I immediately found myself in a world of hurt and never really made money on those investments because I didn't realize how difficult long-distance investing could be when you are not prepared. Therefore, if long-distance investing is in your future, I would recommend picking up a copy of *Long-Distance Real Estate Investing* by David Greene, published by BiggerPockets Publishing. It's a fantastic deep dive into the world of investing from thousands of miles away, and will help you determine which market to look toward and how to build your team there, and tips for making sure you don't get screwed over.

DAVID GREENE

BiggerPockets Podcast ■ Episodes 169 and 257

David Greene started his real estate journey with a huge blow to the ego—and the wallet—when his first rental property tenant forged David's name on a check and stole $7,000 from his checking account. Not a great way to begin a real estate investing career. Further, his difficulties in getting started were compounded because he lived in the Bay Area of Northern California, one of the most expensive markets in the United States. Many people would have simply given up at this point, deciding that it's just too tough to build wealth through real estate when one lives in an expensive market.

But David was no stranger to hard work and tough situations. As a police officer in the San Francisco Police Department, David routinely put in 100-plus-hour workweeks, busting bad guys and chasing down criminals to keep his city as safe as possible. So rather than running from the tough real estate start, David instead began to ask himself, *If my city is getting too expensive, how can I invest at a distance?*

This led David to develop a team-based investment strategy he later coined his "Core Four," made up primarily of a rock star real estate agent, a property manager, a contractor, and a lender. Rather than trying to know and do everything himself, David decided to rely on experts whose job it was to know the market he was considering investing in. "If you were to go buy yourself a car, would you actually open the hood and pore over the engine and read books on understanding how engines work to make sure that a Camry is the best car for you, or would you read a consumer report that compares a Camry to an Accord and to a Hyundai and use that expert opinion to base your decision on?" David said.

For most people, expert opinion is the ultimate guide to determining decisions, so David applied this principle to his investment strategy. He started buying properties in Arizona and discovered he could be receiving cash flow each month without ever needing to step foot in the state. Later he expanded his markets to Florida, Georgia, and Arkansas, collecting impressive monthly cash flow with each purchase and becoming a real estate millionaire in the process. Today, David buys up to two houses each month across the country, relying on his Core Four in a system of checks and balances to ensure deals make sense and no one can rip him off. David also became a top-selling real estate agent and spends his time growing the business so he can buy more real estate at a distance.

And what if something goes wrong? For David, it's simple: You deal with it. "Sure, anything could go wrong, but in those situations, there is someone whose job it is to fix it," David says. "Besides, those things that could go wrong at a distance are the same things that could go wrong right down the street from you. It won't be any different when you're out of state. I haven't come across a thing that's any more unique in a different area than what I have with the rentals I own in California. The same stuff happens and can be solved, no matter how far away you live."

7. Do I Need an LLC or a Corporation to Invest in Real Estate?

How's this for a roundabout answer: You probably don't *need* one, but it might be a good idea. Someday. Maybe. Let us explain!

There are no *laws* that require a person to have an LLC, that is, a limited liability company, or a corporation to invest in real estate. In fact, for most beginners, having an LLC or a corporation can actually make investing much more difficult. But before we dive into the pros and cons, let's take a quick look at what an LLC is and what a corporation is.

An LLC and a corporation are legal entities set up to operate a business. Think of an LLC and a corporation as entirely separate "persons" (owned by you) who could own your real estate directly, instead of you owning it directly. People often open these entities to limit the liability that they would encounter in the case of a lawsuit.

For example, let's say that John and Jane Homeowner created and owned BiggyBird LLC. And BiggyBird LLC owned 123 Main Street. The tenants of 123 Main Street slipped and fell and sued the owner, and the courts determined that the landlord was at fault and ordered it to pay $10,000,000—far more than the insurance policy would pay out, and far more than BiggyBird LLC had in its accounts. BiggyBird LLC went bankrupt. However, if the LLC had been created and operated correctly, this catastrophic event would have left John and Jane financially intact. In other words, if John and Jane owned other assets (properties, stocks, etc.) directly in additional legal entities, those assets would, hopefully, have been safe from the lawsuit and the bankruptcy.

(There are also some other legal and tax reasons for setting up an LLC or establishing a corporation that are beyond the scope of this book. For more on that, pick up a copy of *The Book on Tax Strategies for the Savvy Real Estate Investor* by Amanda Han and Matthew MacFarland, which you can get at www.BiggerPockets.com/store.)

Protecting yourself from a lawsuit sounds pretty good, right? But LLCs and corporations have one major downside, especially for new investors: difficulty in obtaining loans. When you first begin buying real estate, you'll probably buy smaller residential properties with conventional loans. Let's say, you'll get a bank loan and probably buy a single-family house. But most banks do not lend money on a residential property to a legal entity—they only want to lend to a real person. Therefore, a lot of investors end up going through the hassle and expense of setting up an LLC only to find themselves not able to use it on their purchase. This entire situation is swapped, however, when it comes to flipping houses or buying larger commercial real estate properties like apartment buildings. In those transactions, the lenders will often require the individual to own the real estate in a legal entity.

Do you need an LLC or a corporation? You should really check with your legal and tax advisers, as the authors of this book are neither and can't offer legal advice.

Don't let the legal entity issue stop you. As mentioned earlier, this question of "to LLC or not to LLC" is one of the most common questions we receive, but we have a suspicion that this question is actually more of an excuse than a question. In other words, many people refuse to take action on their real estate journey for years because they don't know whether to get an LLC or not; it's *fear disguised as a question*. It's much easier (and sounds better) to say, "I haven't started investing yet because I don't know if I should get an LLC" than it is to admit, "I'm afraid!" Listen: If you feel like you need an LLC or a corporation, go talk to the right people today, get what you need, and move on. But don't let it stop you any longer.

8. Should I Wait to Invest Until the Market Changes?
Probably not.

A lot of investors are looking at the real estate market right now and saying, "Wow, I sure wish I would have invested in real estate back when prices were super cheap! I guess I'll just wait until the market crashes again, and then I'll jump in."

While we understand and respect the sentiments in that statement, let us offer a few pieces of advice on why we think that's a bad idea. When the market does correct itself again (and it will—real estate *is* cyclical, meaning it goes up and down), you need to be prepared and ready to buy. But if you sit back right now, refusing to partake, you won't have the confidence, the clout, nor the collateral to invest. There are deals to be found in today's real estate market—you just have to look harder. This requires that you become an expert at deal-finding, deal-analyzing, and putting together the financing. Is it hard? Yes, often it is.

But consider the baseball player taking a few practice swings before stepping up to the plate. Instead of swinging one single bat, he grabs three bats and swings all of them together. Why? Because his muscles quickly get accustomed to the weight of three bats, so when he drops the extra bats and approaches the plate moments later, the single bat in his hand feels light as a feather, giving him the ability—and confidence—to knock the ball into the left-field bleachers! In the same way, becoming an experienced real estate investor now by developing the skills necessary in today's market will help you knock it out of the park when the market does decline. Your skills will be sharp, your reputation will be solid, and your finances will be in order. You'll be ready to dominate.

And as David Osborn said in Episode 226 of the *BiggerPockets Podcast*, "Don't wait to buy real estate. Buy real estate and wait."

9. Do I Need to Have a Real Estate License?

Definitely not, but it could come in handy. A real estate license is not necessary for investing in real estate. A license gives you the ability to help others buy and sell real estate, but anyone can buy or sell real estate on their own without being an agent.

Just because you don't have to *have* a license, does that mean you shouldn't? Not necessarily. Having a real estate license can come in handy for an investor, for a few reasons:

- **Speed:** In a competitive real estate market, the early bird often gets the worm. As a real estate agent, you can get first knowledge of real estate deals that are listed.
- **Access:** A licensed real estate agent can get into almost any property that is listed for sale with a special key and lockbox. In other words, you don't have to wait for someone else to go with you or give you permission to see a property. If the home is vacant, you can head over any time, assuming the home has the special lockbox present. If the home is not vacant, you can set up a time to view it without having to fit into another agent's schedule.
- **Commissions:** When a home is sold, the seller usually pays around 6 percent to the agents who made it happen. This fee is typically split 50-50 between the agent who listed the home and the agent who brought the buyer. Therefore, as a real estate agent, when you buy a property, you can represent yourself and use that commission toward your down payment or repairs, or to take a trip to Jamaica.

So, what's the downside of getting your license? There are a few:
- **Time:** First, becoming an agent is not as easy as just signing a document. You have to take an extensive class (depending on the state, the class could be up to 190 hours long) and you must pass a difficult test, which may require long hours of studying. This takes away time from actually investing in real estate.
- **Money:** Then, once you become an agent, you'll find yourself paying several thousand dollars in fees each year just to hold on to your license.

- **Paperwork:** Finally, as an agent, you'll find yourself responsible for additional paperwork and disclosures in every deal. If you are representing yourself, you can't simply let your agent do all the heavy lifting, because you are the agent!

Should you get your license? Really, it's up to you. Of the two authors of this book, Josh has had a license, and Brandon has not. There are plenty of examples of individuals who have had a license and found success, and others who achieved greatness without it. But to answer the original question: No, you do not need a license to invest.

Wrapping It Up

Great questions lead to great answers.

It is our hope that addressing these questions head-on, right here at the start, has put some of your biggest concerns at ease. Now with those out of the way, we can move on and help you discover how you should start your real estate journey. And the best way to start your journey actually has nothing to do with houses, apartments, or flips. It has to do with you and your financial foundation. Let's get you ready for a lifetime of financial success.

CHAPTER TWO

Boring Financial Stuff — That Just Might Save Your Life!

Hide your kids and lock the door ... because we're about to tell you a horror story unlike any movie you've ever seen.

The scene opens upon a nice family: two loving adults and a couple kiddos recently added to the mix. The parents wake up each morning, enjoy breakfast, get the kids off to school, and head out the door to their jobs. After an hour-long commute, they spend eight hours— sometimes more—working hard to make their company more profitable. On the outside, they look happy and content. But something evil lurks beneath the surface.

Their *finances*!

Each month, their paychecks are deposited into an account. Then, like a leaky bucket, that money drains out faster than it should. Our cute little couple knows how much they earn at their jobs but base their purchasing decisions on emotion and greed. Their banker tells them that they can qualify for a home up to $250,000, and, shockingly, they've recently purchased a home for $250,000. The couple often needs to make larger purchases, such as nice cars so they can get to work, nice furniture so they can feel "at home," and even good iPads (they're for the kids). They borrow the money needed for these purchases from banks, credit card companies, and anyone else who will throw them some cash. After all, it's just a small monthly payment. They can handle it ... right? Over time, they buy more and more stuff on credit, and continue adding small monthly payments. Their bank tells them they can buy a bigger, nicer, more expensive house ... so they upgrade to a nicer $550,000 home (for the kids, of course).

Although this family has a decent amount of income from both parents working, they have just a few thousand dollars in their savings account, and far less in their checking account. When the wife's debit card is declined at the supermarket due to insufficient funds, she embarrassingly pulls out a credit card and mumbles something about the "bank not working right." Month after month, events like this happen.

"If only I could get that raise," the husband grumbles one night in bed, "we could really get ahead."

Years go by. Raises come. Income rises. The job gets worse; the commute gets longer. And despite the income climbing, our family never really gets ahead. The kids take up sports, which are expensive. Stress from the job makes vacation a must-have quarterly event. Cars need to be upgraded.

Then one day, after serving loyally at his company for 15 of the best years of his life, an economic downturn forces layoffs and our hardworking husband and father loses his job. Three months of lost wages lead to even more debt because the bills need to get paid. Relief is found when a new job is obtained, but the pay is slightly lower than before. So he works longer hours—60, sometimes 70 hours a week. The marriage suffers.

The kids head off to college, but because the parents can't afford to help with the cost, the kids start their own financial journey with six figures in student loan debt. And the cycle continues.

Our beloved couple finally reaches retirement and spend the rest of their days living on Social Security and watching television. When asked how they're doing, they smile and tell everyone, "We're doing great." But inside, they are dead.

At night, while holding each other, the wife asks her husband, "Why is it so hard?"

He replies, "I don't know, honey. I just don't know."

This story is not fiction. This is *life* for millions of people. No matter how much they earn, they spend more. They can't invest in their future because there is never any extra money to invest. The desire for owning more and more stuff hinders their ability to build true wealth and financial freedom. They are trapped. They are dying.

You might have thought the "Save Your Life" part of this chapter's title a bit of hyperbole; let us assure you, it is anything but. Having a strong financial foundation not only helps you build wealth, but it can also help you in almost every area of life.

As everyone knows, a firm foundation is the key to a long-lasting structure. It doesn't matter how great the building looks; if it's built upon a weak foundation, it's going to collapse. So today, right now, it's time to help build your real estate foundation—and it has almost nothing to do with real estate. It has to do with money and your relationship to it. And yes, while we titled this chapter "Boring Financial Stuff," we hope you'll really take the time to read this information because it truly could save your financial life. (And we'll try to keep it from being too boring!)

Knowing Where You Stand

The first step in building a strong, stable foundation is knowing exactly where you stand, financially. That might seem obvious, but the vast majority of Americans have very little knowledge of what their financial position is at any given time. Knowing where you stand comes down to three factors:

- How much you currently have
- How much you currently earn
- How much you currently spend

Smart business owners know these numbers at all times and create monthly financial statements that document every penny. Average people, however, do not. Consider the family from the story we just told. They might have known how much they earned, but the only indication of trouble was a negative account balance. They believed, falsely, that more income was the answer. But let us be incredibly clear here: More income is not the answer to your money problems. More income will be great, but only after you understand the full extent of your financial picture and choose to control it, rather than allow it to control you.

Knowing your financial position is vital to building a solid foundation. Once you have the right data, you can make the right decisions. But those decisions won't always be easy. You might need to spend less, or spend differently. Your spouse might be difficult to convince. Your kids might wonder why Mom or Dad is suddenly saying no more often. You may need to forgo the next vacation or the next car upgrade.

But in the end, it'll be worth it. A little sacrifice now and you can build a lifetime of financial independence later.

So let's start by creating your own Personal Financial Statement on the next page. This financial statement is simply a record of exactly what your financial life looks like, and it should take only a few minutes to fill out. I'd recommend doing so now.

Personal Financial Statement

BiggerPockets®

NAME: _____

DATE: _____

ASSETS		LIABILITIES	
Total		Total	

INCOME		EXPENSES	
Total			

NET WORTH	
Total Assets	
Minus Total Liabilities	-
Total	

PROFIT / LOSS	
Total Income	
Minus Total Expenses	-
Total Profit or Loss	

Total	

Now that you know where your money is going each month, it's time to make some decisions on where it's going to go in the future. This is revolutionary to so many people because, for once, you are actually telling your money where to go, rather than letting it dictate where you go. You have taken back control.

This doesn't mean you can't have nice things. It doesn't mean you can't enjoy vacations, movies, or even new cars. But those items are planned for, and they fit inside your plan.

Showing Your Money Who's Driving

Are you controlling your money, or is your money controlling you?

Or to put it another way, on the road to wealth, who's driving? Who's making the decisions? You probably assume that, since you write the checks and swipe the cards, you are running the show. But chances are, you are simply a passenger on this trip. Most people look at money in the same way as did the couple at the start of this chapter. They buy stuff they want because they want it. Then they pay their bills. Then they might donate to some charities. And finally, whatever is left, they try to save. But, we argue, this is 100 percent upside down. We'll have more on that in a moment. First, let's get on the same page and learn the importance of categorizing your expenses. You see, every expense you have can be placed in a category. Once categorized, you'll see how to take back control.

There are generally five expenses an individual or family has, and every dollar that leaves your bank account can fit into one of the following categories:

1. **Variable Expenses:** Groceries, gas, clothing … these are generally required expenses that don't usually occur on a fixed timeline. When you run out of gas, you fill up. When you need underwear, you buy it. This would also include all those items you pick up from Amazon, Target, Walmart, etc. The cost of living. Again, we'll look at ways to reduce these later, but for now, it's important to simply define them.

2. **Fixed Expenses:** Next, it's time to define your fixed expenses. Certain expenses are more-or-less "fixed" in time each month, meaning they come out each and every month around the same time. This would include things like your mortgage payment, car

payment(s), credit card bills, and utilities. Many of these expenses are, or can be, deducted automatically. While it's possible to decrease some of them (often dramatically), for now it's important that they are simply labeled.

3. **Donations:** Yes, setting aside money that you plan to simply "give away" is important, even when you don't have much (or any) to give. Studies show[3] that generosity leads to an increase in income.

4. **Savings:** This is money set aside each month for the future. It might be inside a retirement account, like a 401(k) or an IRA, or it might be just money you set aside into a savings account.

5. **Fun Money:** Finally, after all the other categories have been planned for, you should have some "fun money" leftover. This is money you can use for whatever you want: vacations, eating out, gifts, a cool new drone, whatever.

---

3 https://speeches.byu.edu/talks/arthur-c-brooks_giving-matters-2/

Now, let's talk about priorities.

Most people, including the family at the start of this chapter, filter their expenses in the following way:

In reality, this is the flow for someone whose money is driving them. They purchase anything they want based on desire, rather than allowance. Whatever they have left, they put into savings. But let's look at how a financially intelligent person manages the flow of their money—notice that it's 100 percent flipped upside down.

INCOME

↓

SAVINGS / INVESTMENTS

DONATIONS

FIXED EXPENSES

VARIABLE EXPENSES

FUN MONEY

The biggest shock to most people is that saving money is the *first* expense that should be accounted for. "But I don't have any money to save!" people shout. *Save anyway.* The money in your budget for savings should never be "whatever is left," though that's how the majority of people view it. Isn't your future, your wealth, your freedom worth more than that? Aren't they the most important things? So give savings the respect it deserves and make sure it is the first expense taken out of your income (except taxes, which you can't do much about right now). For more on the importance of this concept, don't miss the incredible book *The Richest Man in Babylon* by George Samuel Clason. This book was foundational for both of us in shaping our financial outlook on life.

Furthermore, this "expense" should be removed from your checking account automatically. This could be accomplished by opening up a separate savings account at your bank and setting up an automatic transfer, or by opening a retirement account such as a Roth IRA that you could even use to fund your real estate deals in the future (see Chapter Seven for more on this).

So how much should you save? That will obviously depend on your income and goals, but we'd encourage you to make it more than you think you can do. You can always trim expenses elsewhere, or earn more ... both of which we'll talk about later in this chapter. When saving is not prioritized, it doesn't happen. But when saving money is prioritized and automated, the rest of your expenses tend to fall into place.

One of the best ways to categorize your income and expenses is using that Financial Spending Plan, or FSP. On the next two pages, you'll find two identical FSPs so that you can begin, right now, to categorize. Why two? One for "Current" and one for "Future." In other words, take a look at your expenses from last month (your bank statement will work great for this, or access the data from your online portal through your bank) and put each into one of the five categories. Then use the second FSP to declare what you want your expenses to look like in the future, starting now. How much do you want to save each month? How much do you plan to give? How much will you spend on fixed expenses? How much on variable expenses? And then, whatever is left over, place into the Fun Money category. At the end, the five categories should match your income exactly. Because every single dollar must be accounted for.

FINANCIAL SPENDING PLAN™

From BiggerPockets®

INCOME	
Total	

Savings / Investments		Fixed Expenses		Variable Expenses	
Total					

Giving / Donations					
Total		**Total**		**Total**	

Fun Money	

FINANCIAL SPENDING PLAN - SUMMARY	
Savings / Investments	
Giving / Donations	
Fixed Expenses	
Variable Expenses	
Fun Money	
Total Expenses	

FINANCIAL SPENDING PLAN ™

From BiggerPockets®

INCOME	
Total	

Savings / Investments	
Total	

Giving / Donations	
Total	

Fixed Expenses	
Total	

Variable Expenses	
Total	

Fun Money	

FINANCIAL SPENDING PLAN - SUMMARY	
Savings / Investments	
Giving / Donations	
Fixed Expenses	
Variable Expenses	
Fun Money	
Total Expenses	

The FSP exercise is eye-opening because many people have no idea where their money is truly going. But by categorizing your income and creating your FSP, your plan, you are telling your money that *you* are now driving. You are in control. And you are heading someplace wonderful.

Now, one important question: What if your categories, no matter how hard you try, add up to more than you earn from income?

For example, Jerry and Linda (not their real names) created their FSP and it looked like this example on the next page.

FINANCIAL SPENDING PLAN ™

From 🦬 BiggerPockets®

INCOME	
JERRY'S INCOME	$2,100
LINDA'S INCOME	$1,400
Total	**$3,500**

Savings / Investments	
Total	**$0**

Giving / Donations	
Total	**$0**

Fixed Expenses	
RENT RENT	$1200
ELECTRICITY	$100
CREDIT CARD	$100
STUDENT LOAN	$150
CAR PAYMENT	$400
LANDSCAPER	$250
WATER BILL	$100
Total	**$2300**

Variable Expenses	
GAS	$200
GROCERIES	$450
MISC SHOPPING	$300
EATING OUT	$400
CLOTHING	$150
Total	**$1500**

Fun Money	$0

FINANCIAL SPENDING PLAN - SUMMARY	
Savings / Investments	$0
Giving / Donations	$0
Fixed Expenses	$2,300
Variable Expenses	$1,500
Fun Money	$0
Total Expenses	**$3,800**

Notice how Jerry and Linda are currently taking home $3,500 in income, but spending $3,800 in expenses—not including any savings, donations, or Fun Money. Sadly, this is not unusual. In fact, according to a recent study from USFinancialCapability.org, 18 percent of Americans polled currently spend more than they earn.[4]

What then? The obvious answer is Jerry and Linda need to either spend less or earn more. Simple to know, hard to do. But the rest of this chapter is going to help Jerry and Linda maximize their income while reducing their expenses.

But the information that follows is not just for those who find their FSP out of whack. Even if you earn way more than you spend, the following sections are designed to help anyone earn and save significantly more.

How to Save More Money Without Abandoning All Fun

Imagine your finances are akin to a large metal bucket. Each paycheck is a gallon of water dumped into this bucket, and each expense is a hole drilled in the side of that bucket, allowing water to leak out. Some holes are small, some are large, but all allow water to seep out and require your consistent filling. In this section, we're going to focus on seven strategies to find those holes and reduce their size, and even how to eliminate some of them altogether.

Use the Power of the Occamy

In *Fantastic Beasts and Where to Find Them*, the prequel to the Harry Potter novels, J. K. Rowling tells of a creature known as an Occamy. This creature is incredibly powerful, but not because of some unique fighting skill. Instead, the Occamy's power lies in its ability to grow or shrink to fit whatever container it finds itself in. It could shrink to fit inside a teacup or expand to the size of a school bus.

And your finances will do the same.

If your goal is to reduce some of the money that leaks out of your wallet each month, you've made huge strides in this endeavor already. By simply knowing where your money is going, and how much you are allowed to spend (categorizing it), you'll naturally begin fitting items into your plan. Your spending will increase or decrease to the size of the container in which you place it. Whether consciously or unconsciously,

---

4 www.usfinancialcapability.org/downloads/NFCS_2015_Report_Natl_Findings.pdf

we naturally spend around what we earn. I know some people who make $500,000 per year and spend $500,000 per year. I know others who earn $25,000 per year and spend $25,000 per year. With the FSP, then, your mind is retrained to consider only the Fun Money and the Variable Expenses when determining how much to spend, rather than all your income. By paying yourself first and automatically deducting money for savings, you'll naturally spend less. And the interesting part is, you'll likely not even notice.

Kill Your Coffee Habit? Maybe Not ...

You need to stop drinking coffee, eating out, and enjoying life right now.

Just kidding, of course!

Although many personal finance experts will encourage you to stop your weekly coffee habit, the truth is, 80 percent of your losses each month come from 20 percent of your expenses. In other words: Eliminating your three-times-per-week coffee shop habit might help you save $80 a month. But finding a way to decrease your housing expense from $2,000 per month to $1,000 per month or getting rid of a car payment could help you save *ten times* as much money. (We'll talk more about that in a moment.)

This isn't to say you shouldn't reduce your coffee shop habit. Maybe this is the only area of your life where you can easily save some money, and desperate times call for desperate measures. To go back to the leaky bucket analogy, your bucket might have only a few small holes to fix and no large holes, so maybe you need to focus on plugging those small ones. But chances are there are some large holes to tackle first. Most significantly, your housing payment and your car payment. Let's look at each.

How to Live for Cheap (or Free)

The No. 1 most significant expense (outside of taxes) for most people is their housing payment, whether it be rent or a mortgage. Typically, this expense is as high as 50 percent of your take-home pay! Therefore, this "large hole," when reduced or removed, can make the biggest impact on your monthly leakage. But how can you reduce or eliminate this without living in a cardboard box under a bridge?

When I (this is Brandon) was 21 years old, I sold my first property (a fixer-upper house) and, not knowing anything, lucked into purchasing a small duplex (two units on one property). I moved into one unit and quickly fixed up the other. Then something magical happened: The tenants I leased the house to paid me rent of $650, and I paid my bank $630 for the mortgage payment. In other words, I was getting paid to live for free! This strategy is known as house hacking, and we'll talk a lot more about it in Chapter Five. But essentially, the idea is simple: Buy the right duplex, triplex, or fourplex; rent out the other units; live for cheap or free.

While potentially effective, house hacking isn't the only way to cut your living expenses. Renting out a room in your single-family home could also help reduce your load, as would choosing to live in a cheaper location or downsizing to a smaller home. Yes, it might be a temporary sacrifice, but by reducing your highest expense, you can plug the largest hole in your bucket, giving you more income to save or to spend on real estate investments.

Is Your Money Driving Away?

We're about to step on some toes here. Or, more accurately, we're about to *drive* over some toes.

The second largest expense for most individuals is the payment on the car they drive.

"But ... but ... I need my car to get to work." Maybe. But do you need *that* car? You know what I mean—and the anger rising up in you right now is a good indication that you know, deep down, you bought the car you are driving for more reasons than just transportation. A $2,000 vehicle that is ten years old will likely get you to work in the same way, so why do we buy new or slightly used cars? The simple truth: status. The age and condition of our vehicles are outward indications to everyone else our status in this world. Yes, you can justify your purchase with, "Well, I don't want to fix things when they break," or, "I got a zero percent interest loan on the car." But let's recognize this justification for what it is.

Are we telling you not to have a nice, newer car? Not at all. If you are wealthy enough, living below your means, and setting aside a signifi-cant portion of your income for savings and giving, then great. Enjoy the car! But the truth is, it seems the individuals who are living paycheck to paycheck or drowning in debt are the ones who buy the nicest cars. So take an inventory of your vehicle and what you really need. Again, it might be a sacrifice, but if it'll help you shave off decades in your quest for financial freedom, isn't it worth it?

Is There Money "Hiding" in Your Bank Account?

I (Brandon) recently found $365,402 hidden in my bank account. And there is a good chance that there's some cash hiding in your bank account too.

Let me explain.

I decided to take an inventory of my spending, so I printed out my bank statement and went line-by-line through all the expenses, placing each into a category. It had been a while since I had last done this, and I was shocked to find $200 of monthly expenses for things I no longer used. Thirty minutes later, I was $200 per month wealthier. In my case, it was several online subscriptions to software companies I had signed up for months ago and had forgotten about. But maybe for you it's a magazine subscription, an entertainment subscription, or something entirely different. Set a reminder in your smartphone to check your bank statement each and every month for these "phantom" bills.

So, why $365,402? Because $200 invested at 8 percent every month from now until I reach retirement age is $365,402.

Keep in mind, subscriptions might not be the only expense you can reduce. Look at your car insurance, health insurance, home insurance, and other regular fixed expenses, and find ways to reduce those costs. For example, if the commercials can be believed, switching to a new auto insurance plan could save you hundreds, if not thousands, of dollars per year.

JESSE FRAGALE

BiggerPockets Podcast ■ Episode 220

Jesse Fragale caught the real estate investing bug when he met a young and successful real estate investor who was driving his dream car, a 1999 cherry red Dodge Viper RT/10. When Jesse asked his mother what the man did, she told him he was a real estate investor. It didn't take anything more to convince Jesse that real estate investing was the path for him as well.

While attending college in Toronto, Canada, Jesse was renting a room from his friend when it occurred to him that he would rather have people paying him rent than paying rent himself. So, in 2008, while still attending college, Jesse purchased his first property—a student rental property that was being leased to five college women. The success of this deal led Jesse to add other student rental properties to his portfolio.

Jesse quickly realized that real estate investing is not always positive when he encountered, in his words, "the worst day" of his life. One of Jesse's properties suffered from significant water damage and mold, and when his insurance denied covering the cost of the repairs, Jesse was left to foot the bill for a $21,000 repair job. Because Jesse had wisely kept all of his profits from that property in his company, he was able to cover the cost of the repairs without losing his shirt. This experience taught him the importance of being financially responsible and setting money aside for unforeseen capital expenditures and repairs. "You think you're cash-flowing," says Jesse, "but then you get hit with that new roof or furnace, and it just wipes you out."

After years of investing in student housing and acquiring 35 units, Jesse decided that he wanted to try his hand at investing in apartments. Jesse and his coworker John, both of whom are real estate brokers, recently partnered up to invest in an 11-unit apartment building, finding the process significantly easier than his smaller deals. He now encourages others to consider larger deals, saying, "People are a little apprehensive with apartments because they feel they are these big deals that they could never do. But as someone once told me, 'The bigger the deal, the easier it is to do.' I probably could have been accepted for this apartment easier than for a single-family home that I would live in, because the rules for apartments are commercial rules if they are over four units. The building is the critical piece, not just the individual."

Jesse currently has his sights on obtaining 100 units within the next five years.

- - - - - - -- -- -- -- -- --

Bring Your Spouse on Board

While earlier we touched on the fact that the largest holes in your bucket were taxes, housing, and vehicle expenses, the truth is, oftentimes a spouse (or relational partner) might be the largest reason for the expanding holes. In the joking words of Scott Trench, author of *Set for Life*, there are a lot of "cash-flow negative spouses" out there! There are two reasons for this:

1. You want to please your spouse, so you justify your purchases because you know those purchases will make your spouse happier.
2. Your spouse just buys a lot of stuff.

Let's first talk about the wrong way to fix this: "Listen, honey darling baby boo. You have a disease—it's called spending our money. Stop it!"

Bad idea. (Divorce is expensive, too!) So if a head-on confrontation isn't the most advantageous way to fix the problem, how do you best align your passion toward financial responsibility with your spouse's?

First, understand that, most likely, you are using your spouse as an excuse to justify your own spending. Take 100 percent responsibility for your own spending habits, and you might be shocked to find that most of the problem is you. But either way, relationships are made up of two people with independent minds, so getting your partner on board with change will likely help your efforts to reduce spending.

Financial responsibility is a mind-set before it's an action. Therefore, if you can change a mind-set, the actions follow almost naturally. This isn't usually done by lecturing someone into compliance. Mind-sets are changed slowly, and there are three primary ways in which a mind-set is changed:

- **Through Story:** Humans love a good story. Not only does it grab attention, it also changes the way a person thinks. A good story has the ability to change one's mind-set. Tell your spouse a story that can illustrate your goal. For example, the story we told you a moment ago, about Brandon finding $365,402 hidden in his account—what did that do to your mind-set? Did it shift it, just a little bit?
- **By Aligning Goals:** Few people enjoy working out and eating super healthy. Instead, we make these small sacrifices in our day because we want the results. Every result you desire in life involves some sort of sacrifice. Therefore, a great way to get on the same page with your spouse is to define and align your goals. Once your spouse understands the mission—financial freedom—he or she will likely join you on the quest, as long as it's a goal they can get behind.
- **Through Media:** After 300 different interviews on the Bigger-Pockets Podcast, isn't it interesting that 90 percent of the guests

say the same book when asked, "What is your favorite real estate book?" The answer: *Rich Dad, Poor Dad* by Robert Kiyosaki. Why? Interestingly, the book hardly mentions real estate. But this book is continually brought up because it changes one's mind-set in a powerful way. In addition, movies, podcasts, blog posts, and other forms of media can make a big impact. Therefore, a great way to help your spouse's mind-set change is by suggesting books or media. It might be as simple as asking them to read (or listen to the audiobook version of) *Rich Dad, Poor Dad, or The Richest Man in Babylon*, or Dave Ramsey's *The Total Money Makeover*.

How to Cut Your Food Expense in Half

Food is expensive, especially if you have a large family. Add in healthy, organic meals and your food budget could eclipse your house payment. Therefore, finding ways to trim your food expense could save you hundreds of dollars a month—but it doesn't mean you need to sacrifice deliciousness or health. Instead, pay attention to the following tips and you could save 50 percent or more of your food bill each month.

Eating out is becoming more and more prevalent in our lives, to the detriment of our wallets and financial freedom. According to Fool.com, from 2015 to 2016, for the first time in history, Americans spent more money at bars and restaurants ($54.857 billion) than they did on groceries ($52.503 billion).[5]

From time to time, someone will argue that eating meals out is cheaper than what they could cook at home. While this might be true when comparing a $0.99 fast-food burger with a home-cooked one, the medical bills from eating that crap will far outweigh what you spend. But let's get real: When you go out to eat, you likely aren't spending $0.99. Take a look at your latest bank statement. According to TheSimpleDollar.com, Americans are averaging $12.75 per person, per meal.[6] That means a family of four could average $50 while eating out. Multiply that by 4.2, the average number of times Americans eat out each week, and that could push your food expense to more than $800 each month. And I don't think we even need to talk about the insane markup

---

5 www.fool.com/retirement/2017/01/01/heres-what-the-average-american-spends-on-restaura.aspx

6 www.thesimpledollar.com/dont-eat-out-as-often-188365/

on alcohol. For some, that expense alone could save you thousands of dollars per year.

Planning your meals ahead of time can also help you shave a ton of money off your food bill. Busy people push food decisions to the back of their mind and end up going out to dinner more frequently because they don't have anything at home. Take 20 minutes each week to plan out the next seven days of meals. Not only will this help keep you eating at home, but you can plan your meals in such a way to maximize your grocery shopping. For example, we might do "Italian week" or "Mexican week," in which we can remix the various grocery items in a variety of different meals. It's amazing how many different meals can be made from beans, rice, cheese, meat, and tortillas.

This isn't to say you need to cut out all restaurants and foods and drinks from your life, but reducing those expenses by half could help save hundreds with relatively little change to your life. Rather than grabbing that sandwich and drink from the lobby of your office building each afternoon, pack a lunch and enjoy it while taking a stroll around the block. Make more dinners with your spouse. Order a soda water with lime instead of a drink when you hang with friends. Not only will you be healthier, those small changes add up and make you wealthier in time.

You Can Afford Anything ... But Not Everything

Finally, in the words of our good friend Paula Pant from from the website AffordAnything.com, remember: "You can afford anything you want—but not everything you want." Financial responsibility is about making choices and prioritizing desires. People often think of frugality as a bad thing, as saying no to everything and living like a hermit inside a cardboard box. But in reality, frugality is simply making conscious choices to control your spending, rather than letting your desires control you. If you really love to travel, great. Travel! If you love drinking with friends, fine. Enjoy it! If you absolutely need that $100,000 Tesla with Ludicrous Mode that will take you from zero to 60 in 2.3 seconds, fantastic.

But know the cost, weigh the options, and make the necessary adjustments to your FSP. And only spend that money after you've set aside your savings and giving money. Pay yourself first, and enjoy the rest.

At this point in the conversation, the question inevitably arises in most people's minds: *Well, what if I can't save any more money? What if I'm already frugal but still don't earn enough to make any big dent in my savings? How do I earn more money?*

The reason I placed this section at the end of the chapter on personal finance is because earning more money is useless if you don't have control of your spending. If your money is still driving your life around, no amount of extra income is going to make a difference. Millionaires still live paycheck to paycheck all across America. We call this Income Creep.

When you make $12,000 a year, you spend $12,000 a year, avoiding vacations, eating out, and jewelry. When you make $100,000 per year, you stay in nicer hotels, buy new cars, and hire a house cleaner. When you make $1,000,000 per year, you lease a private jet and routinely order $400 bottles of wine at dinner. While you might laugh at this and say to yourself, *I'll never do that,* let's take an honest look at your life: Are you spending more now than you did when you got your first job out of college? Chances are, the slow Income Creep has already begun, and if you don't identify it and rein it in, you'll never out-earn your spending. You'll be a millionaire living paycheck to paycheck ... one bad month from being back where you started.

Is this to say all additional spending is wrong? That you shouldn't improve your lifestyle as your income grows? Not at all. I (Josh) can't imagine having my wife and kids stay at the same roach motels that I was content to stay in after college. However, the key is knowing that the creep exists and actively choosing to contain it like the Occamy. Once you recognize Income Creep and give your finances a container to live within, you can begin earning more money while keeping your lifestyle relatively simple. I've generally aimed to spend half of what I make, no matter how much that is. This way, I can still increase my standard of living (nicer cars, nicer house, etc.) while not falling victim to the Income Creep.

So for those who know how much they spend and have reined in their spending and taken control of their finances, let's talk about the two primary ways to increase your income:

- Earn more at work
- Earn more on the side

Let's dive into each, and we'll show you how to immediately begin driving more revenue into your life, giving you the ability to save more, give more, and invest more.

How to Earn More Money at Work

Not all jobs will give you the ability to earn more. But you'd be surprised at the number of opportunities that exist for most jobs, even those that might not seem obvious at first. It's not just sales or commission-based jobs that offer additional pay. Even teachers, firemen, and police officers have the ability to dramatically increase their income through the jobs they hold when one looks in the right place. Let's look at a few ways to increase the amount of cash you receive from your employer each month.

Work Extra Hours

We'll start with the obvious but most painful one: Work more hours. Put in the extra time needed to increase your paycheck. For example, David Greene (we met him back in Chapter One) worked as a full-time San Francisco police officer but took advantage of every overtime shift he could to double his income, plowing that money into enough real estate investments to quit his job. Teachers can often get paid to lead after-school tutoring.

Get a Promotion

If getting a promotion at work seems like a long shot, you've already lost. Employers want to promote individuals who are making (or have the potential to make) an impact in the company. Most employees draw a line between "management" and "everyone else," and consider promotions to be luck or politics. While those factors might play into the equation, if you can make your company more revenue, decrease the workload for current management, or in some other way demonstrate your ability to make an impact, promotions are possible. Here's a novel concept: Ask your boss what it would take to get a promotion, and then do it. Stop thinking of upper management as the enemy, and instead think of them as the goal.

Get a Higher Degree

In many occupations, obtaining a higher degree (bachelors, masters, doctorate, etc.) can immediately offer a bump in pay. In the tech world, salaries are often based on the specific code learned or certification obtained. Therefore, if taking a six-month intensive course on your weekends and evenings can bump your salary $20,000 per year for the next several years, isn't it worth the investment? Isn't your time better spent learning in the evenings than watching television?

Add Skills

Are there any skills you can add to your current abilities that would help you obtain higher pay at your job? For example, perhaps you are a receptionist at a law firm, bringing in $45,000 per year. Most individuals would consider this a career with a definitive ceiling. However, what if (on the weekends and evenings), you intensely study marketing and copywriting, finding what works well for marketing a legal firm on the internet? You approach your company with a plan to become the company's marketing expert in addition to your current role, which they accept with enthusiasm, offering you a pay bump in the process.

Negotiate for Commission or Profit Sharing

Imagine the scenario we just proposed: you, the legal office receptionist-turned-marketer. What if management didn't want to give you additional pay for your new skills? What if they don't see the value? Consider negotiating for commission or some sort of profit sharing. Commission offers the company a "no-lose" proposition. If you fail to do whatever task you attempt, they lose nothing. But if you succeed, they make extra revenue (or improve in some other way) they would not have had before. Perhaps you, the receptionist, ask for 10 percent of the revenue that comes in directly from the ads you run, with no cap. At first, you make nothing from your ads, but as you tweak and test them, you begin to find messages that resonate with individuals. After one year, you are consistently bringing the company an extra $50,000 in revenue, netting an extra $5,000 per month for yourself. In addition, you now can add *marketer* to your résumé and potentially jump ship to another job entirely.

Be the Best

If you want more freedom or more income at work, become—in the words of Cal Newport and the title of his pivotal book—*So Good They Can't Ignore You*. When you are an average employee, your options are limited because your company can find someone else to replace you. But if you become the best at a specific task, your negotiating power for increased pay or freedom rises dramatically.

For example, let's say you work as a plumber for a large company outside Seattle. If you are an average employee, you show up (usually) on time, get your work done with some grumbling, and leave work when finished. In other words, you are exactly like every other plumber in the company. You are completely replaceable. But imagine, rather, you seek to become the best plumber in the company. You pick up extra skills, you read books and attend seminars on customer service, and you even leave a simple thank-you card for every single property you visit. Soon customers are requesting you, specifically. Your speed and skills and productivity efforts help you accomplish twice as many calls as the next guy in the company. Finally, you spend 15 minutes per day prospecting for new business. In other words, you've moved from "replaceable" to "indispensable" in the eyes of your company. Because you bring in so much revenue and business, you have the leverage needed to negotiate for higher pay and profit sharing.

Jump Ship

Leaving a company is hard, but if you are underpaid at your current job and can earn more elsewhere (or have a better quality of life), consider jumping ship. You could potentially add tens of thousands of dollars to your annual salary for the cost of a couple of hard conversations and a few weeks of getting used to the new job. Best of all, your current company doesn't need to know you are looking, so the downsides are almost nonexistent. If you explore the market and find no benefit to leaving, no harm, no foul.

Become an "Intrepreneur"

An entrepreneur is someone who starts their own business, but an *intreprenuer* (a term coined in 1978) is someone who starts a business *inside* of a larger company, usually taking some sort of financial piece of the revenue to align interests.

For example, perhaps you work for a large consulting firm that helps golf club manufacturers across the world. You also have some additional skills in project management, and you've seen how a certain type of software has helped other manufacturing industries increase their output, but the golf club market currently has no such software. You approach the owners of your company with a plan: You want to build a software business inside the consulting business. If it works, this could become a huge income stream for the company, and it'll be your pet project, and you'll run it as a CEO type, with your salary based on the success of the business.

Unlike when you start a business from scratch on your own, you don't need to worry about finding customers because your company already has them. If your software idea fails, it's a relatively low-risk idea to test from the company's standpoint. You present the idea to the board and the board gives you the green light. You hire a small team, begin building the software, and soon you are running the most profitable division in the company, quadrupling your salary in just two years, giving you extra money each year to invest in real estate.

Ask for a Raise

Finally, one of the fastest (yet scariest) ways to increase your salary or income is to ask. Yes, this might be scary. But there is tremendous upside with almost no downside, so make it a goal to ask for a raise regularly. Most individuals, however, go about seeking a raise all wrong.

Except for a few cases, you do not deserve a raise because of how long you've been at the company. This entitlement mentality can actually work against you. Instead, asking for a raise needs to be thought of as a request for investment. Like any business investment (which, in case you weren't aware, your salary is), a case must be built on why the company should agree to make that investment. Think of it like a request for a new copy machine or company hire. What benefit does the company get from giving you a raise?

In your quest for a raise, be sure that your performance at work is exemplary in the months prior to asking. Find ways to demonstrate the impact you are making on the company, and use data when possible. When sitting down with your boss and asking for the raise, come prepared. Find out what your company values, and show how you've helped. Showcase your past accomplishments. Find ways to demonstrate that you are underpaid compared to similar positions at other companies. And keep it light but serious.

How to Earn More Money on the Side

For those who work a job in which earning more is not possible, or a job where you simply are not happy and don't want to work there much longer, it is still possible to drastically increase your income by making money on the side. There are several ways to do this, but understand that this usually isn't as easy as it might seem. While you can find numerous examples of people who have perfected the following paths and made great side income, you don't often hear of the many, many business ideas that fail. I don't say this to discourage you—many people do find success. BiggerPockets itself was just a side hustle for the first few years. But by understanding the challenges that lie ahead, you will be more prepared for the hard work, persistence, and growth needed. Let's take a look at some of the best ways to earn more money on the side.

We want to start with some general business tips that apply to any entrepreneur, including a budding real estate investor. Then we'll dive deeper into some specific ways to generate side income.

Start a Business

Have you ever dreamed of being your own boss, controlling your own schedule and destiny? If you have the entrepreneur bug, then starting a business could be a great way to increase your monthly income and work for your own success rather than your boss's. For example, perhaps you'll sell sunglasses at the mall, or open a landscaping business, or a bakery, or something completely different. Or maybe you'll open a new branch of an existing business, known as a franchise, in which the branding (logos, etc.) and systems (how the business is run) are already defined and documented for you.

But let us (yes, we've both started numerous businesses) warn you: Starting a business is hard work, with very little chance of success. There is no guarantee of riches. You need to make the *right* business, and more importantly, you need to execute it well. It doesn't matter how great your idea or business model is if you don't take persistent and consistent action to grow the business. Waking up and going to work is easy because, if you don't, the consequences are *immediate*. Entrepreneurs, on the other hand, often find it difficult to get stuff done because the consequences are often not as black-and-white.

If you plan to start a company of your own, consider these 12 principles that have helped us grow multimillion-dollar businesses:

1. **Do Something You Enjoy:** Building a business is slow. Don't start a business you won't want to be doing in five years.
2. **You Won't Know Everything:** Recognize that you are driving through a dense fog of unknowns, and drive anyway. When I

first got into real estate investing, I had no idea how to buy a property, rent a house, or evict a tenant. I figured it all out on the job. You will too.

3. **Finish What You Start:** Many entrepreneurs suffer from the same curse. You like to start things more than you like to finish them. You may have a lot of awesome ideas, and many of them would likely succeed and make you a great deal of money if fully executed, but that doesn't mean you should start them. Pick one and go with it until it dies or it makes you rich enough to buy a private island.

4. **Partner Carefully:** Don't partner with someone because it's convenient; do it because it makes you stronger. The right partner will make you rich, faster. The wrong partner will drive you nuts (and take half the profit).

5. **Learn to Manage:** Unless you are currently a manager and have developed those skills, you'll likely be terrible at managing people. That's okay, we all do at first. But this is one task you must get better at. Hire an assistant right now, even if it's only a virtual one for $3 an hour. It will give you some great training on managing, with little financial risk or downside.

6. **Do What Is Important:** Stop wasting time designing business cards, logos, business plans, and stationery. They don't matter much right now. Go build your business and stop doing busywork that makes you feel like you are accomplishing stuff.

7. **Get Obsessed:** There is a fine line between dedicated and obsessed, but screw the line. Trample right over it. You need to cross that line continually, so never let anyone tell you that you are too obsessed with your business.

8. **Don't Quit Your Job Too Soon:** Yes, by quitting you'll have much more available time to build your business, but let's be honest. There are 168 hours in a week; only 40 are consumed by your day job and another 50 by sleep. You have plenty of time if you would just hustle and turn off Netflix. But conversely, don't be afraid to quit your job if you can afford to.

9. **Focus on Your Higher-Paying Tasks:** Look at all the tasks on your plate each week. Then determine which ones could be outsourced for $10 per hour and which would cost $1,000 per hour. Focus on doing more $1,000-per-hour tasks and fewer $10-per-hour ones.

Mowing your lawn is a $10-per-hour task. Being a world-class salesperson or connecting with the right influencer could help you make $1,000 for that hour of work. Where should you be spending your time?

10. **Keep the Main Things the Main Things:** Your spouse, your kids, your faith, and your integrity matter more than your business. Never forget that.

11. **Read ... a Lot:** Books help reframe a mental state while also teaching new tactics and principles that can grow a business. So read a lot. If you don't have time, listen to audiobooks. And not just business books. Read motivational books, self-help books, success books, fiction books, biographies—whatever. Just read.

12. **Wake Up Earlier:** Waking up earlier might not sound fun, but for many people, it's the most productive time of the day. Get your most important tasks done before the kids are asking for breakfast, the spouse is asking for help with the dishes, and the phone starts ringing. One hour of dedicated morning focus can be worth five hours of afternoon work. Not a morning person? That's an excuse lazy people use. For more advice on this, read *The Miracle Morning* by Hal Elrod. It's life-changing.

Like driving down a lonely highway on a dark, foggy night, entrepreneurship can be a little scary. But keep your foot on the gas anyway. As Mark Cuban said, "It doesn't matter how many times you fail. Each time only makes you better, stronger, smarter, and you only have to be right once. Just once." You might struggle, you might falter, you might fail. But keep going. Entrepreneurship, whether it's through real estate investing or something entirely different, has the power to change your life. You only need to be right once to have a lifetime of financial independence.

The tips outlined above can be applied to all examples in this book to increase the odds of success, so let's talk about some specific side businesses you can build in your life to make more income.

Consulting, Teaching, Tutoring, and Freelancing

In his *New York Times* bestseller *Outliers*, Malcolm Gladwell argues that it takes roughly 10,000 hours of deliberate practice at something to become "world-class." From surfing to stock trading to home decorating, he says that roughly 20 hours a week for ten years is the key to becoming the best. Others argue it can be accomplished in far less time, and some skills might require even more time, but the fact remains: It takes a long time to get good at something. And chances are there is something in your life that you are world-class at.

Maybe it's painting, or project management, or dog walking, or video games, or something entirely different. And because it takes so long to become world-class at something, there are ample opportunities to use your skill to earn side income. By consulting (coaching others to achieve success in a field), teaching (community colleges, online, etc.), or freelancing (working for others on a temporary basis), you can charge high rates for work you are already excellent at.

Sell a Product

Have you ever seen a product for sale and thought, *Hey, I had that idea.* Good for you—a lot of other folks probably did as well. The key, however, is that you didn't take action on it. Ideas are mostly worthless, but for those willing to work hard to implement, selling a product can be a great way to make extra income. Creating products has become increasingly simple to do in our technological society, as websites like Alibaba.com or AliExpress.com can make anyone a manufacturer and an importer, and companies like Squarespace.com or Shopify.com can give anyone an online storefront.

And keep in mind, you don't need to come up with a great idea in order to sell a great idea. Remember: Implementation is what matters, so find someone with a great idea and partner with them to do the implementation.

Blog

In the beginning, no one knew what to call it. *Journaling? Journalism? Online writing?* Finally, the world settled on a term: *blogging.* Blogging is the practice of publicly writing short, essay-style posts on the internet and gaining a following of readers. There are blogs about food, family, business, wealth, and every other topic under the sun. Blogging gives anyone the chance to make public commentary on politics, teach others how to cook, or document their travels with eye-pleasing photos. Put another way: Blogging turns an individual into a media channel. So how does one make additional income from blogging? There are several ways to monetize, but all require a fairly significant amount of monthly traffic, which is the hardest part. With 440 million blogs on the internet,[7] standing out as a fresh, consistent voice is important. Then, monetize by placing ads on the website or selling a product (such as an e-book or online course), or by consulting or affiliate marketing, in which you sell *other* people's products (for a commission) to your readers. BiggerPockets, of course, has an extremely popular blog. You'll find dozens of articles each week from a variety of sources, but at the beginning, it was just me (Josh), plugging away on my computer.

Keep in mind: Blogging is a long-term commitment and a slow way to generate income. If you are hoping to use blogging as a way to quickly build up wealth, pick something else. But like real estate investing, success compounds slowly over many years, and the results can be fantastic.

Lease Out Your House or Car

They call it the "sharing economy," but it's really more like the "leasing economy." Essentially, you can earn extra income by leasing something of yours to others. The most popular way to do this is by renting out space in your home, or the entire home itself. Websites like Airbnb.com or VRBO.com have made this process almost painless. We'll talk more about short-term rentals in Chapter Five, but leasing out your home isn't the only thing you can lease. Turo.com is an app that allows you to lease out your vehicle, by the day, for extra income. If you don't need your car every single day, and you live in a densely populated area, leasing out your car could bring in hundreds or even thousands of dollars in extra income.

Get a Second Job

Perhaps the most unpopular choice on this list, but also the one with the highest chance of success, is simply getting a second job. As discussed earlier, there are 168 hours in a week, so if 40 are spent at your primary job and 50 are spent sleeping, that still leaves 78 hours for extra "stuff." Perhaps 20 hours of that time could be spent on an additional job. It doesn't mean you need to do it forever, but that extra income could be the immediate boost you need to get out of debt or raise extra money for

---

7 www.mediakix.com/2017/09/how-many-blogs-are-there-in-the-world/#gs.8KnwZAs

your first real estate deal. A little sacrifice now can lead to a completely different life later.

Now, let's talk about our two favorite methods for making additional income *through real estate*.

Become a Real Estate Agent

Real estate agents make money when they help someone buy or sell a house. Although there is no law that dictates how much an agent should make on a transaction, most transactions offer 6 percent to the agents who put the deal together: Fifty percent of that goes to the agent who represents the buyer, and the other 50 percent to the agent who represents the seller. Furthermore, an agent typically works "under" another real estate "managing broker," who also takes a cut. In the beginning, that cut might be 50 percent of the agent's portion, but that can be negotiated, and different real estate agencies have different pay structures. But let's assume, as a starting agent, you'll get 50 percent of the commission and then split *that* with your managing broker, leaving you with just one-fourth of the total 6 percent commission. Let's look at an example:

You recently obtained your real estate license and helped your friend buy her first home. The final sale price was $350,000, and the seller offered a total of 6 percent commission on the sale. Six percent of $350,000 is $21,000, which is split between you and the seller's agent, giving you $10,500. Then, you have an arrangement with your broker to split the commissions 50-50 for the use of their marketing, their office building, and their brand name. So, of that $10,500, you personally keep $5,250. But then you'll also need to pay income taxes on that revenue (for example, 20 percent), as well as self-employment tax (15.3 percent) and possibly state income tax (for example, 5 percent). Your take-home pay, after all is said and done, might be around $2,000 (though, the tax liabilities can largely be offset by certain deductions, such as your vehicle, home office, and possibly your phone).

While keeping only $2,000 of a total commission of $10,500 might seem like an unfair deal, that's still an extra $2,000 in your pocket (after tax). For many, that's more take-home pay than they earn at their job in an entire month, and that's just one deal. Imagine doing two, three, four, or five of those each month. Additionally, as an agent, you have the ability to build up a consistent flow of customers, as the average person moves every seven years. In the beginning, it might be tough to find clients, but the longer you are in the business, and the better systems you build, the more income you can earn (and the more passive that money can become). And because agents are typically paid a percentage of the sale, the income you can receive will largely depend on the price range of the homes you are helping clients buy or sell. Six percent of $50,000 is a lot different than 6 percent of a $1,000,000 home.

As with most businesses, success is not spread evenly among the one million-plus real estate agents. Most of the profit is generated by a very small number of agents at the top. In fact, according to the National Association of Realtors, "Twenty-six percent of all Realtors made more than $100,000 last year, while 26 percent made less than $10,000."[8] So how can you find yourself at the top of the heap? By doing the hard work that most agents don't want to do. David Greene, who became a six-figure-earning real estate agent in his first full year in business, says,

"The secret to being a successful real estate agent isn't a secret at all: It's hard work. It begins with following a tested process and committing to a daily regimen of action. Far too many agents rely on luck or happenstance to build a pipeline of buyers and sellers, but top performers work for it, every single day. They do this by making concerted, systematic, and purposeful contact with those that know, like, and trust them. By maintaining relationships and reminding those that matter most they are looking for buyers and sellers, they stay top-of-mind with their sphere of influence when it comes to referring them business.

"Top-producing agents know their database is their databank, and they treat it that way. By systematically adding people to their database and maintaining regular contact with them, they win the contest for the 'mind share' of those they know. Top-producing agents do this through phone calls, emails, text messages, note cards, scheduled lunches, client appreciation parties, and social events. The agents who treat their business like a business are the ones who find massive success. The ones who treat it like a passive hobby experience passive results."

Becoming a real estate agent isn't free, though. Each state has a different requirement for the cost of becoming an agent, typically between $1,000 and $2,000 for fees and memberships (per year). In addition, each state has a required number of "classroom hours" you'll need to take before obtaining your license, ranging from 30 hours to

---

8 https://www.nar.realtor/newsroom/nar-member-survey-shows-more-younger-realtors-entering-the-industry

156 hours, with additional hours needed each year to maintain your license. Luckily, in most states, this classwork can be done online for a few hundred bucks.

Lastly, being a real estate agent has one additional benefit, as we discussed in the previous chapter: the ability to get first dibs on real estate deals for yourself. It's for these reasons that our general recommendation for anyone wanting to quickly earn additional income is to become a real estate agent.

Flip Houses or Wholesale Real Estate

Finally, let's quickly touch on something we'll cover in more detail in Chapter Five: You can also earn additional income—sometimes a lot of additional income—by *actively* investing in real estate. The most common way to do this is to flip houses or become a wholesaler (someone who is paid a fee for finding great deals and passing them on to other investors). If done right, these strategies can help an individual make tens of thousands of dollars in extra income each year, while also giving that person real-world experience in finding and rehabbing properties. These skills can lead to a lifetime of greater success in a real estate investing career.

Wrapping It Up

It is our hope that this chapter has given you the tools needed to build a solid financial foundation for your life. You learned how to examine exactly *where* you are right now, financially. You also learned how to build a solid financial plan, your FSP, to maintain stability as you grow. Then you discovered some easy ways to begin saving more money each month, and we closed with some powerful tips and strategies for immediately increasing the income you earn each month. Are you feeling stronger, financially, just by learning this? Great! But remember, it only matters if you apply it, so make financial responsibility a priority in your life, building the most stable foundation possible. Let's move on to building your real estate empire. But before you can begin studying the specifics of the various niches and strategies involved with real estate investing success, you need to line up some ducks.

CHAPTER THREE
Getting Your Ducks in a Row

"Give me six hours to chop down a tree and I will spend the first four sharpening the axe."

—ABRAHAM LINCOLN

Under the weather. Adding insult to injury. Barking up the wrong tree.

The English language is full of fun idioms that help convey a point. The funny thing is, though, most of us actually have no idea where those phrases come from, nor what they were originally meant to convey. While we all likely know the *meaning* of an idiom, its *origin* is much more elusive.

Take, for example, the title of this chapter: "Getting Your Ducks in a Row."

Some believe this phrase originated from the most literal sense, whereby *ducks* refer to the baby ducklings that follow close behind their mother in a line, a scene common in nature. Others, however, point to the lack of evidence of this phrase being used to discuss ducks anywhere prior to 1970, and are drawn instead to other explanations. For example, bowling pins were once referred to as "ducks," leading some to argue the phrase originated from the need to line up those "ducks" just right to knock them all down with one roll of the ball. Still others point to the world of hunting as the source, referencing an article from 1901 in the magazine *Recreation*, where the story is told of John Mitchell, a hunter whose trick strategy involved "getting the ducks in a row" so he could take down several ducks with one shot. And still others point to games such as pool, where balls that lie just in front of a hole are often referred to as "ducks," or a shooting arcade game where John Wayne wannabes use air rifles to shoot a line of metal ducks.

While scholars and idiom enthusiasts may disagree about the meaning of this phrase, few can debate the importance of the message being communicated. *Having one's preparations laid before beginning an activity or project is vital to the success of that venture.* Your real estate investing is no different. Therefore, this chapter will focus on helping you line up your ducks to get ready to invest. In the pages to come, you'll gain a solid understanding of the principles you needed to make your first investment. We'll give you a close look at the way market cycles function to make real estate predictable yet powerful. We'll talk about the nature of fear and analysis paralysis that nearly every new investor goes through—and how to overcome them. Then we'll look at your real estate team, including discussing the importance of partners and mentors. Finally, we'll dive deep into the murky waters of LLCs and corporations to make sure you are protected no matter what kind of real estate you venture into.

It's time to get your ducks, *whatever that means*, in a row!

Understanding Market Cycles

The real estate market is cyclical—average prices go up and down, largely driven by the general population's fear or confidence in the economy. I'm sure you remember back in 2007 and 2008 when the U.S. real estate market crashed hard, driving prices down as much as 50 percent in some areas. Then we saw an incredible climb from 2012 to 2018, and soon we'll encounter another drop, likely followed by another climb. And on and on it goes. However, lucky for us, while the market does go up and down, it also tends to average upward over time, keeping pace with inflation. To put it another way, while prices may drop for a while, we are confident that, over the long term, our real estate investments will continue to grow in value.

Typically, the terms *buyer's market* and *seller's market* are used to describe the market cycle we find ourselves in. Are prices low, and are there a number of homes available with few buyers? Then, thanks to supply and demand, it's a great time to buy, and it's a buyer's market. Are houses selling quickly, often above asking price? Then it's probably a great time to sell, thus a seller's market. And, of course, the market is often in the middle between those two extremes.

In a perfect world, investors would buy a lot of properties when prices drop, and sell them when prices increase. The problem with this logic, however, is that it is incredibly difficult to understand where we are in the market cycle. Hindsight is 20-20, as they say. However, you can take a look around and try to gauge what kind of market you find yourself in. You might not know if you are at the top of a cycle or the bottom, but you can know if you are in a buyer's or a seller's market, and your strategy may shift depending on that knowledge. For example, if you believe we are at the very top of the market, or nearing it, you may think twice before starting the construction of an apartment complex that will take three years to complete, because if the market drops significantly before that property is complete, you might end up in trouble.

While changes in market cycles may help make one type of investing over another easier, we prefer to simply invest no matter what the market looks like. We're going to buy incredible deals in a "hot market" and in a "not market." We're going to stick to our metrics and buy with the knowledge that the market might decline—because we know it always does. We're not going to buy a rental property that loses money each month just because we believe the market will double the price next year (that's called speculation, and while wealth can be built this way, it's a risky venture that shouldn't be taken by new investors unless they have a lot of money to risk).

Yes, the real estate market is going to decline again. Maybe it'll be a crash, maybe a soft drop. Maybe it'll just keep climbing. Maybe not. It doesn't matter a lot to us. We're going to continue buying based on sound, conservative principles. When prices climb, we'll double our efforts to find great deals. And over time, we know our wealth will continue to grow.

DAVID GUDMUNDSEN

BiggerPockets Podcast ▪ Episode 188

When it comes to knowing market cycles, it's hard to find someone who knows more than David Gudmundsen. He has been actively investing since 1994 and has invested in nearly every form of real estate, buying more than 250 deals since his start. He has seen—and experienced—both the market highs and the lows, and has become an expert in knowing when to buy, when to hold, and when to liquidate. While many of his colleagues on his home turf of Arizona were losing their portfolios during the crash of 2008, he had already safely downsized his portfolio and was just waiting to begin buying again once the market rebounded.

As most investors know and as we've said, the financial market is cyclical with highs and lows. The key to real estate investing is to buy properties when the market is poor and sell when the market is strong. As David says, what's more important than the old real estate phrase "Location, location, location" is the phrase "Buy low and sell high."

What worries many real estate investors is trying to gauge when the market is going to turn. If you sell too early you may make less money, and if you sell too late you could get burned and lose a lot. However, even David admits that trying to perfectly "time" the market is impossible. We can never see the top or bottom while in it, so the most important factor for investing in a property is to make sure the numbers work. "You need to make sure that the money coming in is greater than the expenses, even if the market is down," David says.

David equates the fluctuating real estate market to that of a game of musical chairs. "It's like musical chairs when there's 20 people and 20 chairs," he says. "The music is on, everyone is dancing, lights go off, and everyone is partying. But what the dancers don't realize is that, quietly, chairs are being taken. What I've learned is that it's okay to sit down, take a chair, put your legs up, and relax. Be early in and early out. When the lights go on, at least you aren't one of the 19 people fighting for the few chairs that are left. That's when it gets brutal."

Nervous? Here Are Seven Ways to Overcome Fear

For every successful real estate investor out there, there are dozens who were too filled with fear and uncertainty to ever actually do a deal. If you are just beginning, chances are you have some fear as well—but don't worry; fear is a natural part of life that is designed to help us avoid bad decisions and the consequences derived therefrom.

But fear can also stop you from ever getting started, and as a result, you may find yourself spinning your wheels without getting anywhere. The purpose of this section is to address that fear, to teach you seven ways to overcome it, and to help you succeed in spite of it.

1. Get Off Your Duff

If you are looking to real estate investing to save you from a job you hate, then you had better start working to replace the income from your job with money made from real estate activities. Develop a plan and work that plan every day—just like you would get up and go to work every day for a paycheck. If you expect to do one deal and end up on a beach somewhere with beautiful people all around, wake up. Successful real estate investors work hard, and you will need to do the same. But instead of working for a company you're not fond of, you're working for yourself, which is a blessing and a curse.

2. Commit

Stop buying courses and other materials or seeking out mentors or coaches until you are committed to step number one. If you are not committed, no course, class, or trainer is going to get you any closer to your goal. Almost every real estate course out there focuses on the mechanics, but the real action is what's going on between your ears. When you can get that under control, it won't matter what technique you use; you will find success as a real estate investor.

3. Start Participating

BiggerPockets is filled with knowledgeable real estate investors who are willing to share what they know for free. Sign up for a free account and interact daily. Don't just lurk; participate, ask questions, connect with others, and build relationships. If you are afraid to ask questions now, then you are going to be just as afraid to speak with a seller who needs to sell you their property or to negotiate with a big city developer.

Interactions are part of an investor's life, so the faster you can overcome this fear, the more successful you'll be. Being visible to your peers online and off will ensure you're always at the front of their minds—and that's great for business.

4. Learn the Lingo

Without knowing the lingo of a real estate investor, you will always be afraid of sounding like you don't know what you are talking about. Once you build up your confidence in understanding the lingo, your ability to talk with others and understand what is being discussed will grow exponentially.

5. Learn the Concepts

Once you have the lingo down, you need to start understanding the concepts. If you can't adequately explain what debt-to-income is or why 70 percent ARV is important in a house flip, you need to spend more time learning. Fear is often a result of being unclear. Additionally, once you have a good understanding, help teach someone else. Teaching others a difficult concept will cement that concept into your own mind, helping you to never forget.

6. Watch Others

By associating with investors who are involved in the same kind of investing you want to get into, you will naturally begin to pick up on the traits that make them successful. If this means working nights and weekends for a local investor for free, then that's the price of admission. You will quickly learn to overcome your fear when you help others accomplish success, giving you the confidence to strike out on your own.

7. Overcome Analysis Paralysis

A close cousin of fear is known as "Analysis Paralysis," and many investors end up in this purgatory for years. These are the moments where you research, plan, evaluate, research, plan, evaluate in an endless cycle and are paralyzed from ever actually taking action. It's the problem of reading books without implementing, reading blogs without engaging, and meeting others without interacting. Typically, it's due to fear of screwing something up.

It's easy to convince yourself that you don't know everything you should know before you start taking action. However, you don't need to learn about every single niche buying technique, and you don't need to be an expert before getting your hands dirty. You should focus on one area of investing and become an expert in it, and then move on to the other techniques and areas. We'll cover the various real estate niches in the next chapter.

Once you know where you want to start, you need to learn the ropes. The BiggerPockets Forums are an excellent place to learn everything you need to know about any topic. Ask questions. Learn the basics and start planning. You might feel that you are not completely ready to begin, and you probably never will be unless you take action. It will seem scary, and you probably won't be able to answer every seller and buyer question at first. But because you took action, you will be in a position that will force you to learn the answers to those questions.

When you're fearful, it's so much easier to spend more money and pay for another course or spend another month reading about what other people are doing. Doing so won't get you anywhere. Get educated, get your plan together, and start taking action. As you do, you will quickly start to feel at ease in your new skin. You will actually feel like a real estate investor. Your confidence will skyrocket, and you will become even better at what you do.

All investments have some degree of risk, and real estate investing is no exception. While risk can't be avoided, it can be managed through proper preparation, which you have already begun by reading this guide. The hardest thing to do in any new venture is to get started. At some point, you need to follow the advice of Nike: "Just Do It!"

NATHAN BROOKS

BiggerPockets Podcast ■ Episodes 87, 159, and 232

Nathan Brooks decided to become a real estate investor after overhearing a man in a restaurant talking about it with his friends. Nathan introduced himself to the man, and within a few weeks they were business partners, purchasing two properties that they intended to fix and flip. The plan was for Nathan to be in charge of finding and financing the deals, and his partner, who had a background in construction, would rehab them. It did not take long for Nathan to start realizing that he had made a big mistake: Not only did he not know much about real estate investing, but he also did not know much about his new partner. It wasn't long before his partner stopped showing up regularly to work on the properties and, when he did show up, it was only to ask for more money. Nathan, not wanting to give up so quickly, continued to try to make it work.

With a strong belief that he could still come out on top, over the next 18 months he purchased another six units that he found through an investor on Craigslist. All of a sudden he had $1,000,000 in property that needed major repairs—with an unreliable business partner. He didn't know what to do. With limited structure in place, never-ending rehab costs, continued vacancies, and a shady business partner, it wasn't long before Nathan's real estate empire came crashing down. Banks that had lent him money began demanding payments that he couldn't make. One of his properties was quickly foreclosed on. Another went into short sale. Before long, he was forced to file Chapter 7 bankruptcy. In an instant, all of his investment properties were gone. And to add insult to injury, his business partner skipped town with the business credit card, racking up tens of thousands of dollars in debt for Nathan.

While many would simply throw in the towel after a blow like this, Nathan and his wife decided to use it as a learning experience and get back in the game. With a lot of hard work, they eventually saved up 50 percent for a down payment and, after asking 27 times, convinced a private investor to loan them the remaining amount for their first property after the bankruptcy. They purchased a small three-bedroom, one-bath home for just $21,000, and after a small rehab, rented it for $800. They then refinanced it for $70,000 and used the money to buy another property in the same neighborhood, utilizing the BRRRR strategy (which we'll cover in Chapter Five) to rebuild their empire.

From there, Nathan and his wife began to flip one property after another, building the next deal off of the previous one. With every deal, they would repeat what they did right and continue to learn from where they failed. This strategy has proven to be quite effective. To this day, the couple has flipped more than 200 properties and their business is growing exponentially each year. They have been able to achieve this by building a strong team with a lot of open communication and having a solid plan, clear expectations, and the drive to always do more. One thing Nathan hopes other investors and people in general can learn from his experience is that "it's okay to fail. It's okay to understand where we come from. We can look back on it as long as we're learning from it and making a conscious choice to not make those same mistakes."

Assembling Your Real Estate Team

While as an investor you are required to wear many different hats, you don't need to (and can't) wear all of them. Instead, you need a team. When we refer to "team," we're not suggesting you go out and hire a team of employees to work under you. A team is merely a collection of individuals in various industries that you can rely on to help move your business forward. Here's a brief look at who should be on any winning real estate investing team:

- **Your Mentor:** Every successful entrepreneur needs a good mentor, a guide. By training under the watchful eye of someone smarter than we are, we can only get smarter. This is such an important topic, we'll spend quite a bit of time discussing it later in this chapter.

- **Your Partner:** You don't need a partner to invest, but if you have one, he or she will be a valuable member of your team. So valuable, in fact, that a good chunk of this chapter will be spent on discussing the pros and cons of working with partners, as well as tips for making your partnership prosper. We'll get to that momentarily.

- **Realtor:** An exceptional real estate agent is fundamental in your investing career. You or your spouse may even choose to become a real estate agent so that you can gain access to the incredible tools that agents have. Either way, having an agent who is punctual, a go-getter, and eager, is important. Real estate agents are paid from the commission when a property is sold. Simply put, for the buyer, an agent is free. The agent can be an excellent resource for contract real estate work, which may include the following activities: referring buyers, showing properties, open houses, broker price opinions, etc.

- **Property Manager:** If you don't want to actively manage your properties, a good property manager is important to have. A good property manager can be hard to find, but finding one who can efficiently manage your rentals will make your life significantly easier.

- **Mortgage Broker/Loan Officer:** A mortgage broker is the person responsible for getting you loans—especially if you are going "conventional" (not hard or private money). You want someone who has the experience of working with other investors, and you want that person to be creative and smart. Many loan officers have a pipeline of buyers (or future buyers); real estate investors can use the help of local loan officers to build a list of buyers and lease purchasers for their properties.
- **Real Estate Attorney:** It is important to have someone on the team who can go through contracts and who knows the legalities of all your moves. Don't try to pinch pennies by ignoring this valuable member of your team. You don't need to meet for hours each week with your attorney, but you want someone who will be available when you need them. Having an attorney who is skilled with real estate investing is very important for the success of your career. Keep in mind, attorneys can also be compensated through fees collected at acquisition or disposition of a property.
- **Escrow Officer or Title Rep:** If you live in a state that uses title and escrow companies, your escrow officer or title rep is the person responsible for closing the deal, taking you from "the offer" to "the keys." Having a good one on the team helps to close deals that much quicker. You always want people looking out for your interests.
- **Accountant:** As you acquire properties, doing your own taxes and bookkeeping becomes increasingly difficult. As soon as possible, hire an accountant (preferably a certified public accountant, CPA). Your numbers person should also be well aware of the ins and outs of real estate, and preferably own rental properties of their own. Come tax time, this is the person to help you through the write-offs. A good tax accountant will save you more than they cost.
- **Insurance Agent:** Insurance is a must, and as an investor, you will probably be dealing with a lot of insurance policies. Be sure to shop around for both the best rates and the best service. Do not skimp on getting insurance; you never know when you'll need that policy.
- **Contractor:** A good contractor seems like the hardest team member to find, but can often make or break your profit margin. You want someone who gets things done on time and under budget. Be sure that your contractor is licensed/bonded/insured to protect you. Don't simply hire the cheap person.

- **Supportive Family and Friends:** Having the support and backing of loved ones is important in any endeavor. If your spouse or family is not on board, don't invest until they are.
- **Great Handyman:** Someone to take care of the little things that come up on a daily basis is imperative to have on your team. Ask for referrals from other landlords for the best handymen; they typically don't need to advertise but work almost entirely on referrals from a small group of investors and homeowners.

One of the best sources for finding these team members is through referrals from other investors. In general, other investors will be happy to refer their handyman, mortgage broker, or accountant to you because it reflects well on them and their relationship with that professional. Try asking around at your local real estate investor club or on BiggerPockets, and you'll be well on your way toward putting the pieces in place.

What Makes a Great Real Estate Team?

A great real estate team is defined by its ability to consistently produce reliable results. As you might suspect, that's way more difficult to construct in real life than it is to talk about it.

Investors, especially ones with either large portfolios or those who flip a lot (often both), rely on their team daily. When one member fails, the entire endeavor suffers, sometimes to the point of sabotaging the team's goals altogether. Whether you're serving clients, flipping properties, or keeping track of your rentals, your team must consistently produce and avoid the "excuse train" at all costs. Those who are constantly making excuses will pull you down faster than you can imagine.

People talk a good game, so watch them when it's their turn to produce. A great team member should exhibit certain traits, which are sometimes difficult to see on the surface but can be witnessed through longer conversations and via referrals from others. For example:
- Are they really experts?
- Do they interact well with everyone?
- Are they a pain to contact?
- Do they return calls/emails quickly?
- Do they hit deadlines?
- Do they produce as promised, when promised?
- Can they communicate clearly and efficiently?

Assembling the team will not happen overnight, but once it's together, the group will give you the backing and help you'll need to make your real estate investing dreams come true.

TARL YARBER

BiggerPockets Podcast ■ Episode 189

Tarl Yarber was a typical American college student when he came across the idea of wholesaling real estate. Being young and ambitious, Tarl immediately got to work on trying to make real estate investing his career. He obtained a list of people defaulting on their mortgages and set out on a door-knocking campaign, offering to buy their home and help them out of their situation. After limited success, Tarl knew he needed a better system, so he attended a local real estate club to learn how others found success in the business. One of the individuals at the meet-up took Tarl under his wing and became a partner, helping Tarl get his first deal and enter the world of real estate. But for Tarl, it was something even more: He discovered the power of working on a team.

Tarl's second deal was huge—a $100,000 profit on a single wholesale deal. "It changed everything—financially, my life, everything," he says. And with that, he jumped in with both feet. He quickly moved away from the wholesale model and began to focus on flipping houses—doing full remodels on old houses in the Seattle and Portland areas, making them "look like brand-new houses." Realizing he couldn't do it all by himself, Tarl began to assemble a team to help him scale the business, which included a project manager, an acquisitions manager, an assistant, and more. By utilizing his team, Tarl was able to tackle more projects with less personal involvement, giving him the ability to keep his eye on the big picture. To date, Tarl and his team have completed more than 500 deals and are currently working on 16 rehabs at the same time.

Tarl funds many of these deals by using private investors and hard-money lenders, stating, "The majority of my success has always been networking. Networking. Networking. We've always been honest and up-front with people. And we have built a reputation of always putting our investors first." He has created a very detailed system and has built trust with these investors by showing them his organized portfolio with photos, completed deals, deals in progress, profits, losses, etc. This is vital, he explains, because "it shows you're a professional who knows what you're doing."

Should I Use a Partner or Go It Alone?

Before beginning your real estate journey, you will need to decide if you want to pursue your career on your own or with the help of a partner. This decision is not the same for everyone and depends largely on your knowledge, time commitments, abilities, talents, and timeline. If a partnership is something you plan on pursuing, the kind of partnership becomes important as well. Some individuals choose to invest in real estate with a partner from the start. Others choose to invest with partners on a case-by-case, deal-by-deal basis.

Let's take a look at some of the pros and cons of using a partner vs. going through your investing career alone.

Real Estate Partnership Pros

Team Brainstorming: Two heads are better than one, so ideas can often develop with clearer focus and direction as multiple minds work through the same issues.

Pooling Resources: Real estate investing generally takes a great deal of resources, and can often be too expensive for one person to handle alone. A partnership allows you to pool your resources to get off to a stable start. A solid partnership may also help with bank financing.

Assistance with Analysis: It is important to master the art of deal analysis, and a partner can help a lot. There are hundreds of considerations when searching for your first real estate investment deal, so having someone else looking at your numbers will increase your odds of an accurate analysis.

Complementary Qualities: Different people bring different strengths and weaknesses to a partnership, for example, analytical vs. hands-on, construction vs. financing, time vs. knowledge. Understanding what each person excels at, and harnessing that strength, is key for successfully working with a partner.

Task Division: When investing in real estate, there are many tasks that can easily overwhelm your life. Effectively and fairly dividing tasks can ensure that all partners are able to contribute to the business without feeling overwhelmed.

Expanded Networking: Networking with others within and outside the real estate industry is vital to the growth of your real estate investing endeavors. In a partnership, each partner already comes to the table with their own network of connections.

Accountability: A partnership, if both sides do their part, will help to keep the business moving forward; you've got a built-in accountability partner to keep you to task. When one partner begins to falter, the other can step in and assist to ensure the team is moving forward.

Confidence/Motivation: Starting out in real estate investing can be overwhelming. A partnership can help inspire confidence and motivation when obstacles arise. A good partnership can be revitalizing and motivating.

Split Risk: As with any investment, real estate investing involves a certain level of risk. Having a partner splits the risk (and thus, the profits) and can lessen the fear of loss.

Real Estate Partnership Cons

Personality Conflicts: Partnerships can be difficult because of the possibility of vast differences in personalities. When you are relying on another person to get things done and you don't mesh perfectly, conflict can easily arise.

Difference of Opinion: Everyone has an opinion on how things should be done. If you are in a partnership, you are forced to compromise on many aspects of your business. From paint color to investment type, differing opinions can cause difficulty.

Suspicion/Trust: As with any close relationship, it is easy for suspicion and trust issues to arise, especially when things aren't going well. Trust can be hard to gain and quick to lose. Fraud can also play a role in the demise of many businesses and partnerships.

Delayed Decision-Making: When you are acting alone, you have the ability to make decisions quickly, based on how you want things done. In a partnership, you are oftentimes forced to discuss all decisions—no matter how trivial—with your partner, which can add a lot of time to your dealings.

Smaller Profits: When you form a partnership, your profits, by nature of the agreement, are split. In other words, you will make much less money per deal than if you were doing it by yourself.

Mixing Business/Friendship: Often people get into business with friends or family, and many times that becomes the death of that relationship. Partnerships don't always work out, and when they don't, the relationship is often severed for good. A partnership is very much like a marriage—don't get into it unless you're ready!

Unrealistic Expectations: When you rely on someone else, it's easy to set expectations on how something should be done. However, when the partner doesn't live up to your expectations, it's easy to be bitter and blame the other person.

Responsibility for Partner: While the legal ramifications depend largely on the entity structure you set up, you and your partner are still in business together, which means you are responsible for that person, at least in terms of the business. If they skip town, you are still responsible for the whole business. Make sure your real estate attorney helps you draft any partnership agreements to help protect your interests.

More Complicated Taxes: When it's just you alone, your taxes are much more straightforward than if you're working with partners. The more members you bring on as owners, however, the more complicated the bookwork becomes and the more time-consuming (and costly) tax season is.

Four Tips for a Successful Real Estate Partnership

If you've decided that the benefits of a partnership outweigh the negatives, be sure to follow these four tips to minimize problems:

- *Don't be a jerk:* Treat your partnership with care and have a giving spirit.
- *Learn to compromise:* There will be disagreements and conflicts in a partnership—and there must be compromises.
- *Talk daily:* Talk every single day, when possible. Discussing daily events as well as future goals will keep the relationship stable and validates the reason you are partners.
- *Plan ahead:* Do not start a partnership off the wrong way. Make sure the arrangement is written, well planned, and includes an operating agreement to detail the roles and responsibilities, capital contributions, profit splits, and exit strategies.

The Bottom Line of Using Partnerships

While partnerships have many benefits, they are not for everyone, and if not properly created, they may be a silent killer to your investment plans. If you choose not to become part of a partnership, you are not actually investing alone. There are thousands of individuals in the BiggerPockets community who can help you through any weaknesses you may have. You can also outsource numerous tasks you don't want to do, rather than give 50 percent of your profits away. For example, if you are not good at construction, it may be cheaper to hire a contractor than to partner with an individual who is good with construction.

If you decide to enter into a partnership, be careful from the beginning. Many people simply do not make good business partners. If you decide you would like to pursue a business partnership, be 100 percent confident that you will choose a business partner who will treat you fairly, add value to the relationship, and maintain similar goals to yours. Carefully plan out the arrangement (in writing) and constantly communicate. If both of you remain committed to the business, you will likely develop one that is prosperous for all parties involved.

JOE FAIRLESS
BiggerPockets Podcast ■ Episode 227

Joe Fairless grew up in Texas but moved to New York City after college with dreams of being a successful advertiser. While there, he decided he also wanted to find a way to invest the money he was earning. So he saved up $1,000 and invested it in a CD account. After a year of not being able to touch that $1,000, he made $16 off of his investment—and was then taxed on the profit. Realizing that this strategy would not build him wealth very efficiently, he began to research other methods of investing and decided real estate was the best strategy.

After saving up $20,000, he bought his first house in Dallas, Texas, in 2009—without ever seeing it. He had a real estate agent take a walk-through video of the property and then had it inspected. After receiving the inspection report, he purchased the house. He repeated that same process with three other single-family homes after that. While his single-family portfolio was growing modestly, Joe wanted to grow faster. He attended a real estate workshop and got excited about the idea of investing in larger multifamily properties. "I read probably 80 percent of the books out there about apartments, I began shadowing people who were multifamily investors, and I was incredibly active on the BiggerPockets forum," he says. Around this same time, he came to the realization that he was not feeling fulfilled with his full-time job, so he left it to invest in real estate full time.

Since he knew he was cutting off his main stream of income, Joe began to partner with others who had money and experience. Before he left his job, he had already met a few people who were interested in investing in large multifamily properties, so he was off to a good start. With his newly formed partnerships, Joe began contacting brokers in Tulsa, Oklahoma, with the expectation that it would be relatively easy to find a great deal. Unfortunately, despite putting an offer on nine deals, he came up empty in Tulsa. He struck gold, however, in Cincinnati, Ohio. He, alongside his partners, purchased a 168-unit apartment complex in Cincinnati (where Joe moved to manage the deal). He eventually sold it and then formed Ashcroft Capital after meeting someone who had complementary skill sets. Today Joe and his partners own 3,500-plus units across the country, valued at more than $300,000,000. He focuses on apartment buildings that have more than 150 units, are B class, stable, built in the 1980s or newer, and have value-add capabilities. His goal is to have $1,000,000,000 worth of properties in his portfolio within the next five years, and he'll continue using smart partnerships to get there.

Real Estate Investing Mentors

A mentor is an individual who teaches and instructs you based on that person's firsthand experience; this is someone who has lived the life before—walked it, talked it, and breathed it.

Finding a mentor and learning from those who have come before you are some of the most important steps you can take in your real estate investing education, yet perhaps some of the most misunderstood. This section is going to focus on what a great mentor is and how to find one, and examine the question: "Should you pay for a mentor?"

Non-Real Estate Mentors in Your Life

In your life, who have been your mentors? We're not talking just real estate, but life in general. There are a number of different individuals who may have served in a "mentor" role at one time or another, such as:

- Parents
- Grandparents
- Older siblings
- Professors
- Bosses

Among all these mentors, there exists a common thread: an existing relationship with you. These individuals were first in our lives through an existing relationship, and the mentoring relationship grew organically out of it. It wasn't forced or manipulated. There was no formal "mentorship agreement" written ahead of time, no payment required for mentorship, no force. The only requirement was the relationship. we call this an "organic mentor," and we highly recommend finding one.

How to Find an "Organic" Real Estate Mentor

Newsflash: Mentors don't walk around with a sign hanging on their necks proclaiming their position (unless they plan on charging you tens of thousands of dollars). Instead, you'll find potential mentors by simply meeting people (also known as "networking"). Here are a few great places to find local mentors:

- **Local real estate networking events and clubs:** All over the country, in almost every major city, real estate investors gather frequently to network, learn, and encourage one another. You can find local meetups in your market by going to www.BiggerPockets.com/events or check out Meetup.com. Events may vary, as with many things in life. Some are excellent and some are just sales pitches, so be cautious but proactive in finding groups of real investors.
- **BiggerPockets Forums:** With more than 1,000,000 people hanging out in our forums, it's hard to believe that there isn't some local expert from your market engaging on the site.
- **Your current network:** Head over to Facebook and simply ask your family and friends, "Hey, does anyone know a landlord/flipper/real estate investor in XYZ area?" With 30,000,000 real estate investors in the United States alone, there is a pretty decent chance your Facebook friends know a few local investors.

Why Would a Mentor Help You?

For those who have been taught that the only mentors are the kind that cost $19,997.97, the concept of an organic mentor is a profound thought. After all, why would a seasoned professional real estate investor bother to help a newbie? You might think: *Won't I just be wasting their time?*

There are a variety of reasons why a seasoned real estate investor might choose to help a newbie, but the fact is, many do. Whether it's the dream of passing on a legacy, having someone with similar interests to talk with, or the potential for making future deals, organic mentorships happen each and every day. These mentorships are usually called by another name, though: friendships.

So, will they work with you? Can you really find someone willing to help show you the ropes? It depends on your attitude and how you approach the mentor. Many new wannabe investors tend to approach the relationship as if a potential mentor would be lucky to work with them. This entitlement attitude leads many of these individuals over to the BiggerPockets Forums, where they proudly announce that they are looking for a mentor to teach them all they know, but offer nothing in return other than the privilege of working with them.

Put another way: "Hi, my name is (so and so) and I'm looking for someone to invest a significant portion of their time and energy telling me how to get rich. I offer nothing to this relationship but expect you to jump at the chance because you probably have nothing better to do. Most likely, I'll just disappear once I realize I can't get rich overnight, leaving you exhausted and irritated. So, who's first?"

If you would like a mentor to come into your life, instead of your search being all about you and what you need, seek ways to grow a mentorship organically. Try these tips for building those relationships:

- **Focus on relationships:** Concentrate first on establishing relationships with seasoned investors whom you would like to learn from. A mentor doesn't need to be an internet celebrity. A mentor can be the investor down the street who owns half a dozen rentals and works a full-time job, or an active BiggerPockets member who donates his or her time to answering questions in the forums. The key is finding an individual you want to learn from in the field you want to enter. While you can glean a lot of information from any successful investor, attempting to build a deep mentorship with a mediocre house flipper—when all you want to do is buy and hold small multifamily properties—is probably not a great first step. Seek out individuals who are doing what you want to do.
- **Become valuable:** Make yourself valuable in a way that is meaningful (profitable) to the other person. What can you offer the other person you want to learn from? Do you have a free weekend that you can offer to help clean up a vacant unit? Do you have web design skills or cold-calling skills? Value is found in many different forms to many different people. Make it your goal to provide solid value to every relationship you have. Additionally, you don't necessarily need to do everything for free for that person. If you are handy, perhaps just being a dependable maintenance person who doesn't rip the would-be mentor off is enough to build that relationship. Maybe a well-designed website could be your value proposition. Whatever it is, remember: Provide value.
- **Don't expect anything in return:** You didn't build your early mentorships (parents, grandparents, etc.) by expecting something in

return. You built them because you were simply going through life. Provide value, and in return, you may receive something back—but don't expect it.

- **Always think win-win:** Don't simply focus on what's in it for you. Your mentor may be far more successful than you, but that doesn't mean you can't help that person become even more successful. As the popular phrase goes, a rising tide lifts all ships.

- **Work hard:** Most successful investors are willing to help, but only after you have proven that you are worthy of their involvement. A mentor does not want to waste their time. Being a mentor is a huge undertaking for both sides, and no one wants to devote a significant amount of time and effort building a relationship, only to have it fall apart when the student gets bored. Prove that you are in this for the long haul through persistence, building knowledge, and actively growing outside the relationship you are building.

- **Start small:** Imagine you are sitting at a bar, and you see a cute guy or girl across the room. You casually saunter over in their direction, hand them a drink, and loudly ask, "Hey! Would you like to get married and have four beautiful children together?" Hopefully your dating skills are better than this, and your mentor-seeking skills should be better as well. So rather than approaching a stranger with a huge request (like, "Will you be my mentor?"), start small: Ask a simple question about something you honestly need help with or clarity on (preferably a question that could easily be solved by searching Google). For example, when I (Brandon) found my real estate mentor Kyle, I simply asked him, "So how did you buy all these rentals?" Later I asked, "Do you have any local banks you like working with?" And still later, "What do you think of XYZ neighborhood?" These simple questions were easy for Kyle to answer and showed I was genuinely curious about his business. And remember: Almost everyone likes to talk about themselves. So ask questions about the person, not just about your own situation.

Should You Pay for Mentorship?

The role of a mentor is to make the journey from point A to point B a little quicker and a little easier. For many wannabe investors, paying for a mentor is the quickest and easiest way to find one. But should you? If you've been around BiggerPockets for any length of time, you'll understand that it is our core belief that you do not need an expensive paid mentor or guru to help you succeed. There is a vast amount of information out there, most of it free, that you can use to learn and grow as a real estate investor. Furthermore, places like the BiggerPockets Forums give you the ability to ask *almost any* question you want and receive answers back from many actual seasoned real estate investors. Think about it: There are more than 1,000,000 people on the site (and counting!), and many of them are active on our Q&A forums. So you can find some get-rich-quick guru and pay thousands of dollars for them to maybe answer your questions ... or you can just ask it for free and get answers from many of your peers who are active in the field. We tend to believe that the input of many is certainly superior to one person's opinion.

With that said, the choice to pay for mentorship or training is not always bad, and is 100 percent up to you. The role of a product or training from a guru should be to improve your processes and make your journey easier, not necessarily shorter. The theory is, if you spend $500 on a product that helps you achieve $1,000 in profit, then the product is worth it. The problem is that most individuals simply choose to buy a product looking for a shortcut and do not actually put into practice the lessons taught. Furthermore, most real estate gurus are not $500 ... they are more like $35,000.

Before you ever pay for training, we recommend that you first exhaust all options for finding a local mentor, as we discussed previously. A paid mentor will most likely be unfamiliar with the intricacies of your local real estate market, while a local mentor will usually have a much better grasp. If you cannot find a local mentor, seek out knowledge via books, forums, blogs, and other sources. Besides gaining knowledge and pointing you in the right direction, the quest will also help guarantee your full commitment. After all, you don't want to pay hundreds (or thousands) of dollars just to lose interest next week.

When you have a firm grasp on the type of investing you want to get into, then, and only then, should you consider paying for mentorship. Before you do, however, be sure to check out the Guru Review Forum on BiggerPockets, as well as the Better Business Bureau. Be very wary of shining online reviews from members who show up on a site just to defend some program (these are often paid members of the organizations themselves). Additionally, there are many gurus out there who simply exist to repackage free information and sell it for exorbitant amounts, claiming to have secrets or some new methodology. Do your research ahead of time to avoid working with these scammers.

Finally, before paying for a mentor or program, follow this one final step: Wait! Often, pitches and pressure applied from the individuals promoting a program are effective at striking the emotional nerve, and, as a result, can encourage you to buy out of fear or excitement, rather than prudence. Wait a few weeks to see if you are still as interested. Many times, when the daze from the salesperson's endless success stories wears off, the program is suddenly not as appealing. After all, there is a reason they want you to "sign up *today*."

Paid mentors can provide accountability ("I spent thousands ... I better make it worth it!") and good information that is neatly packaged for easy consumption. Many investors do find success working with paid mentors. Many others, however, do not. By focusing on finding local mentors, building your knowledge, and researching your potential paid mentor before paying, you are able to increase your chances of finding success and avoiding failure.

And finally, remember: There is not a product, coach, or mentor who can make you successful. That is strictly up to you. A mentor—paid or not—is merely a guide to help you navigate the path as safely and quickly as possible. The choice to do so is up to you.

Real Estate Networking

One of the most important marketing tactics you can implement today is networking. Networking is simply the process of getting to know others for the purpose of moving both individuals forward. It doesn't need to be a formal thing, but your day-to-day interactions should be part of your networking strategy. Networking often happens at an event, where dozens of people get together and mingle, exchange cards, and tell industry-specific stories. While, yes, this is a form of networking (most often seen at conferences and meetings), networking is actually a lifestyle.

Some of the most noteworthy connections you'll make will come from impromptu conversations about your real estate investing. We're not suggesting that you simply walk up to strangers and start telling them about your dreams and goals, but take advantage of talking about your business when the opportunity presents itself. You'll be surprised at how many people are interested in real estate and how often one quick mention of real estate leads to an entire conversation.

Not only is networking valuable for meeting people and businesses that can move your business forward, but it's also effective for building your real estate team (which we covered extensively earlier in this chapter). No person can succeed entirely on their own, so finding the best people to work with is one of the important tasks you can do at the start.

One of the best places you can start networking is your local real estate investing club. There's one located in nearly every major city. People gather at these clubs on a regular basis to discuss current market trends and investing strategies, to swap tenant horror stories, and to make connections. Many of the most important people on your team will probably come from your local investment club. These clubs can differ dramatically in size and quality, so if there are multiple clubs in your city, be sure to check them all out. For a list of local real estate investment clubs, see the BiggerPockets Events page. If there is a group in your area, check it out. If not, consider starting one. By starting your own networking group, you become the "hub" and the person everyone knows.

A final note on networking: Get yourself some professional business cards. While many aspects of "old time" marketing are fading away, the business card remains a staple in the real estate industry. Be sure that your business card contains the following information:

- Your Name
- Your Company Name
- Your Company Position Title
- Your Website
- Your Phone Number
- Your Email Address
- Your Wants/Needs if Applicable (We Buy Homes, or We Sell Properties, etc.)

Entities: LLCs, S Corps, and C Corps

Back in chapter one, we addressed the question, "Do I Need an LLC or a Corporation to Invest in Real Estate?" To summarize what we told you then, it's highly unlikely you'll *need* to have an LLC or a corporation at the beginning of your investment career, but you might *want one*, thanks to the potential asset protection (meaning, if you get sued, you won't lose everything) and possible tax benefits.

In this section, we want to dive a little deeper into the different entity options you have and explain why you might choose one over another. Keep in mind, each state has its own rules regarding entities, so we really do believe you should talk with an attorney and a CPA to help you set up the perfect structure for your business. The goal of this section is not to tell you exactly what to do for an entity, but to give you the whole picture so you know all the options and can make a decision for yourself—or at least you can ask the right questions of your attorney and CPA.

But let's first talk about why entities matter. For instance, you own a very nice fourplex and rent it to some nice tenants. You own this property as a "sole proprietor," which is a fancy way of saying you own it yourself, with no entities. Your personal name is on the title. When you refuse to fix the broken stair at your rental property, and your tenant falls and breaks their leg, they would be able to sue the owner of the property to collect damages. (Of course, you aren't going to be a slumlord, so you'll fix that stair, right?) While you better have insurance to cover this event, the penalty could end up higher than your insurance will cover, thus leaving the balance up to the owner. In this case, you could be stuck with a million-dollar bill and, if you don't have that cash just lying around, there goes your life. The courts take your personal house, your Tesla, your kids' Hot Wheels, and the big-screen TV you bought on Black Friday last year (in addition to forcing you to sell all your other real estate deals). Now, you and the family are living in a van down by the river, eating from garbage cans, and dreaming of the life you once had.

But what if the *owner* of that property wasn't you? What if a company owned the property, so when the company was sued, the company could file for bankruptcy, and the owner of that company could walk away without his other assets being affected. Little Johnny could keep his Hot Wheels collection and you could keep the TV. This is one of the primary reasons real estate investors set up entities: to separate assets in case one gets sued or something terrible happens. Of course, if you have adequate insurance, hopefully this will never be a problem. But you never know, and that's why we have entities.

Another reason for establishing an entity for your real estate business is to take advantage of possible tax benefits. We'll discuss this in more detail momentarily, as we explore each of the most common entity types. But know that the right entity could save, or cost, you a lot of money in taxes each year, so definitely consult with a CPA on the best strategy.

Entities also allow an owner to maintain strict separation between business and personal assets. One common mistake many new investors make is simply running all of their "books" through one checking account. They get paid from their job ... it goes into their personal checking account. They get rent ... and they deposit it into their personal checking account. They flip a house ... personal checking account. No, no, no! As an investor, you must maintain strict separation of business and personal assets, both for legal and common-sense reasons. A legal entity can help an investor "mentally separate" the two in their head, as it's very clearly a separate business.

Also keep in mind: If you have a legal entity and you *do* commingle funds (like using the business account to pay for personal stuff), a judge could declare that it doesn't really exist, and completely ignore all the legal separation you worked hard to create. This is known as "piercing the corporate veil," and you don't ever want that to happen. So keep your personal and business expenses separate, 100 percent of the time.

Finally, one more reason to establish an entity: Your lender might require it. This is far more common with commercial investments than residential. Some commercial lenders, including hard-money lenders for house flippers, will require that the property be held in an LLC or a corporation of some kind.

Interestingly enough, most residential lenders require the opposite. It's actually highly difficult to obtain a conventional residential loan (to buy a property with one, two, three, or four units) inside of an LLC or a corporation. They flat-out will not allow it. That's why many investors will purchase those residential properties in their own name (as a sole proprietor) and then, after the purchase, will transfer the property into their corporation. Seems simple enough, but this also presents some risk because of a clause in nearly every mortgage known as a "due on sale clause."

The due on sale clause essentially says, "Hey, if you sell your home, then you need to pay us back." This makes a lot of sense; if you sold your house, of course you should pay the bank back what it is owed. So why is the due on sale clause important in this discussion? After all, you may not think you are *selling* the property, you're simply *transferring* it into an LLC, right? Technically, yes; but in the eyes of the lender, a transfer into an LLC could be considered a "sale" and, thus, could trigger that clause. In fact, some mortgages specifically state that transferring to an LLC would violate the clause.

Does that mean you are breaking the law? Unlikely—it simply means that the bank would have the option of calling your note due and demanding that you pay them back. The key word there is *option*. Having your note called due is not a situation any investor wants to find themselves in, and, in truth, neither of the authors of this book have known anyone to whom this has happened. Many, many real estate investors purchase residential properties with conventional loans, transfer the property into an entity, and simply live with the potential risk. We can't say that a bank has never called the due on sale clause because of a transfer to an entity, but we haven't experienced it. Some argue that when interest rates begin to rise, banks will "encourage" borrowers to refinance and will begin causing a stink about all the entities. Definitely possible. Therefore, deciding whether to place your property into a legal entity will depend on the property, your attorney's advice, your CPA's advice, and your risk tolerance.

Next, let's dive into the most common entities one by one, so you can get a good overview of each.

LLCs

An LLC, short for limited liability company, is probably the most common entity used by rental property investors. The primary reason to set up an LLC is for asset protection, not tax benefits, because an LLC is known as a pass-through entity. In other words, the IRS requires that you "pass through" the income that an LLC earns, and it is accounted for on your normal personal tax return. (As opposed to a corporation, which may pay its own tax with its own tax returns.)

It's fairly easy to get started with an LLC, and it generally costs less than $800 a year to set up and maintain if you do it yourself, and much cheaper than that in some states. If hiring an attorney, you might spend $1,000 to $2,000 to set it up the first time, and then a few hundred bucks a year to maintain. There is ongoing maintenance required in the form of paperwork, and if you don't do it right, your entity might go bye-bye.

Furthermore, if your LLC has more than just your spouse inside of it (this is known as a multi-member LLC), you must file a separate corporate tax return for that business, which could add on a few hundred or even a few thousand dollars to your tax-prep fees each year. If it's just you, or just you and your spouse, no corporate tax return is needed.

When setting up your LLC, you'll also want to set up a bank account under that LLC, in addition to obtaining a FEIN number from the IRS. A FEIN number is like a Social Security number, but for businesses. It's free and mostly painless to obtain on the IRS website or through your CPA.

Corporations

Depending on your business type, your CPA or attorney might suggest that, instead of an LLC, you set up a corporation, probably for the tax savings. There are two primary types of corporations: C corporation and S corporation.

A C corporation is a legal entity that is taxed as if it were a completely separate person, and the tax rate is based on the government's corporate tax rate, which is currently a flat 21 percent at the U.S. federal level (in addition to any state corporate tax).[9] Then, any profits given to the investors or owners (namely, you) get taxed again at your regular tax rate. Yes, that means you might have to pay taxes twice on the income received. Doesn't sound ideal, does it? That's why most real estate investors don't choose the C corporation, except in unique circumstances. Instead, many "active" real estate investors (flippers, wholesalers, and other non-rental property investors) opt for the S corporation.

The S corporation is similar to a C corporation, except it allows the company profits to be "passed through" to your personal tax return, much like an LLC does. S corps are most common for active investors like house flippers and wholesalers because of some special tax benefits. When you invest in flips or other real estate that you hold on to for less than one year, in the eyes of the IRS, you are not "investing" in real estate, but rather you are "self-employed" in the business of real estate. As a self-employed business owner, you are responsible for paying "self-

---

9 www.taxfoundation.org/us-corporate-income-tax-more-competitive/

employment tax" (currently 15.3 percent)[10] on the money you earn.

We'll show you a real-life example of this—but first, let's look at how taxes are normally calculated when you make money in the United States. If you have a job, you've probably noticed that your employer takes out some money labeled "FICA tax" from your paycheck. This tax totals 15.3 percent of your earnings, split evenly between you and your employer. You are pitching in 7.65 percent, and your employer is paying 7.65 percent of your income toward this tax. The FICA tax was established to help fund Social Security and Medicare, primarily to financially help elderly and disabled Americans.

If you are a self-employed business (you are a consultant, you run a cleaning business, mow lawns, etc.), you don't have an employer to chip in half of the tax, so you are responsible for the entire 15.3 percent, which is commonly referred to as the "self-employment tax." Essentially, 15.3 percent of everything you earn as a self-employed individual is given to fund Social Security and Medicare. In addition, you'll also pay the normal state, federal, and local taxes, which will differ based on your tax bracket (income level) and location.

One final piece to the puzzle: Corporations can issue "dividends" to their shareholders anytime they like. It's basically a way for the company to distribute profits. This income is not subject to the FICA or self-employment tax (though some state/federal/local taxes probably do apply). This is important, so tuck it away in the back of your mind.

Now, back to real estate. If you invest in rental properties and hold on to them for many years, you are obviously not self-employed. It's an investment. There aren't a lot of reasons to put your properties into an S corp, but rather a lot of reasons why you shouldn't. However, if you buy and sell real estate while holding the properties for less than one year, the government considers you self-employed, and now an S corp could save you a lot of money. To illustrate this point, let's use an example.

Let's say you earned $100,000 this year from your house-flipping business. Besides the normal taxes due (state and federal, which we'll ignore for now), you also need to pay this self-employment tax of 15.3 percent. That's $15,300 out of your pocket.

Remember a few moments ago when we mentioned that dividends are not subject to self-employment tax? If so, you might be wondering:

---

10 https://www.irs.gov/businesses/small-businesses-self-employed/self-employment-tax-social-security-and-medicare-taxes

Why not just pay yourself the $100,000 all as a dividend and pay no self-employment tax? One reason: The IRS doesn't like that. You'll likely get audited, and they'll penalize you because you *are* working in the business. Dividends are, essentially, meant to be passive investment income.

So now we get to the fancy strategy that makes S corps popular. Many active investors choose to split their income into two parts: earned income (subject to self-employment tax) and dividends (not subject to the tax.) Essentially, they become an employee of their company and pay themselves a "reasonable" salary that would make sense if they were ever audited. In this example, you, the house flipper, might take that total $100,000 income and pay yourself a salary of $40,000 per year (which is subject to the 15.3 percent tax, or $6,120). The remaining $60,000 would be given out as a "distribution," which does not require the self-employment tax. So rather than paying $15,300 in self-employment tax, the investor would pay just $6,120, a savings of more than $9,000. (Remember, this is in addition to any federal, state, or local tax you might owe.)

As you can see in this example, choosing to operate your active real estate business inside of an S corp might be advantageous to you. But again, please consult with a CPA who specializes in helping real estate investors. There may be other strategies that will work better.

A Final Note on Entities

Here's the thing I've noticed: People like to set up entities because it makes them feel like they are taking action. They aren't. In fact, the idea of an LLC is probably the number-one excuse people have for not taking action. I see it almost every day on BiggerPockets. "I want to invest in real estate, but I don't know what to do about a legal entity." How absurd! The truth is: People use the "entity dilemma" as an excuse so they don't have to get out there and take action.

It's easier to say, "I don't have an entity yet, so I can't buy a property" than it is to say, "I'm scared." But this is often the truth. Yes, entities are valuable. Yes, they can help you reduce risk and save you money (when used correctly). Yes, we have them. Yes, we recommend talking with someone about setting one up at some point. But entities are no substitution for taking action.

Wrapping It Up

How are your ducks? All in a row? We hope so! And after a doozy of a chapter like this, it's a testament to your dedication that you are still with us. But getting those ducks in a row *is* important for the next stage of your real estate education: picking your niche. Let's go to Chapter Four and look at the different niches you can begin investing in. Chances are there are a lot more options than you realize.

CHAPTER FOUR
Real Estate Investment Niches

Have you ever received a box of chocolates as a gift over the holidays?

There are always so many choices, and sometimes you need to take a little bite of each one to figure out exactly what you're going to find inside. In a way, learning how to invest in real estate is like that box of chocolates. There are dozens (if not hundreds) of different ways to make money as a real estate investor, and it's up to you to choose the niche you want to get into.

You might absolutely love some niches, while others might make you shudder. However, unlike with that box of chocolates, as an investor you are able to get a full taste of the many different options available to you, and you can then choose the one(s) that you enjoy the most.

Best of all, you don't need to choose them all. Learning how to successfully invest in real estate is about choosing one niche and becoming a master of it. This chapter is going to open up that box of chocolates for you to sample and let you see some of the most common niches you can get into when investing in real estate. You'll discover the most common property types that you are likely to deal with as a real estate investor. Each of these has many subsets as well, but remember, you don't need to know them all. This is merely a list to help you begin to understand what options are available from a 20,000-foot view.

Raw Land
Raw land is, well, dirt.

Land on its own can be improved to add value, and it can be leased or rented to create cash flow. Land can also be subdivided (split apart) and sold as separate parcels for more profit. Some investors choose to buy raw land with hopes (or plans) that someday the land will become much more valuable because of external developments, like the construction of a freeway or from a development being built nearby.

SETH WILLIAMS

BiggerPockets Podcast ■ Episode 39

There are many ways to make money, especially when it comes to real estate investing. Seth Williams chose to take a road less traveled, and it has turned into a great opportunity for him. While most investors focus on houses or apartments, he went back to the basics: vacant land. After taking a home study course on investing in vacant land, he was amazed to see how simple and relatively inexpensive this strategy was. Rather than worrying about raising capital, expensive rehab costs, filling vacancies, and angry tenants, he just needed to have a good idea of how much a vacant lot was worth and then buy it at a low enough price that he could resell it quickly and make a profit.

How does he find these cheap land deals? He often starts by contacting the county office of his preferred location to buy in and requests a list of property owners who are close to losing their real estate due to unpaid taxes. He then mails these individuals, asking them if they would like to sell their property. If they respond to his inquiries, and the property looks like a good opportunity, he will make an offer to buy their property for pennies on the dollar. "I'm looking for apathetic landowners who want an easy button," Seth says. "They just want the property out of their life, and I'm offering them a convenient solution."

Once he purchases a property, he will turn around and sell the vacant land as quickly as possible. Not wanting to be stuck with a property for a long time, he often prices it well below market value to ensure a quick sale. "My goal is to turn around and sell it right away. If I have a property valued at $100,000, I might list it for $40,000 just to move it quickly. Since I'm buying these properties for such a low price to begin with, I can offer a better value than anyone else in the market when I sell, and I'll still make a very nice profit," Seth says. Typically, he can get properties sold within a month or two, and sometimes within a few weeks or even days. Many times, he will offer seller financing (which we cover in Chapter Eight) to sell his properties quickly, which also generates additional cash flow each month.

There are numerous benefits to investing in vacant land. One of the primary attributes that attracted Seth was the lack of competition. When fewer investors are in the space, Seth doesn't have to worry about the price increasing from a bidding war. In addition, Seth can often purchase vacant land at a much cheaper price than residential or commercial property, giving him the ability to buy these vacant properties outright with his own cash, without relying on a loan (thus, no monthly payments with high interest rates while the property is being resold). Finally, Seth loves land investing because he does not have to worry about renovations, tenants, and many other headaches that come along with residential and commercial properties. He just finds good land, buys it cheap, and sells it again.

- - - - - -- - - - - -

Single-family Houses

Perhaps the most common investment for most first-time investors is the single-family home (also known as a single-family residence or SFR). Single-family homes are relatively easy to rent, easy to sell, and easy to finance.

Benefits of single-family homes include:

High inventory: You can find single-family homes in almost every location on earth. There are hundreds of millions of homes, which means you shouldn't have a problem finding them. And people love to live in homes rather than apartments. For most people, especially Americans, living in a single-family home is the top of the real estate food chain.

Easy to understand: Chances are great that you live in a single-family home right now, or have in the past. And even if you haven't, understanding how they "work" is fairly straightforward. No one looks at a house and says, "But ... what is it?"

Easier to sell and rent: Because so many people want to live in single-family houses, these types of investments can often sell or rent much faster than other property types. For example, when I (Brandon) list a home for rent, it typically rents faster and for more money than my multifamily properties.

Financing is simple: Most banks can finance a single-family home without a lot of trouble because they do so many. In 2017, more than five million properties in the United States were bought and sold,[11] so banks have a lot of practice with this kind of financing.

Cash flow and appreciation: If you buy right, renting a single-family home can provide great monthly cash flow and tend to climb in value over time, resulting in your equity climbing higher and higher.

Simple to manage: A single-family home can be fairly simple to manage because there is just one tenant living inside. Generally speaking, we've also found that single-family houses tend to attract a higher caliber tenant who takes better care of the house.

Simple to rehab: Most contractors can handle remodeling a single-family house, and there are few surprises inside (despite what the flipping TV shows would have you believe). Sure, you might encounter some weird and/or dangerous things like aluminum wiring, asbestos, or a failing foundation, but even these are common in the world of construction problems. A local home supply store will likely have all the materials you would ever need to rehab a home, and for fairly low prices.

So what's the downside?

Well, first: scalability. A single-family home is just one property that will require its own financing, its own rehab, its own management. And *one* single-family house is unlikely to make anyone rich or provide true financial freedom. Therefore, if you buy single-family houses, it may take a large number of them to reach your financial goals. That's why many investors who start with single-family houses end up jumping into other, more scalable niches, as it can take about the same amount of work to buy a 50-unit apartment building as it does to buy a single-family house.

Another downside is competition. Because everyone wants to own or live in a single-family house, when you shop for homes you are competing not only with other investors but homeowners who are willing to overpay for properties because they are emotionally attached to the deal. This can make it tough to find great deals that actually produce the kinds of returns you want (tough ... not impossible).

---

11 www.nar.realtor/research-and-statistics/quick-real-estate-statistics

JOSH RANDALL
BiggerPockets Podcast ▪ Episode 242

Josh Randall owns and operates a printing company in Central City, Kentucky. Josh was working furiously to grow the business but was still having difficulty saving for retirement. His friend Tim Shiner (a successful business owner and real estate investor we interviewed on episode 221 of the *BiggerPockets Podcast*) convinced him to start investing in real estate, encouraging him to set lofty goals and reward himself generously once he achieved them. Josh took this to heart and set a goal and a reward: When he made $20,000 in real estate, he would buy himself a brand-new Corvette.

It wasn't long before he found and purchased a mini-mall in his area for $40,000. He sold it soon after purchasing it for $120,000, and made $80,000 in profit off the deal. He had partnered with his father, so they each walked away with $40,000. Josh got his Corvette, but more importantly, he found his future. He was hooked on real estate.

Having reached his first goal, Josh set a new goal: to retire by age 48 and to back out of his printing company. In order to do this, he would need to invest in a lot of deals, but working 12-to-15-hour days managing his 70 employees at the printing company didn't give him much time to focus on real estate investing. His solution was simple: Utilize the help of others. He currently owns about 50 houses and 40 apartments, and his wife helps him manage them. "It is actually easier to manage my properties than my 70 employees," he says. He also has built a small team around him, including a project manager to handle the management of his rehabs.

Having a solid team in place gives him the ability to buy a house about every four to six weeks. Initially he would look for deals by "driving for dollars" on Saturdays. Once he even knocked on the door of a house that he drove past on his way to and from work every day and asked the owner to let him know if he ever wanted to sell. The owner was willing to sell it to him on the spot. That same day Josh was talking to a coworker about the deal, and that coworker agreed to buy the house from him. He ended up wholesaling that deal for $10,000, which he used to buy a pontoon for his family. All it took were a couple of conversations and the courage to have them.

As time passed and Josh's portfolio grew, he became known around his area as "the guy who buys real estate." He now gives low offers but is still able to make a lot of deals because he doesn't need to buy, pays in cash, and is often the seller's last resort. Once he purchases the property, his team will fix it up and/or add additions to increase its value, and then he will quickly rent it out. He has no trouble filling vacancies and finds most of his tenants through a Facebook group that he created. He will often have a vacancy filled within an hour of posting on the group page.

To keep himself and his family sane, happy, and healthy with this heavy workload, Josh treats his family to frequent vacations, paid for by the properties. He even financed a brand-new Chevy Camaro for his wife by purchasing a house and using the cash flow to pay the monthly payments on it. Even after the car is paid off and has likely depreciated in value, he will still be making money off of the property.

--- --- --- --- --- --- --- --- --- --- --- --- ---

Small Multifamily

Small multifamily properties are any residential property that has between two and four units. Yes, that means a duplex, triplex, or four-plex (also known as a "quad"). These property types are slightly harder to find than single-family houses, but exist in almost every residential area of the world.

To a bank, small multifamily properties are no different than single-family houses. The same lending rules and guidelines that govern SFRs also govern small multifamily properties, as long as they don't have more than four units. This means that some of the great loan programs available for single-family houses are also available for small multifamily properties, including the ability to house hack, which we'll look at in the next chapter.

Furthermore, small multifamily properties can cash-flow quite well, assuming you don't overpay. And because fewer homeowners are looking to buy a small multifamily property to live in, there is often less competition than you'd run across bidding on single-family homes.

Another perk of the small multifamily property is the ability to take advantage of "economies of scale," as only one loan is needed to buy the two, three, or four units in the property. In other words, an investor can add up to four units to a portfolio with a single loan.

DARREN SAGER

BiggerPockets Podcast ■ Episode 48

Darren Sager was attending college when he learned that one of his professors was a real estate investor. Interested in this, he met with the professor outside of class and learned about real estate and the 1 percent rule (more on this later). After he graduated from Boston College in 1997 with degrees in both accounting and marketing, Darren immediately began to work for Deloitte in its real estate practice in Manhattan, wanting to gain as much knowledge as possible. Soon he made the jump and bought his first income property using a loan from his mother and a piggyback loan for the 20 percent down payment. With his mother as a cosigner on the primary loan, he purchased a duplex in Maplewood, New Jersey, for $235,000, with each unit renting out for about $1,200 per month. Darren quickly moved into one of the units, cutting his commute time by 66 percent. After learning that another duplex down the road from his was being rented out for a significant amount more, due to an added half bath, Darren moved out, added a half bath to each unit, and raised the rents to $1,600 per unit. He still owns that property today and rents out each unit for more than $3,000 per month. He enjoys figuring out ways to add value to property in the most cost-effective way.

After that first property, Darren focused on more properties with the plan to buy and hold them. He prefers multifamily properties that have three or more bedrooms in each unit—in the hopes that they'll attract longer-term families to reduce turnover—which are located within a short walking distance to train stations (a unique selling point for those who are commuting to New York City for work). He also looks for properties that need a lot of rehab, knowing he can get a much better deal when the property needs repair, and that he can, in turn, increase the rent of the rehabbed units and doesn't have to worry about larger capital expenditures if the home has been brought up to date.

Darren also understands that one of the largest expenses with many rental properties is the natural wear and tear from tenants. Therefore, when he rehabs a property, he chooses to go the higher-quality route and does his best to make it "tenant-proof." Examples of this include quartz countertops, porcelain tile floors, thicker drywall, soundproofing, and extra coatings of varnish on hardwood floors. While the outlay is more expensive initially, the amount he saves by not having to do as many repairs more than makes up for it. "We don't aim for trendy, we aim for timeless," he said. "We want our units to still look and function great 25 years from now."

Darren is currently renovating homes for resale, which is enabling him to purchase smaller multifamily homes near train stations. In addition, he's a full-time real estate agent who focuses on working with other real estate investors to find potential buy-and-hold investments as well as flip opportunities.

Large Multifamily

While small multifamily buildings are made up of between two and four units, large multifamily properties have five units or more. This could mean a simple $200,000 fiveplex or a $200,000,000 500-unit, A-class behemoth. Due to their size and cost, these properties can provide massive cash flow and potential for appreciation when they are purchased correctly. However, these apartment complexes typically require a larger down payment and net worth to purchase, and the loans can be difficult to obtain for those without significant real estate experience.

Instead of being priced based on the average amount that other apartments have sold for, the value of these properties is based on the income they bring in. This creates a huge opportunity for adding value by increasing rent, decreasing expenses, and managing effectively. These properties are a great place to utilize on-site managers who manage and perform maintenance in exchange for free or decreased rent.

ANDREW CUSHMAN

BiggerPockets Podcast ■ Episodes 170 and 279

Andrew Cushman was a chemical engineer for nearly eight years but had always wanted to be an entrepreneur. He and his wife attempted many small business ventures but nothing seemed to click—or make enough profit for them to leave their jobs. After stumbling on to the idea of real estate investing, Andrew and his wife decided to jump in. But it didn't come easy. Andrew explains that it took 4,576 phone calls to get his first deal. While most would have given up much earlier, Andrew (alongside his wife) persisted until he obtained his first deal. Having a strong belief in himself and his system, he knew that if he kept going and constantly improved his process, he would eventually reach his goals. Finally—success! Andrew purchased his first property, a condo flip, and after making more money from this deal than he did in a year at his job, he immediately decided to leave his job and do real estate full time.

After flipping 24 properties during their first four and a half years, Andrew and his wife decided to transition from house flipping to investing in apartment complexes. There was just one problem: They didn't know anything about investing in apartments. So Andrew went back to what he did when he started flipping houses—he approached a mentor and asked for help. Soon he was able to buy his first apartment building: a 92-unit residential complex that had low occupancy and needed a significant level of repairs. After a lot of hard work and money, Andrew was able to rehab the building and fill it with tenants, and discovered his true passion. Now, six years later, Andrew owns nearly 1,800 units.

Another key to Andrew's success was his focusing on building a strong team and a smooth system for rehabbing properties. After a little trial and error, they found a great general contractor who could complete the work exactly as they wanted (they do exist!), gave him autonomy, and paid him well. They then did the same with their real estate agent. "If I expect someone to perform really well for me, then I should pay them really well," Andrew wisely reasons. This strategy has worked effectively for them, freeing him and his wife up to be able to do what they do best: find amazing deals.

So how does one go about finding great deals on apartment complexes? Rather than placing thousands of cold calls like he did with the house flips, Andrew simply uses brokers. "These brokers have spent their lives building relationships with the owners of these apartment complexes," he says. "Why am I trying to replicate that? The more effective way is to build a relationship with that broker so that I can leverage his relationships."

Finding a great deal is one thing, but where does one come up with the money for these $1,000,000-plus apartment complexes? Andrew chose to go with syndication—a group of people who are willing to pool their money to obtain a property that they normally wouldn't be able to get alone, and then sharing the benefits. "I acquire the property, come up with the business plan, and then go to our investor pool and say, 'Alright, here's the property, here's the business plan, the projected returns, and we have this much equity available. You can invest from $50,000 up to whatever you want,'" explains Andrew. When the property is refurbished and released, Andrew either sells or refinances it with a bank, returning the investors' money with a healthy return and then holding for cash flow (which investors continue to receive as well). Then it's on to the next investment.

- - - - - - --- - - - - -

Commercial

Although larger multifamily properties can also be considered "commercial," what we're really talking about here is nonresidential commercial investments. These commercial investments can vary dramatically in size, style, and purpose, but ultimately involve a property that is leased to a business.

Some commercial investors rent buildings to small local businesses, while others rent large spaces to supermarkets or big-box megastores. While commercial properties often provide good cash flow and consistent payments, they also may carry with them much longer holding periods during times of vacancies; commercial property can often sit empty for many months or years. Therefore, commercial investments can require more experience and a stronger position of wealth to begin investing.

DAVID PUCHI

BiggerPockets Podcast ▪ Episode 253

As a lawyer in a Denver-area attorney's office, David Puchi jumped ship and began doing private legal work for a local real estate developer, learning the ins and outs of the commercial real estate world. Looking to diversify and increase his income, David capitalized on his experience and opened a commercial property management company, managing retail, industrial, and office buildings for investors. When one of his clients sold a building and began searching for another, David and his business partner teamed up with their client to purchase and manage the new building. The deal worked out well, so they continued to invest in commercial buildings together.

Eventually David discovered his niche, specializing in neighborhood shopping centers in Midwestern states. David believes that this is the "sweet spot" for commercial real estate investing because of the affordability, lower competition, and profitability. David makes a strong case for the viability of these shopping centers due to their "recession and internet-proof nature." Barbershops, gyms, nail salons, restaurants, liquor stores, and drive-through coffee shops are his ideal vendors because people still get haircuts, buy alcohol, work out, and drink coffee, even when the economy is bad. Furthermore, these types of businesses can fit in well in any neighborhood, whether poor or wealthy.

In addition to the recession-proof nature of strip malls, David also argues that they make a great investment because the properties typically come with a "triple net lease," meaning the tenants pay rent, their share of the taxes, and upkeep—such as parking lot and roof maintenance—as well as most other expenses that could pop up. Furthermore, David loves the stability and ease of tenant removal found with these retail shopping centers. "If they stop paying rent, we can essentially kick them out. Obviously, we will try to work with them if something came up like a death in the family or an illness, but if the business is just failing, then we can evict them pretty easily. Once a tenant is done, they're done. But that rarely happens. Typically, if the business is doing well, the last thing they are going to do is stop paying rent," he says.

His investing strategy focuses on purchasing C- or B-rated shopping centers owned by individuals who are nearing or are in retirement. He has found that often the owners are eager to sell because they would like to retire with the money, and their kids usually have no interest in running a shopping center. David uses a team of people who connect with brokers, owners, and other real estate professionals to find and manage these deals.

Once the shopping center is purchased, they then make renovations and bring in tenants that will help create synergy and high traffic volume. "The due diligence is absolutely huge," David says. "You have to make sure they fit your model. We have a 100-point due diligence list that we go through." Factors that David's team looks for include the ease of access, signage, traffic, the condition of the buildings and parking lot, and what the neighborhood looks like.

Mobile Homes and Mobile Home Parks

Mobile home parks, also known as trailer home parks, were popular to build in the middle of the last century, but fewer are being created today. However, a large segment of the U.S. population still chooses to live in this property type, as it is often the most affordable housing they can obtain.

There are several unique ways a person can invest in mobile homes, from renting to flipping, usually at a significantly lower price point than many other investments (often below $10,000 *total* for a mobile home). Many of the strategies used in other types of real estate investing can be applied to mobile homes, whether in a park or on their own land.

In addition to investing in mobile homes, many investors (including me, Brandon) today are investing in mobile home parks for a few powerful reasons, generally focused around the idea that with an ideal mobile home park, the tenants own their own homes and simply rent the land. This encourages the tenant to stay longer while decreasing the repairs required on the homes.

JEFFERSON LILLY

BiggerPockets Podcast ▪ Episodes 111 and 262

Jefferson Lilly worked for tech start-ups in the San Francisco Bay Area for a decade before taking the plunge into real estate. He had started investing in the stock market at the age of 17, and as an adult, he wanted to diversify his public market investments into real estate. While researching the potential of investing in small multifamily homes and apartments, Jefferson stumbled across mobile home parks and realized the potential was huge. He discovered that not only are the cap rates—the ratio of Net Operating Income (NOI) to property asset value— potentially higher, making the investment more profitable, but tenants inside tend to stay much longer than other residential rental properties. Tenants often own their mobile homes; thus, they are responsible for the upkeep of the proverbial "leaky toilets and leaky roofs," and park owners' repair and maintenance expenses are significantly lower.

Jefferson made contact with numerous mobile home parks nationwide as part of his industry research and created an "unofficial advisory board" of about ten park owners so he could ask them due-diligence questions. After 17 months of learning and searching, he purchased his first mobile home park. He continued to work his day job for the first year of owning this investment, but then switched careers to focus his efforts on being a full-time mobile home park investor.

Most of these homes are owned by the residents, but in one of Jefferson's more recent purchases, he and his team brought in several new mobile homes and offered new residents the option to begin renting-to-own mobile homes in his park. This is a win-win, because Jefferson and his investors receive monthly cash flow from these mobile homes and the tenants become homeowners in three to ten years.

Jefferson has now been investing in MHPs for 11 years. Along the way, he has scaled up by joining forces with a business partner and raising more than $20 million of equity. Together they have purchased 23 mobile home parks coast-to-coast (although most are in the Midwest) and are planning further expansion.

Private Notes

For those who have a bit of cash lying around, investing in private notes can be a great way to get your money working for you without needing to get your hands dirty. Rather than investing in a piece of real estate, you are investing in a piece of paper. Essentially, you are creating an IOU—officially known as a "promissory note"—to someone else, and each month that person (usually an investor, but sometimes a homeowner) pays you instead of a bank. So basically, with note investing you are the bank!

A note (combined with a document known as a "deed of trust") gives you, the lender, the right to receive monthly payments from the borrower until the loan is paid off. The note states all the terms that were agreed upon, and also gives you the legal right to foreclose on the property if the borrower stops paying. If you have ever purchased a home for yourself to live in, or an investment property, and you used a bank, you signed a promissory note in all that paperwork at the closing. If you stop paying, as millions of people did back in 2007–2012, the bank could foreclose and take back the property.

Interestingly, notes can be (and are, every day) purchased and sold just like physical real estate. Some investors' entire business is in the trading of private notes. Let's say you made a loan to a friend for $100,000 and he's been paying you 10 percent interest every year for a few years now. You can sell that note to me, an investor, and then I will receive that 10 percent each year (but paid monthly). Sometimes notes are purchased at a discount, depending on the condition of the payee. Imagine if your friend hasn't paid you anything in over a year and has refused to accept your phone calls about the money. Do you imagine I, a note investor, will want to pay full price for that note? I might, instead, offer you $80,000 for that $100,000 note, and take the risk that I can either get the borrower back on track with payments ... or maybe I'll foreclose, take the property, and sell it myself (though, that is generally not what note investors want to do, given the level of legal work required for such an action).

Private notes can be one of the most passive ways to invest in real estate as, ideally, your job is simply to collect a monthly check. Recently, a friend of mine (this is Brandon talking) wanted to flip a house, but he didn't have the cash. So I lent him $86,000 at an 8 percent interest rate. Each month he paid me $573.33 until the house was fixed up and sold. It was true "mailbox money" because all I did was walk out to my mailbox and deposit the check each month. (Until, of course, I switched him over to an automatic deposit into my checking account. Now that's passive!)

Note investing can be done on a one-to-one level or through larger institutions designed to facilitate such transactions. Perhaps a friend or colleague approaches you with the need for a loan, and you allow an attorney or title company to handle the note paperwork. Boom! You're a note investor. To learn more about note investing, be sure to pick up a copy of *Real Estate Note Investing* by Dave Van Horn at www.Bigger Pockets.com/store.

REITs

REIT stands for real estate investment trust. In the most simplistic definition, a REIT is to a real estate property what a mutual fund is to a stock. A large number of individuals pool their funds together, forming a REIT, and allow the REIT to purchase large real estate investments, such as shopping malls, large apartment complexes, skyscrapers, or bulk amounts of single-family homes. The REIT then distributes profits to individual investors. This is one of the most hands-off approaches to investing in real estate, but do not expect the high returns found in hands-on investing. You can buy shares in a REIT via your stock account, and they often have a relatively high dividend payment. If you invest in a REIT, you'll find it very similar to investing in a stock or mutual fund. In fact, they are almost indistinguishable.

Crowdfunding

Crowdfunding is a relatively new concept that has been growing rapidly over the past few years. Before crowdfunding, investors purchasing large real estate deals (like apartment complexes or commercial buildings) had to utilize banks to get loans, but often ran into trouble due to the complexity of borrowing from a bank. In addition, many banks refuse to lend on properties that are not in perfect condition, thus making it difficult to purchase many of the best deals out there. Crowdfunding has emerged as a solution for those investors, while also giving normal everyday people a method for directly investing in deals and, ideally, the ability to achieve higher-than-normal returns.

There are a variety of crowdfunding companies operating today, and each has a unique approach to how they operate and how they use investors' money. For example, some companies pre-vet each deal that comes through, where other sites allow any deal to show up on their platform. Some companies invest only in the "debt" side of the deal (meaning, the money you give them is only part of a loan, a promissory note, and your return is made from the interest on that loan). Other crowdfunders invest in the "equity" side of the deal as well, which means they also share in the profits from the deal after the deal is eventually sold or refinanced. Additionally, some crowdfunders allow anyone to invest inside the deals, while others only take investment money from accredited investors. An accredited investor is a distinction made by the U.S. Securities and Exchange Commission (SEC) as someone who is sophisticated and "rich enough" to invest in outside-the-box deals. Specifically, an investor is accredited if that person has a net worth of at least $1,000,000 (not including the value of their primary residence) or have income of at least $200,000 each year for the past two years (or $300,000 combined income if married) and plan to have the same income going forward.

The crowdfunding business changes often, and the field is relatively new, so we've decided not to include the names of the top crowdfunding companies here in this book. But head to BiggerPockets and check out our frequent resource updates for more information on crowdfunding!

Wrapping It Up

We just covered a lot of different real estate niches. But remember, as we said in the beginning, don't think that you need to master them all. The purpose of this book is to give you a variety of different options so you can make the best choice for you, your family, and your goals.

However, it's not enough to simply know about the different property types that an investor can buy. You need to do something with those investments. And for that, we need to move to the next chapter to talk about the most common real estate strategies. After all, it's not what you have, it's how you use it!

CHAPTER FIVE
Real Estate Investment Strategies

The year was 500 B.C. and the Persian army, which had conquered much of the known world, had a problem: The city of Babylon was in open rebellion against the Persian king and had successfully kicked out the Persians, regaining control of their city. After an unsuccessful siege lasting 18 months, the Persians decided they needed a change in *strategy* to win this war.

Enter: Zopyrus.

Zopyrus was a Persian nobleman who decided the only way to defeat the Babylonians was from the *inside*. But in order to gain their trust, he'd have to go to extreme measures. So one morning, Zopyrus showed up at the Babylonian city gates soaked in his own blood. That day, he had cut off his own ears, cut off his nose, and had himself whipped nearly to the point of death, blaming his leader, King Darius, for the horror show and convincing the Babylon leadership that he was defecting to the side of Babylon because of this supposed punishment from the Persian king. The Babylonian leaders bought the rouse hook, line, and sinker, inviting the mutilated man into their inner circle and eventually putting Zopyrus in charge of the army, allowing him to weaken their defenses, which led to the recapture of Babylon by the Persians.

In this case, as in many stories of war, the number of soldiers in the battle played a far smaller role than the *strategy* behind the soldiers. Sun Tzu, author of the military and business classic *The Art of War*, put it this way: "The expert in battle seeks his victory from strategic advantage and does not demand it from his men."

Numbers matter, but it's more about what you do with the numbers that determines victory or defeat. A sound strategy can lead to tremendous victory, and a weak strategy can cause ruin.

So, what does your strategy look like?

The previous chapter focused on a variety of investment niches that you can use to invest in real estate, from single-family homes to commercial properties to notes and more. However, when learning how to invest in real estate, it is not enough to simply *know* what these property niches are. You need to know what you are going to *do* with them to make money. As an investor, you will use a variety of strategies when dealing with these investment niches to produce wealth. This chapter will explore some of the most popular and powerful ones.

Buy and Hold

Perhaps the most common form of investing, the "buy and hold" strategy involves purchasing a property and renting it out for an extended period of time. It's probably the most simple and purest form of real estate investing there is. This can be done with single-family houses, apartments, mobile homes, commercial buildings, retail spaces, industrial centers, and much more.

Essentially, a buy-and-hold investor seeks to create wealth by accessing most or all of the four "wealth generators" of real estate:

1. **Cash flow:** When you buy and hold real estate, most investors want to see a monthly profit, known as cash flow. This means, if the unit rents for $5,000 per month and all of the bills add up to $4,000, the investor keeps $1,000 in cash flow each month.

   Although it's entirely possible to invest in buy-and-hold real estate without cash flow, and many do, I don't recommend it. Some investors may choose to forgo cash flow and instead rely on the hope that the prices will skyrocket over time. While this can, and has, worked, this kind of investing—known as speculation—is best left to individuals who have deep pockets.

2. **Appreciation:** The second reason to buy and hold real estate is for the appreciation. No, we're not referring to the admiration of the building (though we do appreciate a good deal). Instead, we're talking about the fact that real estate tends to rise in value over time. This increase is known as appreciation, and it's one of the

greatest wealth generators on earth. In January 1988, the median price for a new house in America was \$119,000.[12] Thirty years later, in April 2018, it's \$314,400.[13] That 264 percent increase is known as appreciation, and it's largely driven by inflation. (After all, in 1988, milk was \$1.89 a gallon, a movie ticket was \$3.50, and a new car was \$10,400.[14] Those were the days!) But appreciation isn't just based on the natural rising of prices in an economy. It's also based on supply and demand, and can also be forced up by making the right repairs to a property.

3. **Loan paydown:** Imagine a simple real estate deal: You purchase a home for \$200,000 that provides no cash flow and no appreciation. Each month you break even on the deal, and in 30 years, the house is worth exactly what you paid for it. Not a great investment, is it? However, what if, when you bought the property, you took out a loan from a bank that slowly pays off that \$200,000 over the course of 30 years, the typical length for most mortgages in America. At the end of 30 years, how much "equity" do you have in the property? That's right—\$200,000. Because although the price of the property has not increased at all (which is unlikely, but this is hypothetical), and even though you've made no profit during those 30 years, at least the loan is paid off and now you owe \$0 on a property worth \$200,000. This is a good example of the third wealth generator of real estate: the loan paydown. Essentially, if you have a loan on a property, the balance is being paid down each and every month by the money your tenants are paying you. Of course, hopefully, you don't buy real estate that never produces a profit, but this simple example illustrates how the loan paydown benefit works!

4. **Tax benefits:** Finally, there are significant tax benefits to owning real estate that may offset your regular income from a job. For example (and without trying to drown you in tax laws), your rental properties may earn you a slight profit each month, but on paper (legally) the IRS may see that property as a loss due to something known as "depreciation." Depreciation is, essentially, the government requiring you to "write off" a certain portion

---

12 www.census.gov/const/uspricemon.pdf

13 www.census.gov/construction/nrs/pdf/newressales.pdf

14 www.thepeoplehistory.com/1988.html

of the properties, even though you never actually spent that money. Depending on your current income level and tax situation, this "paper loss" might help you pay less taxes from your day job, but be sure to consult with a CPA for more specifics of your situation. In addition, income received from rental properties is taxed differently than income earned at a job or from being self-employed. For example, if you made $100,000 from your job as an underwater basket weaver, your mom made $100,000 from her self-employed business of selling water buffaloes, and Bob earned $100,000 in income from buy-and-hold rental properties, who do you think gets to take home more money? That's right: Bob.

Buy-and-hold investing, when you buy the right deal, can incorporate all four of the strategies into one powerful investment.

The largest downside with this plan, however, is that it takes *time*. No one gets rich overnight, as sometimes wealth can take decades to build with this strategy. And sometimes the market does decline in value, and the house you paid $200,000 for might be worth $150,000 the next year. But for a true buy-and-hold investor, the market declines are just part of the picture. If history has anything to teach us, it's that the market will always climb back.

Ultimately, there is much more to buy and hold than meets the eye, but if you can learn how to evaluate and buy good deals, find quality tenants, and manage properly, you're going to be on your path to running a successful business. To learn more about the buy-and-hold strategy, be sure to pick up a copy of *The Book on Rental Property Investing* by Brandon Turner.

TIM SHINER

BiggerPockets Podcast ■ Episode 221

Tim Shiner is what some would call a go-getter. He loves to make lofty goals and achieve them. As a teenager, he created the goal to be a homeowner by the age of 20, and he achieved this goal by purchasing his first home at age 19. It was a cheap two-bedroom, one-bathroom house in a shady part of town that ended up getting robbed twice, but buying that home taught him two things: the value of real estate investing and that it is better to invest in higher-quality properties, which won't have as many problems.

Tim owned a company selling high-end security equipment, and even though that paid the bills, he wanted to increase his streams of income. "My goal is to have as many checks coming in the mail each month as I can," he says. One of his preferred streams is investing in high-end real estate in areas that are going to appreciate quickly.

Tim claims there are three ways to make money in real estate. You can buy it for a low enough price to make it a great deal, which occurs only once; do debt reduction, which takes 20–30 years; or utilize appreciation. Tim chooses to focus mostly on appreciation. For example, over time he bought $5,000,000 worth of property in Southlake, Texas, and it appreciated 20 percent last year, netting him $1,000,000 in increased net worth. Many investors warn about the dangers of focusing only on appreciation, because property values can tank if the market crashes, but Tim disagrees. "The iconic areas are always going to go up," he says. The secret, according to him, is to invest in properties in neighborhoods that have great school systems and are likely to continue to grow over time.

Tim buys high-end single-family homes in booming towns and rents them out to wealthy families who are moving to that area because of the great school system. Tim knows many of his tenants plan to eventually purchase their own home, so he makes an arrangement with the families who rent from him that he will cancel their lease if they decide to purchase a house through his wife, who is a real estate agent. "They are going to leave me either way," he says. "I would prefer that they leave and give my wife 3 percent commission rather than leave and we get nothing."

In addition to owning high-end single-family homes in Texas, Tim also invests in lower-income areas that are likely to appreciate over time. During the recession, he began to invest in rural towns in Kentucky on account of the lower purchase prices. Since then, he has purchased many properties, including a 24-unit apartment building, a 27-unit apartment building, a 24-unit trailer park, and a 48-unit apartment building, as well as a few single-family houses and other businesses. Tim currently owns 153 properties and plans to hold on to them. His two children plan to get their real estate licenses when they turn 18 and join the family business.

Buy-and-Hold Math

You don't need to be a college calculus student to understand buy-and-hold math. In fact, most of the math you'll need is grade-school level. This section is going to quickly touch on some of the basic terms and math formulas you'll need in your buy-and-hold investing career, including some simple rules of thumb that you can start implementing right away.

Income

Income is the amount of money that comes in from a property. This math is perhaps the easiest of all: Simply add up the amount of rent and any additional fees that come in.

For example, you own a rental house. The home rents for $1,000, and the tenant also pays $25 for the use of the garage. Your total income is $1,025. Income could also include late fees, application fees, pet fees, laundry or other vending machines, or any other value you receive from your rental.

Expenses

Expenses are simply the things that cost you money on an investment. For example, the garbage bill for a home is $50 per month, the loan from the bank is $500 per month, and maintenance is $100 per month. The total of these three expenses is $650.

Keep in mind that there are many other expenses you'll face as a real estate investor, such as taxes, insurance, management, holding costs, and capital expenses.

Cash Flow

Cash flow is the amount of money left over at the end of the month after all expenses are paid. To determine the cash flow, subtract the total expenses from the total income:

For example, on the fictional property we've been discussing, the income we saw was $1,025, and the expenses were $650. This means that the total cash flow in the above example property is $375 per month, because:

$$\$1,025 - \$650 = \$375$$

Equity

Equity is the term used to describe the difference between how much a property is worth and how much debt you have on the property. For example, if you own a house that is worth $100,000 and your current mortgage is $70,000, you have $30,000 of equity because:

$100,000 - $70,000 = $30,000

(Of course, this isn't to say you would necessarily make $30,000 if you sold the property, as you would encounter several thousand dollars in expenses if you sold, including closing costs and real estate agent fees.)

Total Return on Investment

Your Total Return on Investment (also known as Total ROI) is a fancy way of describing the percentage of your investment you are making back on your money from the start to the finish.

For example, if you invested $100,000 and made back $10,000 in profit (thus ending up with $110,000), that would be a 10 percent ROI.

Or another example: If you invested $250 and you made $250 from that investment (for a total of $500) over the course of one year, you would have made a 100 percent ROI (return on investment).

Now let's get a little technical, but stick with me on this. It's actually much easier than it might first appear when we start using "math teacher talk."

The actual calculation for return on investment looks like this:

$ROI = (V_1 - V_0) / (V_0)$

V_1 is the ending balance and V_0 is the starting balance.

A simple example for using this ROI equation to calculate an investment return would be as follows: On January 1, you put $1,000 into a bank account. Five years later on January 1, you cash out the account for $1,500. Your ROI on the investment is:

$ROI = ($1,500 - $1,000) / ($1,000) = .50$ (or 50%)

You start with $1,000 and end up with $1,500 after five years for a return of 50 percent. However, because total return on investment doesn't look at the length of time you hold an investment, it's rarely used. After all, is a 10 percent total return good? Well, if you got that in six days it would be amazing, but six years? Not so much! For that reason, total return is often looked at as an annual percentage, known as annual return on investment.

Annual Return on Investment

We're getting a bit into the weeds, so if you aren't a math nerd and you want to skip this short section and head down to "Cash on Cash Return," feel free.

But for those who really want to know, the annual return on investment is similar to the return on investment we just looked at, but it takes a look at the entire, total return on investment and determines exactly what kind of annual return you would have received each year to achieve the total return. In other words, it's useful in looking at an investment after it has been paid out completely and finished, so you can see how it compares to other investments you might have made. While it seems you could simply take the total return and divide it by the number of years, this is incorrect (though, admittedly, what most investors actually do). The true and correct way to calculate annual return on investment is confusing and next to impossible to do without a fancy calculator because the equation is:

Annual Return = (Ending Investment / Beginning Investment) ^ (1 / # of years) − 1

So if you invested $1,000 and, after five years had made an additional $500 for a total of $1,500 (the same numbers we used earlier to discuss total return), we would see the following:

Annual Return = ($1,500 / $1,000)^(1/5) − 1

= 0.08447 or an 8.45% Annual Return.

If you aren't confused enough yet, let us further muddy the waters: Typically, when someone says *return on investment* in conversation, they are actually referring to *annual return on investment,* but these two terms are not the same, which is why we like to differentiate between them. Furthermore, sometimes when someone says return on investment they are actually referring to the cash on cash return on investment.

Cash on Cash Return on Investment

Similar to return on investment, cash on cash return on investment (also known as COCROI or just cash on cash return) is the interest that you receive on the cash flow from an investment, not other pieces of potential profit or losses like appreciation, the loan being paid off, or the tax benefits.

So, the equation is simply:

Cash on Cash Return = Annual Cash Flow / Total Investment

Let's do a really basic example together, to make sure we're all on the same page with this:

John bought a duplex as a rental property and, in total, he invested $100,000 to buy the property, including repairs and closing costs. In the first year, John received, in cash flow, a total of $12,000. So his cash on cash return was 12 percent because:

Cash on Cash Return = Annual Cash Flow / Total Investment

Cash on Cash Return = $12,000 / $100,000

.12 = $12,000 / $100,000

These simple concepts present the foundations upon which almost all other real estate calculations are based. The rest will come in time, but most calculations are related to these.

The Buy-and-Hold Rules of Thumb

There are some rules of thumb that investors can use to quickly screen through deals to make guesses on whether to pursue them or not. But an important disclaimer here: Notice that we did *not* say "There are some rules of thumb that *can help investors make purchase decisions.*" Because rules of thumb are *not* meant to be hard-and-fast rules. They simply help an investor get a quick-and-dirty opinion on some valuable metrics. Here we've outlined several of the most common real estate math rules of thumb so you can begin practicing them in your own analysis of properties.

The 2 Percent Rule (aka the "1 Percent Rule" or the "2 Percent Test")

Perhaps one of the most common rules of thumb used by rental property investors is commonly known as the 2 percent rule, but because it's not a "rule," we like 2 percent test better. Essentially, this rule of thumb looks at the monthly rent divided by the value, in a percentage form. For those who just got confused, let's make this super simple:

If a property rents for $2,000 per month, and the value is $200,000, then:

$2,000 / $200,000 = 1%

In this example, the property does not pass the 2 percent test, but it does meet the 1 percent test exactly.

Or what if it's a property that rents for $1,500 per month and costs $180,000 to buy?

$1,500 / $180,000 = .8%

This definitely falls short of the 1 percent test.

Or what if the property rents for $1,500 per month but is worth $120,000?

$1,500 / $120,0000 = 1.25%

Okay, so you get how the math works, but what does it mean? The 1 or 2 percent test gives us a quick view on whether or not the property will produce positive cash flow. Of course, as it's just a rule of thumb, it isn't always precise, but generally speaking, the higher the percentage, the better the cash flow. This also depends greatly on location, price, and how much the expenses truly are on the property. But the rule of thumb can help an investor make some decisions on whether or not to pursue a property.

For example, we know that most properties that fall short of 1 percent will likely never produce positive cash flow. If it's between 1 and

2 percent, they probably will. And if it is above 2 percent, we're almost positive they will.

So, if a real estate agent tells us that they have a perfect rental house for us to buy, and we see that the purchase price is $125,000 and we find that it will rent for $1,000 per month, we can make a very quick decision and know that, most likely, the deal won't provide cash flow because it falls short of 1 percent:

$1,000 / $125,000 = .8%

In a case like this, we probably won't spend much more time looking at the deal if we were only interested in cash flow.

The 50 Percent Rule

While the 2 and 1 percent rules of thumb we just mentioned can help you make a "go, no-go" decision on whether or not to look further into a rental property, it doesn't really tell us how much cash flow we might expect. For that, investors often rely on the 50 percent rule of thumb.

The 50 percent rule states that, on average and over time, half of the income a property generates is spent on operating expenses. "But what are operating expenses?" you ask. Good question! Operating expenses are all of the expenses involved with running a rental property— except the loan payment. It includes taxes, insurance, utilities, repairs, vacancy, and other metrics that leave the landlord's checking account each month or year. The 50 percent rule can help an investor quickly estimate the cash flow of a rental property because it combines all of the expenses, except the loan payment, into one easy number: half.

Imagine a property rents for $2,000 per month. The 50 percent rule says that half of this, $1,000, will be spent on expenses. This means we're left with $1,000. But then we need to make a mortgage payment on the property (unless you paid cash for it). With the $1,000 remaining, let's say the mortgage payment is $600. How much do you have left? $400.

$2,000 x 50% = $1,000

$1,000 - $600 = $400

That remaining value, $400, is your estimated cash flow.

Of course, that 50 percent estimate on operating expenses can vary wildly, depending on the property. In some areas, taxes and insurance might be incredibly high, but in other areas, they might be much lower. Some properties require that the landlord pay all of the utilities, where other properties allow the tenants to pay their own. These and other property-specific details demonstrate the weakness in the 50 percent rule.

And while inherent weaknesses do exist, the 50 percent rule does have value. When you are looking at a property that rents for $1,200 per month and you know the mortgage payment would be around $1,000, you can almost guarantee that the property won't produce a positive cash flow, because $200 is not a lot of "room" for all those expenses.

$1,200 x 50% = $600

$600 - $1,000 = -$400

The 50 percent rule helps keep real estate investors in check and reminds us that there are numerous expenses that, over time, add up. Yes, a new roof is only needed every 20 years, but if you divide a $10,000 roof into 240 months, that roof is actually costing you $42 every single month. These operating expenses add up and, as most investors have seen, they tend to settle around 50 percent given a long-enough time frame.

An Easier Way to Analyze

At this point, unless you are a math nerd like we are, your eyes are probably glossing over and you are looking for the nearest exit sign. But wait! We want to show you an easier method for analyzing deals that makes life much easier: The BiggerPockets Real Estate Investment Calculators. At BiggerPockets, we created a set of calculators for real estate investors to use that make running all of the numbers, including the above calculations (and many more calculations) significantly easier, faster, and with less chance for error. Try it today at www.Bigger Pockets.com/analysis.

What Kind of Metrics Should You Aim For?

Whenever we discuss cash flow, return on investment, cash on cash return, or any other similar metric, we inevitably get the question, "Okay, but what's a good number to shoot for?"

And that's an incredibly difficult question to answer for other people, because everyone has their own rules and requirements. What might make you happy could be very different from what makes either of us happy. Ultimately, the metric you should aim for is the metric that helps you accomplish your long-term goal. But let us try and clarify.

When I (Brandon) want to buy a property, I primarily look at four separate metrics and try to aim for all of the following:

- **Cash flow:** For a single-family house, I try to achieve $200 per month in cash flow; for a multifamily property, I aim for $100 per month, per unit (so a fourplex should make at least $400 per month in cash flow). Keep in mind, however, that this is applied to properties that I can purchase relatively cheap. If I bought a million-dollar home, it better provide more than $200 per month in cash flow.

- **Cash on cash return:** Over the past 100 years, the stock market has averaged a return of 6 to 7 percent.[15] I decided to almost double that and aim for around a 12 percent cash on cash return.

- **Equity:** I don't like owning real estate that has no equity. If the market dips, I want to be sure I'm not going to be "underwater," where I'll owe more than the property is worth. Therefore, I aim for a minimum of 20 percent in equity in any deal I do. If the property is worth $100,000, I don't want to owe any more than $80,000. This can be done in one of two ways:

  - I could find a really good deal that I can purchase (and rehab) for 80 percent of the value.
  - I could put up a down payment of 20 percent, giving me the required equity.

- **Total return on investment:** Finally, I try to average around 15 percent per year, or more, over the life of a real estate deal. Remember: This includes the profit when I sell the property someday. I might get only a 12 percent return each year from cash flow, but if I sell the property for a profit down the road (as the property rises in value and the loan is paid off), I want to average 15 percent each year when I look back (or when I estimate forward).

---

15 www.thesimpledollar.com/where-does-7-come-from-when-it-comes-to-long-term-stock-returns/

Again, this doesn't mean you must hit each of these metrics for the deal to be great. Maybe you are 100 percent happy with an 8 percent cash on cash return, or maybe you need 17 percent. Maybe you'll buy a house only if it can give you $500 in cash flow, or maybe you'd be fine with $100. The point is: Establish some metrics so you can take the emotion out of doing a real estate deal. It's just a numbers game.

House Flipping

One of the most popular tactics for making money in real estate quickly, due largely to the numerous shows on cable TV that promote it, is flipping. House flipping is the practice of buying a piece of real estate at a discounted price, improving it in some way, and then selling it for a financial gain. Some argue that house flipping is not even investing but simply a business, as it more closely resembles the "buy wholesale, sell retail" model of most retail businesses like clothing, toothbrushes, cars, and almost everything else a person can buy. But because it involves the buying and selling of houses, we'll include it under the real estate investing umbrella.

The most popular type of property to flip is the single-family home, and one of the key factors in flipping a house is speed. A house flipper will attempt to buy, rehab, and sell the property as quickly as possible to ensure maximum profitability and to avoid many months of expensive carrying costs. These carrying costs include monthly bills such as financing charges, property taxes, condo fees (if applicable), utilities, and any other maintenance bills required to keep the house in good financial standing.

Flipping is not a "passive" activity, but instead is just like an active day job. When an investor stops flipping, they stop making money until they begin flipping again. Many investors choose to use flipping to fund their day-to-day bills, as well as provide financial support for other, more passive investments. In other words, flipping houses can help you make big money to invest in other deals.

How to Flip Houses: Step by Step

1. Do your market research
Take a look at the market and decide where the best place to flip will be.

In some areas, $200,000 for a home would be absurdly cheap, where in other areas this $200,000 would be absurdly expensive. Every market is different, so you need to have a good handle on the market you plan to flip in. Ask yourself these questions:

- How much are average homes selling for?
- How much are bank real estate owned properties selling for?
- How fast are properties selling?
- What areas seem to be selling the fastest?
- What property types/sizes/layouts seem to be selling the fastest?

Do a thorough job of understanding and honing in on your local market. Walk through as many open houses as you can, and meet with local experts to discuss the state of the local economy.

2. Arrange your flip financing

At this point, I know you are excited to get started, but let's not put the cart before the horse. You first need to ask yourself a very basic question: *How am I going to pay for this flip?*

There are many different strategies you can use to finance your next house flip. Here are a few of the more common methods:

- **All cash:** If you have the cash in your bank account, you can simply write the check. This is obviously the easiest solution, but for most folks, this is not likely.
- **Conventional financing:** Some people utilize a normal bank loan to flip houses, but this can be difficult if the house is not in great shape (most banks won't lend on unfinished homes).
- **Home equity loans/lines:** If you have a large amount of equity in your personal home, you may be able to tap into this equity in the form of a home equity loan or line of credit. If you are interested in more of these strategies, talk to your local bank or credit union.
- **Hard-money lenders:** A hard-money lender is a private individual or company that lends on high-risk loans (like flips), and charges high fees and interest to get the money. Hard-money loans are ideal on flips because they typically have a one-year-or-less maturity date.
- **Partners/private money:** If you know people who have money to lend, they may be interested in partnering or lending their cash

at a certain interest rate. Private money can be one of the cheapest sources for funds, though raising private money can be difficult and legally cumbersome.

- **Combination:** Finally, you can mix and match nearly all of the above methods to finance your next flip.

You have a lot of different options, but you'll need to pick one in order to move on. Finalize whatever source you plan on using *before* shopping for your investment property. Try to get a loan commitment if you plan on using any of the loans listed above, so that when you find a property, you can quickly jump on it. In today's hot market, speed is key in getting a great deal.

3. Learn to run the numbers

One of the fun things about flipping is the ability to work backward from the future sales price (the "ARV"—after repair value) to determine exactly how much you can pay for a potential deal. J Scott, author of *The Book on Flipping Houses*, calls this process the Flipping Formula, and it looks like this:

ARV – Rehab – Fixed Costs – Desired Profit = Max Purchase Price

In this case, fixed costs are items like the costs associated with holding on to the property, purchasing the property, and selling the property. So, for example, let's assume we are looking to flip 123 Main Street. Based on information on other similar properties that have sold recently, we believe the ARV to be $300,000. We have determined that the rehab should cost about $50,000 and that the fixed costs will run about $30,000. We have decided to try and earn $35,000 on this flip. Therefore, our flip formula looks like this:

ARV – Rehab – Fixed Costs – Desired Profit = Max Purchase Price

$300,000 - $50,000 - $30,000 – 35,000 = $185,000

For the above example property, we could pay $185,000 and, assuming all our numbers turn out to be accurate, walk away with $35,000 in pretax profit at the conclusion of the flip.

4. Find a great deal

Now that you know how to identify a great deal and how you'll finance it, it's time to begin finding leads and working your system to buy an incredible deal. We'll talk about this system in more detail, as well as 27 different ways to find deals, later in Chapter Six.

5. Fix and flip it

Finally, after you land a great deal, it's time to get the contractors into the property to fix it up on budget and on time. When flipping houses, there are numerous variables to control and things often go wrong, so it's vital that the flipper stays on top of the people, the process, and the profit throughout the flip. Then it's time to sell the home for top dollar and hopefully reap the rewards when the home is sold.

J SCOTT
BiggerPockets Podcast ▪ Episodes 10 and 63

J Scott, along with his wife, Carol, both worked corporate jobs in Silicon Valley, but when it was time to start a family, they knew the 100-hour workweeks just couldn't continue. So the couple packed up their stuff and moved home to Atlanta without a plan for how they would make it financially. But they quickly discovered the incredible power of house flipping. After working with a shady wholesaler for six months in 2008, J and his wife finally purchased their first flip. But things didn't go as smoothly as they do on the television shows.

"It did not go well," J says. "We made pretty much every mistake a rehabber could make. First, we paid too much. We knew we were paying $5,000 more than we wanted, but we were desperate to buy something and didn't negotiate very well. Then we spent $10,000 more on the rehab than what we anticipated. We put it on the market, but we gave up selling it after six weeks. It was the middle of winter, we didn't know what we were doing, and we freaked out a little bit." J ended up doing a lease option on the property, until the potential buyers trashed the place and moved out in the middle of the night. Ultimately, J did a second rehab on the house and sold it, making a very tiny profit for a whole lot of work. A hard lesson, but they learned from their mistakes and continued their flipping dreams with renewed vigor. Soon, J and Carol were flipping dozens of homes each year.

J and Carol quickly decided they needed help to scale their business, so they hired a project manager to oversee the projects. They also reformed how they operated, dividing the company into three segments: acquisition, rehab, and marketing/sales. J, who is a self-proclaimed "numbers guy," focuses on finding and acquiring the properties; his project manager (who works on base pay plus commission) handles the rehab; and his wife runs the marketing and selling of their properties. J believes that some of the keys to their success are their emphasis on finding a great deal, keeping rehab costs down, and then selling their properties a little cheaper than their competition. The quicker they are able to sell their properties, the quicker they can turn around and acquire more.

When asked what advice he would give to first-time house flippers, J wisely states, "You need to come up with a plan and write it down on paper." He explains that it doesn't have to be fancy, but writing it down does three things. First, it gets you to really think about whether you actually want to follow through with the project. Second, it forces you to figure out the financial piece—where is the money going to come from? And third, it helps you visualize your gaps—in which areas are you deficient and will need help with?

J also has gone on to write an incredibly popular series of real estate books, *The Book on Flipping Houses*, *The Book on Estimating Rehab Costs*, and *The Book on Negotiating Real Estate*, helping tens of thousands of others learn how to flip houses as well.

- - - - - - ━━━━━━━━━━━━━━━━━━━━━━━━━━━ - - - - -

The 70 Percent Rule for House Flipping

Earlier in the chapter, we looked at a few rules of thumb for buy-and-hold investors. But what about house flippers? For them, the 70 percent rule can be helpful in determining just how much to pay for a property.

The 70 percent rule states that the most you should pay for a potential flip is 70 percent of the after repair value (ARV)—what it would sell for when it's all fixed up—minus the repair costs.

So, if a home would sell for $300,000 all fixed up, and the property needed $50,000 worth of work to get it there, then:

$300,000 x 70% = $210,000

$210,000 - $50,000 = $160,000

According to the 70 percent rule, the most someone should pay for this property would be $160,000.

But there are problems with the 70 percent rule. This rule of thumb assumes that 30 percent of the ARV will be spent on holding costs, closing costs (on both the buyer's and seller's side, such as commissions, taxes, attorney fees, title company fees, and more), the flipper's profit, and any other charges that come up during the deal. This works well in many markets, but it has severe limitations.

For example, the 70 percent rule doesn't work as well for a property with a low ARV, such as $50,000. As mentioned earlier, the 30 percent deducted from the ARV includes the holding costs and closing costs, as well as the profit the investor or flipper wants to make. However, 30 percent of $50,000 is $15,000, so following the 70 percent rule, all the fees, costs, and profit add up to only $15,000. If the fees and holding costs were to total $10,000, that would leave just $5,000 in profit for the house flipper—and I don't know any house flipper who will take on the risk of flipping for just $5,000. So, following the 70 percent rule, a flipper or wholesaler would pay far too much for the property in this case. An investor flipping houses at this level might require far less than 70 percent—perhaps 50 percent or even lower.

A similar problem with the 70 percent rule exists for more expensive properties. The 70 percent rule would dictate that a home with an ARV of $700,000 that needs $50,000 worth of work should produce a maximum allowable offer of $440,000. In most markets, however, finding a $700,000 property for $440,000 is simply not feasible. A person who sticks exclusively to the 70 percent rule will likely never find a good enough deal to ever wholesale or flip a single property. In this case, 80 percent or even 85 percent might be good enough.

Furthermore, some investors may spend more or less on fees and costs because of their particular life situation or location. For example, in some states, purchasing a home may require $3,000 in closing costs, while in other states it might be $6,000. Some investors may have a real estate license, which saves them tens of thousands of dollars in commissions, whereas other investors may need to pay commissions when they sell.

How should the 70 percent rule be valued? Carefully. It's a quick and dirty way to guestimate the approximate amount you should pay for a property, but as with all rules of thumb, no concrete decisions should be made unless you've run a real analysis on a property.

Wholesaling Real Estate

Imagine with us this scenario. Your next-door neighbor decides to sell his nasty house, and tells you that he will take $190,000 for it. You know this is a great deal, so you go ahead and sign a contract that gives you the right to buy the property. But you don't have the time needed to put this deal together, so instead you and I have lunch and you tell me about the deal. I'm a local house flipper and I'm looking for a deal, so I agree to pay $200,000 for that property. A few weeks later, I buy the property for $200,000, the seller gets his $190,000, and you get a cool $10,000. Not bad for a few weeks of work.

The situation outlined here is known as wholesaling, and it's often touted by internet gurus as the best way for a new investor to get started. Wholesaling is the process of finding great real estate deals, writing a contract to acquire the deal, and then selling the contract to another buyer. Generally, a wholesaler never actually owns the piece of property they are selling. Instead, a wholesaler simply finds great deals using a variety of marketing strategies (see Chapter Seven), puts them under contract, and sells that contract to another for an "assignment fee." This fee is typically between $500 and $10,000 or more, depending on the size of the deal. Essentially, the wholesaler is a middleman who is paid for finding deals (although practicing real estate without a license is illegal in all 50 states, so be sure to double-check that you're within legal boundaries when wholesaling).

Most wholesalers sell their contracts to other real estate investors— usually house flippers—who are typically "cash buyers" (which means they don't need to take out a loan from a bank, with all the baggage that accompanies loans, to buy the property). When dealing with these cash buyers, a wholesaler can often get paid within days or weeks with very little drama.

Sounds pretty ideal, doesn't it?

It can be, and some investors make a killing by wholesaling real estate. There are, however, a few major issues with this strategy that must be addressed.

- **Difficulty:** You may be wondering, in the previous example, if the neighbor's house is worth $200,000, why would the neighbor sell it for $190,000 to you? Why not just sell it for $200,000? Great question! That's what makes wholesaling so tough—you have to find great deals before anyone else does and you have to pay less than others because you need to work your own fee into it. Therefore, it can be tough to find deals when there are other investors who can pay more out there looking for deals at the same time.

- **Constant marketing:** Wholesalers must continually seek out the best deals in order to have inventory to sell to others, and they must have a well-designed marketing funnel (you'll read more about this later) to continually attract these leads. Wholesalers also must continually seek out buyers for the deals they acquire. While promoted as a strategy that anyone can do—even someone with zero money—you ultimately do need to have financial resources to build your marketing funnel. That said, those who persist in developing their wholesaling skills often find great success and a good source of income while they grow their knowledge of other, more profitable strategies.

- **Often illegal:** Finally, wholesaling is often illegal. In some states, there is no question of its legality and in other states, it's a gray area. The essence of the debate on whether wholesaling is illegal revolves around the term brokering. Although each state has its own definition, a broker is someone who helps put a deal together. Those who argue that real estate wholesaling is illegal claim it to be so because the wholesaler is acting as a broker in the deal without being licensed. Those who defend wholesaling without a license say that wholesaling is not brokering, but simply signing a contract and then assigning that contract to another, and therefore the law doesn't apply to this situation. They are not selling a property, but simply selling the ownership of a real estate contract.

To further complicate the situation, there is the issue of "marketing" a property that you do not currently own. Most states also include marketing a property as brokering. For example, let's say Jim, the wholesaler, buys a property from Deborah and then sells it to Tom. If Jim put an ad for the house on Craigslist or elsewhere, is he marketing the property? Most definitely! But what if he wasn't marketing the property? What exactly defines marketing? If Jim knew the cash buyer, Tom, and told him about the deal, is that marketing?

If you were to ask ten different lawyers, you might get ten different answers. However, it is the opinion of these authors that the methods used by wholesalers in many states could be considered illegal. Putting a deal under contract, marketing the deal all over Craigslist, and then assigning that deal is a fast way to get fined by your state government and get a nice misdemeanor on your record. So, what's the right way to wholesale? While talking with an attorney is vital, here are two common suggestions to consider:

1. **Get your license.** No one can accuse you of brokering without a license if you have your license. Yes, this might cost you a couple grand, but it's better than getting a penalty from the state for breaking the law.

2. **Buy the property and then sell the property.** Rather than sell the contract and never own the property, you could simply buy the property and then immediately resell it. The downside of this, however, is needing to pay the closing costs twice, which can take away several thousands of dollars in profit. But there is a cost for doing business, right?

The truth about wholesaling is this: Whether or not wholesaling is illegal in your state, it definitely flirts with a line. If you want to see how close to that line you can get, fine. That is your choice. However, if you want to be sure that you are operating your wholesaling business as pure and solid as possible, get your license, or physically close on the property, take title, and then sell it after.

BRETT SNODGRASS

BiggerPockets Podcast ■ 231

Brett Snodgrass grew up in a middle-class family in Indiana. With two teachers for parents, Brett felt destined for the same path. But after starting down that path, Brett quickly realized teaching wasn't for him … he wanted to become an entrepreneur. So after leaving his teaching position, he tried his hand at buying DVDs in bulk and selling them individually, but when an attorney knocked on his door and notified him that he was being sued by a major movie studio, that business quickly died.

That's when Brett saw that there was a house for sale on eBay for the ridiculously low price of $9,000. Brett and his father pooled their money together and bought the house with the goal of fixing it up and reselling. There was just one problem, though: They didn't have any extra money to rehab the house. So Brett went and cleaned up the house, took a few pictures, and listed it online as is. Surprisingly, the house quickly sold for $16,000, and the father-and-son team made close to $6,000 in profit after fees. That's when the light bulb went off for Brett that he could do this full time. He could become a real estate wholesaler.

Brett began reading books and learning about wholesaling while looking for similar deals in his area. He and his father were able to buy ten deals that first year. The next year, in 2008, with the recession hitting hard, Brett was able to do 158 deals and found a business model that worked.

Today Brett and his company average 25 deals per month, using direct mail marketing to drive many of the leads into his pipeline. Brett paid a friend of his $0.25 per letter, and they started sending out 250 per week. Pouring their profits back into more letters, their direct mail marketing now totals about 30,000 mailings per month. Brett also uses online advertising and a website, as well as other local wholesalers, to find deals.

Rather than go the "traditional" wholesale route of taking on assignments or charging finder's fees, Brett decided to buy each property outright and then resell them quickly, just as he did with his first eBay house. He explained that he treats his house wholesaling business like he would a wholesaling business for any other non-real estate product: buy low, and then resell it higher. Brett prefers this method because he doesn't want to confuse the seller with assignment contracts and inconvenience them with potential buyers coming and going, feeling it is easier to just buy the property, make small repairs if necessary, and quickly sell it again. Not only is it a smoother and easier process, but Brett says they have now built up a solid reputation with sellers and wholesalers, so these people come to him first with deals.

Brett and his team of nine other employees tend to sell the majority of properties to three particular turnkey companies, averaging just 30 days between acquiring, listing, and selling the home. He and his team focus more on high volume than higher profit margins, so their average profit per deal is about $7,000, although he states they are investing in higher-value properties more and more as their company grows. Brett says he hopes to continue to grow his business and eventually use the profits to fund a religious ministry.

- - - - - - ─── - - - - -

Real Estate Development

When an individual buys a piece of property and builds something on that property, it's known as "development," and it's one of the more profitable, albeit risky, strategies for wealth creation through real estate. In a way, it's similar to house flipping, where someone buys a house, fixes it up, and then resells. But development usually is done to raw land (or to land where a structure is demolished and made to be just land).

When developing land, there are five distinct stages:
1. Land acquisition
2. Permits and planning
3. Site preparation
4. Building the structure
5. Property management or sale

Some developers choose to work all five stages, from finding the land, to getting the city to allow the build, to preparing the land (both physically and legally), to building the structure, and then they hold on to the property or sell it. Other developers instead choose to focus on just one or two of these stages. For example, one developer may specialize in finding great land deals and getting the site plans drawn up, choosing to then sell the property to another developer who specializes in just building the structure and is happy to avoid the red tape of planning.

The risky part of real estate development comes in the length of time it can take to work through all five steps. Depending on the type of property and the location, this entire process could take many months or even years to complete. If the real estate market sees a sharp downturn during this period, the investor may end up halfway through a development with no exit strategy. For example, let's say you decide to build a community of 25 houses. You find a plot of land, purchase it, get the permits and plans finalized, build the roads and infrastructure (like water, power, sewers, etc.), and start construction on the homes. Maybe you were hoping to make $40,000 per house in profit, giving you a nice $1,000,000 in profit for your hard work in running this development deal. Sounds nice, doesn't it?

But what if the market begins to drop during the middle of building the first home? Suddenly your projected per-home sales price of, let's say, $300,000, drops to $250,000. Now your $40,000 per house profit projections have dropped to a negative $10,000. You might be forced to hold on to that property until the next real estate cycle, hoping your loan and financial position is strong enough to weather the storm. While this might sound like a far-fetched scenario, it happened to many, many developers back in 2008–2012, and many are still digging out of the rubble.

Our hope is not to discourage you from development, as many fortunes have been made in this strategy. Just be sure to weigh the pros and cons, as well as know where you stand financially, before venturing in. And as with all real estate investments, seek to become an expert at this strategy by talking with others who have been there, done that.

DEVAN MCCLISH
BiggerPockets Podcast ■ Episode 180

Devan McClish is not your average real estate investor. By age 23, Devan had already completed 58 real estate deals, 42 in one year alone. Devan's interest in real estate began at age 18 when he asked his friend's father how he could afford his large house and lavish lifestyle. His friend's father informed him that he was a commercial real estate investor and gave Devan a few books to read on the subject, encouraging him to get into residential real estate investing to get started. Devan read the books, took action, and fell in love with the idea of being an investor.

But like many investors, his career started off rocky. Devan spent three years jumping from method to method, and nothing seemed to work. "I was very inconsistent," he says. "If there was one thing I would stress to new investors, it would be to stick with one thing." When he would find deals, they would often fall apart before he could close on them. Rather than giving up, though, this tenacious young man decided to focus on one method and put all of his money and energy into it. It turns out this was the best decision he could have made.

Devan decided to focus his attention on direct mail marketing and eventually with the financial backing of his mother, he was able to purchase a four-unit property. He bought the property for $110,000, put $40,000 into rehab, and rented it out for a monthly cash flow of $2,800.

With the success of his first deal, Devan kicked things into overdrive and started making deals left and right. In the span of just one year, Devan completed 42 transactions: ten wholesales, six rehabs, 17 new construction developments, and nine rental units. Since then he has developed more than 100 new homes. Devan clearly didn't let his young age and lack of experience hold him back. "Experienced investors love to help younger investors out," he explains. When he didn't know how to do something, he would simply find someone with a lot of experience and partner alongside them on the deal.

This is exactly what he did when he started focusing more on development, building new homes. After seeing investors in his area buy his wholesale deals for $5,000, and then make more than $100,000 in profit after completing the project, he knew he wanted a bigger slice of that pie. He went to the top developers in his area and asked if he could partner with them on a deal. "I would rather have 50 percent of the profits from a deal, than have no deal," Devan says.

Today he and his company of seven employees have 65 homes in the works, currently totaling more than $26 million in developing assets. He and his team are currently running a general contracting company, a property management company that is managing 45 units, a wholesaling/developing company, and a realtor business. Some of the properties they own include 11 single-family/small multifamily units; two apartment complexes totaling 41 units; three Airbnb vacation rentals; and a retail strip with laundry, cash advance, and storage.

What's in the future for this young man who is already crushing it in the real estate market? According to Devan, "more deals and more growth." Devan says he hopes to make $1,000,000 in income in the coming year, and have at least 30 employees and $10,000,000 in the bank by age 30.

- - - - - - ————————————————————————————— - - - - -

Turnkey Investing

No, not turkey (*gobble, gobble!*) investing, though we're sure there are people who make money off the Thanksgiving bird. We're talking about *turnkey* (often written *turn key*) real estate investing.

Turnkey real estate investing is an investment strategy in which a particular company finds, buys, rehabs, and manages a property, and sells the "finished product" to (usually) out-of-state investors. The turnkey company's goal is to make the entire real estate investment process as simple as possible, so all you need to do is "turn the key."

So you, the real estate investor, would contact one of these companies and purchase a nicely packaged property, usually a single-family home, and they would take care of nearly everything. You might obtain a loan, or you might pay cash, depending on the deal or the company. Keep in mind that there are hundreds of turnkey real estate providers in America (and across the world), and no two companies are exactly alike. Some will buy, rehab, rent, and then sell a property to you, the investor. Others will simply help you find the property and let you do most of the heavy lifting on the rehab side (if there is any rehab to do), then manage the property for you. Again, each company runs its operation a little differently, so if you decide to go with a turnkey company, it's important that you do some in-depth research on exactly what that turnkey company will and will not do.

Turnkey investing can be an exciting option for some, especially those who live in real estate markets where cash flow is difficult to obtain (as most turnkey providers focus on cash-flow heavy locations, mostly in the U.S., Midwest and Southeast). In addition, turnkey businesses provide a few other benefits, including unique insight into their local market, professional staff who have been there, done that, a consistent method for finding great deals (probably better than you, an outsider, can find), reliable construction crews and the management of those crews, and experienced management of the tenants. And, of course, simplicity. The investor hardly has to do a thing.

Sounds pretty perfect, doesn't it? Well, as with all things in life, there is a trade-off, and it's usually found in the return on your investment. A turnkey company is a business that needs to make money, and they do this through several methods. First, turnkey companies often buy the property at a discount and sell it to you, the out-of-state owner, for a higher amount, essentially "flipping" the property to you for a hefty price. Often the price you pay for the property is the same, or greater, than you'd pay by just finding a property yourself (although this depends highly on the turnkey provider). Additionally, the turnkey provider brings in monthly revenue by managing the property for you, but that's a charge you are likely going to pay no matter where you buy (unless you buy local and manage yourself).

The key to investing in turnkey real estate is to always do your own math. Remember: The turnkey company's best interest is in selling you the property for the highest amount possible because that's how it makes a profit. Many turnkey companies are "soft" on the math when they present the deal to you; they often ignore important metrics in their math (like repairs or management fees) in order to make a deal look better. Before choosing to invest with a turnkey company, always do your own math and make sure the deal really is a deal.

And finally, the greatest risk when choosing to invest in real estate through a turnkey company is the level of trust you must place in this provider. After all, you are relying on their knowledge and expertise to choose a location, choose a property, choose a tenant, and manage that tenant. That's a lot of confidence you are placing in someone else who gets paid whether or not you make a good investment. It would be fairly easy for a turnkey provider to take advantage of out-of-state investors by encouraging them to buy bad properties in bad locations. In fact, we've heard many stories from investors who have purchased turnkey properties only to discover soon after that it was a "pig with lipstick" that immediately began costing the investor a lot of money in repairs. Do your due diligence on both the numbers and the property itself, and make sure it's truly a deal worthy of purchasing.

Turnkey can be a fantastic option for many investors, but it isn't without its risks and responsibilities. Navigate these correctly, and you'll find an endless supply of deals to invest in no matter where you choose to live.

DR. KENYON MEADOWS

BiggerPockets Podcast ▪ Episode 219

Dr. Kenyon Meadows is a radiation oncologist with a strong desire to grow wealth, but because of his demanding career, he focuses on making his investments as passive as possible.

His first attempt at real estate investing came in the form of lending money to house flippers and buy-and-hold landlords who had exhausted their supply of traditional loans. Once he was comfortable with the process and terminology, he began to expand his efforts, focusing on finding a few solid borrowers and creating great win-win lending relationships. "If you find reliable people up front," Kenyon says, "you can maintain that relationship for years." He typically lends to real estate investors who are doing at least 15–20 flips a year because they know what they are doing and are okay with dropping the price of their property to sell it quickly and move on to the next. He generally prefers them to invest some of their own money into the deal and make monthly payments because it creates an incentive to get the job done quicker.

After being the passive private money lender for some time, Kenyon decided to start investing in buy-and-hold properties himself, but found himself reluctant to pull the trigger due to the time and hassle needed with many hands-on rental properties. Instead, Kenyon decided to test out the idea of buying turnkey properties, as this strategy generally requires less hands-on work because the property is already in great shape and (hopefully) has great tenants occupying the units.

Kenyon met his first turnkey provider when he was lending private money so they had an established secure relationship, but he encourages new turnkey investors to really do their due diligence when vetting their provider. Today he also prefers to invest in properties in his area so that he can easily visit them before purchasing and thereafter.

When analyzing turnkey properties, Kenyon strives to stick to the 1 percent rule in blue-collar neighborhoods. He will typically purchase a home for around $80,000, which will rent for $800–$900 per month. He currently has seven turnkey properties, and is always on the lookout for more deals. The first couple of properties he purchased with his own cash, and then he raised private money from friends and family for the others. He recently started working on utilizing cash-out refinancing to continue to grow his portfolio.

Along with investing in private money lending and turnkey properties, Kenyon also invests in crowdfunding platforms for real estate investors and small business loans. He said that when he first got into it a few years ago, he was getting a 12–13 percent return on his investments, but now that they are more popular, he consistently gets about an 11 percent return on his investment. In the 35 crowdfunding campaigns that he has been a part of, only three have fallen in default, and those platforms are working on getting him his investment back.

Nowadays, while Kenyon continues to work on growing his investing streams, he also devotes his time to educating others about the benefits of alternative investing. His goal is to help others like himself avoid the potential risks and pitfalls, and enjoy the rewards.

- - - - - - - ———————————————————————————————— - - - - - -

House Hacking

House hacking is one of the most popular strategies for first-time real estate investors, and also the way I (Brandon) started my rental investing career, so it holds a very special place in my heart.

House hacking is the strategy of purchasing a small multifamily property—usually a duplex, triplex, or fourplex—using one unit to live in and renting out the other units. By purchasing a great multifamily deal, the rent that your tenants pay each month can cover all of the expenses for the property—and maybe more. For example, if you buy a fourplex, live in one unit, and rent each of the other units out for $500 a month, you could be making $1,500 per month in income (because 3 x $500 = $1,500). If your loan, taxes, insurance, utilities, and other expenses come to just $1,200, you could get paid $300 a month just to live in the home. Even better—when it comes time to move out into your future home (the banks require you to commit to staying for at least a year), you can rent that fourth unit out for even more income.

Of course, house hacking doesn't always mean you can live for free, but it could mean living for less than what it might normally cost. I'm working from Kailua, Hawaii, one of the most expensive real estate markets in the U.S., where the average cost of a home is nearly $1,000,000. How can most of the residents, who earn a median income of just $69,964 per year, afford to live in such a market? Many do so by house hacking. In fact, this strategy is so powerful, the Hawaiian government recently passed legislation making an official process, legal allowance, and special financing for residents to add an accessory dwelling unit (ADU) to their property, so they can rent that small unit out to help offset their payments. It's state-sponsored house hacking! Someone can purchase a home for $1,000,000, making their mortgage payment $4,500, but add an ADU and rent it out for $3,000 per month, taking the homeowner's "out of pocket housing cost" from a crazy-high $4,500 to a much more reasonable $1,500. The Hawaiian government gets it, and I'm guessing you are starting to get it also.

Let's talk about some of the other benefits of house hacking:

- **Low (or no) down payment financing:** When you plan to live in a property for at least one year, financing becomes much more friendly for the borrower. For example, an FHA loan allows for just a 3.5 percent down payment, and the USDA (United States Department of Agriculture) loan allows for $0 down if you are buying in a rural area. Traditional 20-percent-down loans also work in this pricing structure and can do even more for your wealth-building plans. And yes, these loans allow for single-family houses as well as duplexes, triplexes, and fourplexes.
- **On-the-job training:** House hacking is a great introduction to the world of landlording. You buy the property, and suddenly you are a landlord—so you'll learn very quickly what to do and what not to do.
- **Can keep an eye on your investment:** When you live in your investment property, keeping an eye on the property and making sure it's running at peak performance is easy. It's unlikely that the lawn will get overgrown, the tenants will move in a pit bull, or maintenance will go unreported for months.
- **Saved expenses:** Let's be honest. The best thing about house hacking is the ability to save money. First, depending on the deal and your market, you may be able to live for free, or far cheaper than normal. This means you can save all the money you normally would

have spent on a mortgage and use it to pay off debts or buy other real estate deals. Additionally, because you live on the property, you can manage the other tenants yourself and can save on the cost of property management, increasing your cash flow even more.

We talk a lot about house hacking because we've seen investors succeed time and time and time again. While it might not be for everyone, we highly recommend you consider this strategy to see if it's the best option for you. If you want to get an even deeper look at house hacking, I'd recommend picking up a copy of *Set for Life*, written by Scott Trench.

SCOTT TRENCH

BiggerPockets Podcast ▪ Episode 223

Scott Trench found himself trapped in a life he didn't want: working a 9-to-5 job at a Fortune 500 company where he was simply a cog in a giant machine, making no real difference to his life or anyone else's.

Spurred by the idea of finding early financial freedom, Scott stumbled across a blog post on BiggerPockets about the power of house hacking (written by yours truly, Brandon). As a financially savvy person, Scott realized that housing was his largest expense and the biggest roadblock to his achieving financial freedom. This article on house hacking showed him a simple strategy for reducing that cost to almost nothing while also getting a solid investment property in the expensive and fast-growing market of Denver. He reasoned that if he could purchase a multi-unit property and have his tenants cover the expenses, including the mortgage, then he could live for free and put all the money that he would have spent on rent toward his retirement plan.

Knowing it was easier for him to save money than make additional income (and knowing that the type of house he wanted in his city would be costly), he spent a year cutting as many expenses as he could to save as much money as possible. He stopped eating out at restaurants, rode his bike to and from work, and kept his costs for social activities down. At the end of that year, on a salary of $50,000, he had saved up $20,000—enough to put a payment down on a home. He connected with a real estate agent he found on BiggerPockets and soon had his house hack completed, a duplex he purchased for $240,000 using an FHA loan.

After completing a quick rehab and finding tenants, Scott found himself living for free with a mortgage payment of around $1,500 per month, rent of $1,100 on the second unit, and a roommate that paid $550 per month. Without a monthly housing expense, Scott was able to save even more for his next investment, another duplex in Denver. Going forward, rather than looking for properties that he can buy and flip for a quick buck, Scott's strategy is to invest in properties in locations that are going to be potentially great for the next 20–30 years. He has the long game in mind, and his house hack is making it all possible.

- - - - - - ——————————————————————————————————— - - - - - -

Short-Term (Vacation) Rentals

One strategy that has exploded over the past several years is the "short-term rental," also known as "vacation rental" strategy. And it's popular for good reason: It can make an investor a lot of money, especially in areas where cash flow is normally difficult to find.

What Is a Short-Term Rental?

Short-term rentals are usually privately owned properties where the owner leases out a furnished home or condo (or yurt, boat, tent ... seriously) by the night, much like a hotel. The guest might stay for one day or maybe several weeks (or longer) while on vacation or on a business trip. Although the ability to rent a home has been an option for travelers forever, recent technological disruptors (such as, Airbnb, VRBO—we'll talk about them in a moment) have made this practice simple, affordable, safe, and accessible for nearly everyone. In fact, right now you could turn your own home into a short-term rental property, and while you gallivant across the country on a road trip, someone might be sleeping in your bed. Weird? Maybe, but hundreds of thousands of people are doing it.

Of course, it doesn't just have to be your own home—many investors are getting into the short-term rental business because they see the profits coming in. The retail business concept of "buy by the yard, sell by the inch" is perfectly at play with this type of investment. As mentioned earlier, this can often be the only way to get cash flow from an area where prices are just too high.

Do Vacation Rentals Have to Be in Vacation Areas?

No, but it helps to be in an area where people visit. Maybe for weddings. Maybe for funerals. Maybe for work. But you need a steady supply of people to make sure you are getting the property filled. Unsure if your area will support a vacation rental? Head to one of the vacation rental portals, like Airbnb or VRBO, and see what other listings are in your area. You can even check the availability of some of your "competition" to see what's happening for them. Although you won't get a perfect picture, you can get an overall view of the potential.

Short-Term vs. Long-Term Math

To illustrate the power of short-term rentals, allow us to show some basic math on a recent short-term rental Brandon purchased and rented out via Airbnb, compared to what it would have been as a traditional rental property:

Regular Rental Property

- Total Potential Income: $750
- Mortgage Payment   -$400
- Taxes   -$75
- Insurance   -$50
- Repairs   -$50
- Vacancy Allowance   -$35
- Total Pretax Monthly Profit $140

Short-Term Vacation Rental

- Total Potential Income: +$3,000
- Mortgage Payment   -$400
- Taxes   -$75
- Insurance   -$50
- Repairs   -$50
- Vacancy Allowance (30%)   -$900
- Water/Sewer   -$150
- Garbage   -$50
- Electricity   -$200
- Cable/Internet   -$125
- Total Pretax Monthly Profit $1,000

As you can see in the numbers above, this property produced $860 per month more income than a traditional rental. However, this does not include additional management costs (which could be several hundred dollars per month if you choose to hire someone else to manage the property) nor the additional taxes due on a short-term rental. Most areas add on a "hotel tax" since, essentially, you are running a small hotel.

Seems like a no-brainer, right? Why would anyone choose to rent a unit as a traditional investment? Well, there are some significant downsides.

The Dark Side of Short-Term Rentals

- **Extra work:** The first thing I, Brandon, discovered when I ventured into short-term rentals was the extra work involved on a day-to-day basis. Guests struggled to find the home, they didn't know how to use the coffee maker, they couldn't figure out how to use a keypad to open up the house, they wanted to know if I accepted pets, they wanted to know how soft the beds were, they wanted to know if I would give them a discount ... and so on and so forth. It was exhausting. Then there was the coordination with the cleaner each time a guest vacated. Luckily, the guest typically pays for the cleaning, so at least this wasn't as much a financial drain as it was a time drain. When my typical cleaner was out on vacation or sick, I had to scramble to find others. Now if that list tires you out just reading it, understand that, with time and practice, you can build systems around these issues. There are managers who can handle the day-to-day interactions. Software exists to help automate a lot of the communication with guests. You can improve your listings and slowly raise your rates. But it takes time and diligence, as with any strategy.
- **Taxes:** Short-term rental properties are taxed differently than traditional rentals. Without my diving too deep into the weeds on this, just understand that a short-term rental property's income (especially when guests stay fewer than seven days) may be seen as business income, not investment income, which would require you to pay self-employment taxes on profits (15.3 percent). In addition to federal taxes, you may also have state and/or local taxes, including income tax and/or hotel tax. In some areas, this could add up to 25 percent more in taxes. Using the example above

with the $1,000 "profit" on the short-term rental, depending on the location, an investor might end up giving almost half of that profit away to the government.

- **Legality:** Finally, many short-term rentals are, simply, illegal. Because of the drastic increase in popularity of this strategy, many local governments are taking notice and cracking down on their existence. Opponents claim that short-term rentals raise property values and rents too high (by removing traditional rentals from the market, thus driving out the poor and the middle class) and also don't have the same safety requirements as traditional hotels. Supporters argue that it is simply the hotels that are playing politics because they are losing business. Whatever the reason, just know that you must learn the laws related to short-term rentals and abide by them (or find a friendlier area to own them in). Trying to build a real estate business by hiding from or skirting government laws is like building a house directly on the sandy beach. It might look good for a while, but it'll quickly crumble when a storm comes, leaving you back where you started.

ZEONA MCINTYRE
BiggerPockets Podcast ▪ Episode 229

Zeona McIntyre had it all planned out: She was going to school for massage therapy and would do whatever she could to "retire" early and enjoy the lifestyle of her dreams. While on this path, a friend of hers repeatedly talked about how he was making great money while traveling the world because he was renting out his apartment through a website called Airbnb. Once Zeona discovered her friend had earned $50,000 in just one year from his one property, that was all the convincing she needed to start doing it herself.

Zeona started off small by renting out her own room through Airbnb when she was away, and soon added her roommate's room whenever the roommate left for a trip. Pretty soon she was renting out her room full-time and staying with friends. That's when she decided to double-down on her efforts and acquire more properties to offer as short-term rentals. After attending a friend's wedding in St. Louis, Missouri, Zeona was shocked to find that some of her friends in St. Louis were paying mortgages as low as $300 per month. She returned home to the Denver area and began researching properties in St. Louis. Within a month, she had closed on her first property there—a three-bedroom home for $72,000. Despite not living in the area, Zeona started making around $1,100 a month in cash flow from that property, convincing her to buy even more.

Today Zeona owns and manages multiple vacation rental properties in several states. She looks for locations that are near big colleges and hospitals, as these tend to attract visiting families. She is also beginning to focus on attracting traveling nurses who will rent for three months at a time. Her current plans are to continually improve her systems and automation, allowing her to have more time to do what she loves, such as traveling the world and exploring other real estate investment strategies.

Live-In House Flips

We already discussed house flipping as a viable strategy for building quick cash through real estate investing. But one related strategy many investors use to get started in real estate is flipping the house they live in. That means buying a fixer-upper home and either fixing it up right before moving in (and then moving in after rehab) or, more likely, buying a fixer-upper and living in the home while remodeling it. Many live-in house flippers tend to do much of their own work to the property to save (and make) even more on the flip, though it's definitely not required.

Live-in house flips can be a great way to get your feet wet without the risk of flipping a vacant house. After all, because you live in the property, if the rehab takes longer or the house doesn't sell as fast as you'd like, it's probably okay because you need to live somewhere no matter what.

Perhaps the greatest benefit to the "live-in flip" is the potential tax benefits, thanks to the "home exclusion" loophole in the tax law. Essentially, this IRS rule allows an individual to pay zero taxes on the sale of their home, as long as they've lived in the home two of the past five years, and the profit is no greater than $250,000 for single homeowners or $500,000 for married (and filing jointly) homeowners. (There are a few other requirements, so be sure to do some research before jumping into this strategy.) A few months ago, I (Brandon) walked into my bank with a check for $86,000 from the sale of a house—and that money was 100 percent mine. I owed $0 in taxes on that profit, and that is a great feeling.

Furthermore, homeowners can do this strategy over and over and over again, as long as they abide by the rules. Imagine buying a fixer-upper home every two years and making a profit of $100,000 each time. That's an average of $50,000 a year—tax-free! And that's exactly what many investors do.

The difficulty in live-in flipping is obvious: needing to live in a property that's being rehabbed. But if you make quick work of the project and buy the right deal, you can live in a remodeled house for most of those two years and make a tax-free killing when it comes time to sell. That's a win-win in anyone's book.

It's important to note, however, that making a huge profit on a remodel is not a guarantee. Perhaps you'll spend more on the rehab than anticipated (which is easy to do when living in the home, as you'll likely make choices based on personal preference, not return on investment), or perhaps the market will drop significantly when you are ready to move. Therefore, a live-in flip is not a guarantee of success. But this strategy can be a powerful way to enter and succeed in the real estate investing game.

MINDY JENSEN
BiggerPockets Podcast ■ Episodes 129 and 261

Mindy Jensen is a third-generation "frugal mastermind." Her grandparents, who grew up during the Great Depression, raised her parents to be frugal and they, in turn, raised her to be frugal. Mindy defines frugality as "saving where you can, so you can spend where you want." She drives a used car, purchases clothing and housewares from secondhand stores, and is always on the lookout for a great deal.

Mindy's frugality has also been applied to her real estate investing career. Mindy and her husband, Carl, had a desire and a plan to be financially free so she could be a stay-at-home mom and so they could retire early. To achieve those goals, this husband-and-wife team has perfected the art of live-in house flipping. The duo will purchase a distressed property that needs renovations and live in the property while they fix it themselves. Mindy says they attempted to hire general contractors to do the rehab on two separate occasions, but ended up firing both of them because they found they could do a much better job themselves at a much lower cost. They will hire workers for larger external projects, such as adding an additional story, siding, and/or a roof, but will otherwise complete the work themselves, including doing the electrical, plumbing, flooring, sheetrock, and painting. In her mind, doing the work yourself is not as complicated as most people think, especially with the help of YouTube videos. "If you can swing a hammer," Mindy states, "you can install wood flooring."

Mindy and Carl have now completed five live-in flips, averaging more than six figures in profit each time, and are currently working on and living in their sixth. They will typically live in each flip for two to three years (to save on the taxes due when selling) before moving on to the next one. This couple has found that they have been able to reach their financial and lifestyle goals through live-in house flipping. Although Mindy no longer *has* to work, she now *gets* to work, making a difference in the lives of millions as the community manager at BiggerPockets. Her real estate investing career has allowed her to spend more time with her kids, enjoy activities such as snowboarding and bicycling, and given her the ability to travel wherever her heart desires.

- -

BRRRR INVESTING

BRRRR is an acronym for a popular investment strategy that involves buying fixer-upper rental properties, repairing them, leasing them out to great tenants, refinancing to get your money back, and then repeating the process over again and again. Combining the benefits of house flipping with the wealth-building characteristics of rentals, this can be a powerful strategy because of the ability to acquire numerous properties without running out of capital to invest.

Specifically, BRRRR stands for:

- Buy

- Rehab
- Rent
- Refinance
- Repeat

Let's break down the strategy step-by-step.

1. Buy

When looking to start a BRRRR deal, the first step is to find a great deal and purchase the home, usually with "short-term" money. We'll talk more about financing in the chapters to come, but because most banks do not want to lend on nasty properties, you'll need to find a more creative way to finance the deal, such as cash, a partner, or a hard-money lender. Again, we'll talk about these strategies in more detail soon, but just know that you will probably need to buy the property without a traditional bank. (Don't worry—it's easier than you think. Stick with us.) Furthermore, you can't just buy "any old property." You need to find a great one. Great location, great neighborhood, but a fixer-upper house.

BRRRR investing is very similar to house flipping; in fact, it *is* house flipping, but rather than selling the house, you are going to rent it out after fixing it up. The same principles that go into house flipping are needed here.

2. Rehab

The next phase in the BRRRR strategy is to fix the property up and make it shine, ready for tenants to pay top dollar. The key to rehabbing a BRRRR property is to make the property as "tenant proof" as possible, using materials that will last a long time and won't need to be redone later. And it's important to rehab with the goal of getting the highest property value and the highest rent possible. For example, if you can turn a two-bedroom home into a three-bedroom home, do it. This can potentially add hundreds of dollars per month in cash flow and tens of thousands in equity.

You could, of course, do all the work yourself if you wanted, or you could hire it out. That's up to you, and dependent upon your skills, availability, and desire. DIY can save you a lot of money, increasing the odds you'll find a deal with numbers that work. But it will also take a lot of weekends and evenings.

3. Rent

After the property has been rehabbed, it's time to rent it out to great tenants. Because you just bought real estate in a great location and rehabbed it to look incredible, finding incredible tenants to rent it should not be tough. You might choose to hire a property manager, but because you already rehabbed the property and because you are renting to high-class, great tenants, managing a BRRRR deal shouldn't be too hard if you want to save the money and do it yourself.

Furthermore, because the property was rehabbed at the start, your repairs on the property should be fairly low for the next few years. Everything has already been fixed.

4. Refinance

Now comes the confusing part that makes everyone run for the hills (just kidding!). A moment ago, we mentioned that it's tough to get a traditional bank loan on a fixer upper, so you would have to buy the property with more creativity. Yet, conventional mortgages are really nice, thanks to the low interest rates and the long fixed-terms. Put another way, a conventional mortgage is likely going to give you the smallest payment of all your financing options. So the fourth step in the BRRRR strategy is to refinance (meaning: pay off the first loan with a brand-new loan) into a nice conventional mortgage after the property has been fixed up. If you bought a really good deal, you should be able to get all or most of your short-term money back, which means it's time to ...

5. Repeat

The final R in the BRRRR strategy is to repeat the process again and again. After all, it worked once, and you got all your short-term money back, so why not do it again? And again? And again?

Sure, at some point the bank will stop refinancing the properties for you. And maybe you'll need to find another solution, like a portfolio lender or a partnership. Or maybe it's time to venture into bigger commercial deals (like apartments). But it can be done, and it is being done, over and over, by investors across the world.

Depending on the strength of the deal you bought, a perfect BRRRR should give you extra profit each month from the cash flow, and you should have a sizable chunk of equity in the home. This can be a great way to build up cash flow toward financial freedom, and BRRRR investing can make you a millionaire faster than you thought possible. But all strategies have their drawbacks, right? Let's take a look at the big one with BRRRR investing.

Drawbacks of BRRRR Investing

There are a few significant ones to be aware of before venturing into your next BRRRR deal. Most importantly, if you are unable to refinance the property to get your money back out, you are in a tough situation, with your first loan coming due and no way to pay it back. For example, let's say you used a hard-money lender (who typically lends at high rates and high fees for no longer than one year) and you can't get a refinance from a traditional bank after the rehab (maybe your credit is shot, or you don't have enough income, or the property isn't worth enough). You still need to pay off the lender, and you might find yourself stuck between a rock and a hard place. But if you bought correctly and stayed on budget, you should have enough equity to turn around and sell the property, turning your BRRRR into a good ol' house flip. (Having multiple exit strategies is always a great thing and one of the perks of the BRRRR method.)

To prevent this refinance denial, visit a few local banks before you buy a property and make sure you are qualified to get a loan. Have them run your credit and check your income, and then have them give you a preapproval letter. Although this letter doesn't guarantee they'll fund you, it does tell you that you are likely worthy enough for a loan.

The BRRRR strategy has a lot of moving parts, but if you work it right, it can be a powerful ally in helping you build some serious wealth. Following this strategy can help you combine the equity growth of flipping with the tax benefits, cash flow, and appreciation of rental properties, maximizing your profit at the end of the day. But it's not without significant work, risk, and dedication.

IAN REEVES

BiggerPockets Podcast ▪ Episode 237

Ian Reeves wanted to improve his life, and after reading *Rich Dad, Poor Dad*, he decided that real estate would be the ticket to financial independence.

Doing research for his first deal, Ian stumbled across BiggerPockets and began to consume as much information as he could. Four months later, he took the plunge and purchased his first property, a duplex in Shawnee, Kansas. He decided to house hack. "If I could go back ten years and give myself one piece of advice, it would be to house hack," Ian says. "House hacking is the single biggest piece of financial advice that I could give to someone."

After finding a like-minded partner through BiggerPockets, Ian decided to focus his efforts on fixer-upper rental properties, utilizing the BRRRR strategy to quickly scale. They immediately went and bought two properties in their area, rehabbed both, found excellent tenants to rent each, and obtained a refinance to put the homes into long-term mortgages. With their capital freed up, they were able to start the process over again (and again and again!).

To give an example, Ian recently bought a house through a wholesaler for $29,000 and put $12,000 into the rehab. The house appraised for $70,000, so he and his partner refinanced the home into a long-term commercial mortgage. They were given 80 percent of the value of the property, which more than covered their initial investment. That property now brings in $975 per month after a $400-per-month mortgage plus other expenses including capex (capital expenditure), maintenance, and property management.

Ian also has begun to expand his business into commercial real estate, buying a small commercial strip mall in Missouri. The previous owner of the property had recently passed away, and the children wanted nothing to do with it. Ian picked up the property, which contained 17 commercial spaces and a vacant plot of land, for $1.26 million. When he had the property appraised, the value came in at $2.4 million, for an equity position of $1.14 million shared between him and his business partner.

Finally, because of his success as a real estate investor, Ian was recently able to cut down his hours at work to just three days a week, allowing him to spend more time investing in real estate. In addition to finding BRRRR deals, Ian also helps others on their journey. "Just last week," Ian says, "I had one guy from BiggerPockets who wanted to meet up for coffee, and I said, 'I can do one better than that. Next weekend I have to go check on some of my rehabs, so why don't you just come along with me for half a day?' He told me afterward that he learned way more from that than he would have over coffee."

Student Rentals

Toga! Toga! Toga!

Although the words *student rental* might conjure images in your brain of frat houses, beer-guzzling teens, and trashed properties, student rentals can actually be a unique way to generate profits through real estate investing. After all, even students need a place to live during college, and with the right systems in place, an investor can ensure above-market rents, possibly guaranteed by the parents.

Student rentals are generally operated like any other rental property, but due to the type of tenant, some unique management strategies can be employed. For example, many student rental owners charge by the room, rather than by the entire unit. This way, they can rent out numerous bedrooms to unrelated students, maximizing their profits. Many student rental owners also ensure positive behavior on the part of the student by requiring the parent to cosign on the lease. If troublemaker Johnny decides to throw a party, and his guests pour liquor all over the carpet, the landlord can hold Johnny's mom or dad financially responsible.

Obviously, to begin investing in student rentals, one must invest near a college. And while large public or private schools with tens of thousands of students might work great, there are thousands of community colleges and other small schools around the country that may have a housing need. Talk with the admissions office at your local college to gauge the housing demand, and, if you find a shortage, you may have stumbled across a great niche in your local market. Just be prepared for higher-than-normal turnover. College kids move almost every year.

BILL SYRIOS

BiggerPockets Podcast ▪ Episode 140

After a near-disastrous start, Bill transitioned from campus pastor to campus real estate investor in the early 90s. He also left behind a laissez-faire mentality of treating real estate as a hobby. Adopting a business mind-set "meant getting business cards, getting a business name, meeting tenants in a professional setting—not at my home, but at an office. Now, granted, my office in those days was Wendy's restaurant."

Through it all, Bill realized one simple truth that has guided all his investments to date: the riches are in the niches. And the first niche he chose to focus on was student rentals. Why? "When done right, it gives you very high rents, no vacancy, and no loss of rents," he says. "I can deal with some parties. I can deal with a heavy turnover. I would say the kinds of rents and the lack of vacancy issues make student housing very attractive for a real estate investor."

Additionally, Bill was drawn to the student rental strategy for its ability to maximize income because of how college students think of bedrooms. "When it comes to campus houses, it's all about the bedrooms," explains Bill, whose company, Stewardship Properties, is near the University of Oregon in Eugene.

While expansion is not usually possible with apartments, if you can carve out another bedroom or two from existing square footage in a house—think: a formal dining room, garage, downstairs, family room, etc.—you can significantly increase rents. "Think of a campus house like a small apartment building," Bill says. "Every bedroom is potentially worth $450 or $550 or $650 per month, whatever the going rate is of your particular campus and location." Additional bedrooms can be huge "value-adds" for campus rentals.

Like any niche, student housing has its particulars. And it is those particulars that can make focusing on a niche so powerful and lucrative. If you can master your niche, you will have the ability to see things others don't. For example, Bill figured out that the best place to find properties was just outside the normal distance to campus. Rehabbing such properties with students in mind could bring in nearly as much rent as those closer to campus, but at a much lower purchase price.

Bill says, "If you gain expertise in one niche, it can serve as a financial foundation to focus on another niche, and then another." Currently, he considers "his niche" as partnering with younger investors across the country, including his two sons, Andrew and Phillip, in Kansas City (check out Episode 121 of the *BiggerPockets Podcast* for their interview). His company provides access to capital, marketing, systems infrastructure, and even a consistent software and website presence. His "boots on the ground" partners work hard at building up a portfolio of properties. These younger investors live in such places as Portland, Oregon; Kansas City, Kansas; Dallas, Texas; Emporia, Kansas; Indianapolis, Indiana; Louisville, Kentucky; St. Louis, Missouri; and Las Vegas, Nevada.

All of these partnerships, with their wide variety of niches, Bill said, were made possible by the financial foundation built on one initial niche—student housing. Bill's advice: Pick a potentially lucrative real estate niche, become an expert in that niche, and over time use your success to develop additional niche markets. And, through it all, remember the threefold key to business development: 1) a big-thinking mind-set, 2) highly productive teams, including key equity stakeholders who are partners, and 3) a concentration on systems that make it possible to not just work *in* your business, but to work *on* your business, refining it to reach its full potential.

Is it Okay to Invest in Multiple Niches and Strategies at the Same Time?

"Don't be a donkey."

That was the four-word answer Derek Sivers (TED talk giver, entrepreneur, philanthropist) gave when he was asked about the advice that he would give his 30-year-old self.

He went on to tell a short story in which a hungry and thirsty donkey was taken out to get some food and water. On the donkey's left sat a bowl of food, and on his right, a bowl of water. The donkey looked longingly right, then remembered his hunger and turned his gaze left. Then he looked back to the right. Then back to the left. Then right. Then left. Soon the donkey died of both starvation and thirst. Sivers's point was simple: By focusing on multiple desires at the same time, we often destroy the opportunity found in both.

What does this have to do with real estate? Well, the last two chapters we focused on a variety of niches and strategies that a person could engage in to create and grow wealth. But inevitably, the question arises: Is it okay to invest in multiple strategies and niches at the same time?

Yes, eventually it's fine to invest in numerous strategies. Most successful investors dabble in more than one niche and one strategy ... in time. There is nothing wrong with trying to flip houses *and* buy rentals. Or to invest in notes while also syndicating an apartment complex. Or owning the nine-bedroom rental house for beer-keg-standing students while also putting your money into an A-class retail strip center across the country.

However, the problem is that most new investors find themselves in the same position as the donkey. They look left, they look right, and left, and right, and up, and down, and soon they find that their enthusiasm is gone, and they've never purchased a single property. Therefore, in the beginning of your investing, find one strategy and one niche, and pursue it until you have it mastered. Perhaps you decide you are going to flip a house. Then become an expert at that. Focus all your efforts on that. Do a flip. Get a firm understanding of the process. Then, and only then, consider other niches.

BEN LEYBOVICH

BiggerPockets Podcast ■ Episodes 14, 61, and 152

Ben Leybovich was born in Russia and moved to the United States with his family in 1989 at the age of 13 with the goal of becoming a professional violinist. While he was attending graduate school, well on his way to achieving this goal, he was diagnosed with multiple sclerosis and everything changed. Doctors advised him to consider other opportunities to make income because, depending on how his condition developed, he might not be able to play the fiddle at the same high level for much longer. This life-changing event started him on the path to investing in real estate.

His first deal was a house that he planned to flip but, because he didn't have enough money to buy the property and pay for the rehab, he tried to partner with a friend. Rather than partnering, however, Ben's friend said he was looking for a nice rental and paid him $20,000 for the deal. "That first deal was the easiest deal I have ever done—by far," he says. He then went on to buy three single-family homes before he switched techniques and began to invest in multifamily properties.

"I am a buy-and-hold guy and I prefer multifamily," Ben proclaims. He also adds that, "It doesn't take any more time and effort to put together a $500,000 deal than it does for a $50,000 deal. The numbers are bigger is all it is. Real estate isn't about numbers; it's about people and stories. It's true that we use numbers to tell those stories, but fundamentally, that's what it's about."

Ben used to find deals by sending out direct mailers, but over time he has developed a positive reputation, and as a result, people now bring deals to him. "This business is about reputation, and eventually it catches up to you," he advises. Today, as he inspects potential properties to invest in, he continually asks himself, *Would I want to live here?* If the answer is no, he knows he is going to have the hardest sales job ever. "I want the units to sell themselves. It's a much easier job to landlord if people want to be there." He manages his own properties and hires out any maintenance issues that arise, so the fewer tenant issues he has, the better.

Unlike other multifamily investors who have a lot of capital to invest, Ben relies on creative financing to fund his deals. "I define creative financing as a combination of tools, techniques, terms, and approaches, which allow us to gain ownership of assets without access to cash," Ben says. He went on to explain how he purchased a ten-unit apartment in Ohio for $373,000, using a commercial loan to cover 70 percent, private money to cover 25 percent, and his own money to cover the remaining 5 percent. But after using the proration of rents and assignment of security deposits, he was left to pay only $5,300 at closing, which came out to 1.5 percent.

Ben and his wife recently moved to Chandler, Arizona, where he purchased a home that has an attached additional unit, called a "casita," which they rent out as a short-term vacation home. This pays most of the cost of their mortgage, and they live almost for free. Ben has also shifted his gaze toward buying larger multifamily properties, aiming to become a real estate syndicator with 100-plus-unit buildings. And while his niches and his location have changed, his ultimate goal hasn't: He wants to continually grow his portfolio and increase his passive cash flow but still have plenty of time to do what matters the most to him— spending time with his family.

Wrapping It Up

The past two chapters looked at the various niches and strategies you can get involved with as a real estate investor. It's our hope that after reading this surplus of options at your disposal, something powerful stood out to you. As mentioned before, you now have a broad overview of how each works, but you don't need to master them all. Pick one niche and one strategy to start with on your journey. Maybe that means you will focus on flipping single-family houses. Maybe you want to house hack your next deal with a duplex. Or maybe you'll invest in private notes and hold them long-term. Whatever your choice, make a commitment to learning all you can on that subject. A book as broad as this one can never give you all the knowledge needed on each topic, so your education must continue beyond.

Now that you have an idea of the kind of investing you want to embark on, perhaps a nagging voice has popped up in the back of your head. *Great*, it says, *but the market is crazy competitive. Everyone is getting into real estate. How am I going to find a good deal?* Well, in the next chapter, not only are you going to discover 27 tactics for finding great deals in any market, but you'll also learn a powerful strategy that will make sure your deal pipeline never sits empty.

CHAPTER SIX
27 Ways to Find Incredible Real Estate Deals

Did you hear the one about the man who lost his car keys outside his favorite restaurant?

It was late at night, and he was on his hands and knees looking for those keys under the glow of a streetlight.

As he searched, a woman who was walking by took notice and began to help in the search.

They looked in the grass.

They looked in the gutter.

They looked under the bushes.

Finally, after an hour of searching, the woman said to the man, "We've been looking for your keys for over an hour. Are you sure you lost them here?"

The man looked at her and said, "No, I lost them three blocks up the street. But it was too dark to look up there, so I've been looking down here under the light."

Although this joke is good for a chuckle, it also illustrates a point about real estate investing. People often don't know where to look. They know the goal, but they are looking in the wrong place.

We want to help you look in the right place. But to do that, we first need to separate the two sides of deal acquisitions:

- The Framework (a way of thinking about finding deals)
- The Tactics (the specific methods used to get leads)

You see, we could throw a million different tactics at you, but without the proper framework, you'll be relying on luck to get a deal. In fact, we would argue that the lack of a solid framework is the No. 1 most common reason people struggle to find deals and, inevitably, quit their pursuit of financial freedom through real estate. As entrepreneur Derek Sivers aptly put it, "If more information was the answer, we'd all be billionaires with rock star abs." We'll give you the tactics (27 of them!) in just a moment, but first, let's nail down the framework that will get you more deals than you ever thought possible.

We call that Framework the LAPS Funnel.

The LAPS Funnel

Every single successful real estate investor follows the same process for finding deals.

Yes, every single one—whether they know it or not.

And those who buy a lot of real estate deals have simply found better ways to work this process. Those who work it don't complain about "not having any deals" because they have more deals than they know what to do with.

Wouldn't you like to know the exact process now, so you, too, can get an unlimited number of deals to buy?

Good, because that's exactly what you're about to learn.

As an investor, your job is not to buy every property you come across. In fact, your job is to disqualify as many properties as possible until you are left with the very best. This is known as a "funnel." (Because it's wide at the top and narrow at the bottom.)

You might start with thousands of possible deals, which we call "leads," but might buy just one of those. Or maybe you'll start with ten leads and buy three. The numbers will differ based on a million factors, but the funnel exists regardless. And it's all based on the principle of the Home Run Deal.

A Home Run Deal is simply any deal that is good enough to fit into your financial freedom strategy—and every property out there, no matter what, has a number that makes it a Home Run Deal.

Maybe a Home Run Deal is a house flip that will make you $25,000 in profit. Or maybe it's an apartment complex that will give you a 10 percent return on investment. Or a single-family rental that brings in $300 per month in cash flow. Whatever your goal might be in purchasing a property, there is a purchase price that would help you achieve it. Of course, sadly for us, most property owners won't sell their properties for that number. But that's okay—you don't need them all. We need to find the needle in a haystack, where our Home Run Number is also the seller's agreed-to sale price. And to find that sweet spot, you need to work the LAPS funnel.

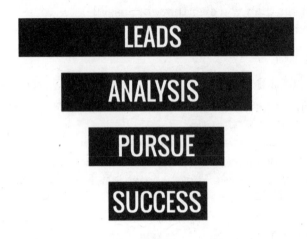

LAPS is an acronym that stands for:

- Leads
- Analysis
- Pursue
- Success

Let's break this funnel apart:

1. Leads

Your funnel begins with your options, or leads. A lead is any property that could someday become a deal for you. These leads could come from a variety of tactics, which we're going to cover in just a moment. Maybe they come from the Multiple Service Listing (MLS), a list purchased from a direct mail list provider, driving for dollars, or something else. No matter how they cross your path, any potential deal is a lead.

Some of your leads might be fairly "cold," like a house you drove by that looked interesting but you don't know anything about, not even if the owner wants to sell. Or a lead could be hot, like a seller who calls you up and says, "You need to buy my house right now; I'm done!" Leads come in all forms, and as you get better at executing the tactics that bring in leads, you can get warmer and warmer leads. But since we're going to spend the majority of this chapter on those tactics, let's move on to the second stage in the LAPS funnel: the analysis.

2. Analysis

As mentioned previously, every property has a Home Run Number, a value that will make it worth buying. Your job is to discover that number, and the only way to do this is through an analysis of the lead. You need to determine if it's worth pursuing, and you need to get the dead leads out of your funnel.

While an analysis includes a detailed look at the profitability of the deal, analyzing a deal actually begins earlier than this. What about the neighborhood? The property type? The condition? If something doesn't meet the criteria you are looking for, dump it from your funnel. For example, you sent out some letters to landlords and received back 100 phone calls, but 50 of them might be worthless, leaving you with just 50 to analyze deeper.

A deeper analysis involves looking at the metrics to determine just how much you should pay. But no matter how you run your numbers, still continue to run your numbers. Don't rely on your "gut" or on "intuition." Rely on the facts. Rely on metrics.

After analyzing those leads, it's entirely possible to submit an offer on every single one. Some investors do work this way. But in all reality, you probably will discover that some just don't make sense to waste time on. Maybe they are asking $200,000 for a duplex, but, when you analyzed the deal, you discovered that the Home Run Number is just $50,000. Or maybe the Home Run Number is actually a negative number (meaning they would have to pay you to take the property off their hands—unlikely).

This is why only a certain percentage of the deals you analyze will likely result in your making an offer, which is our next step in the LAPS funnel.

3. Pursue

You'll never get married if you don't pop the question, and you'll never get a deal if you don't make an offer. That's why the third step in the LAPS funnel is to pursue the deal.

Notice that we call this step *pursue* and not *offer*, because not every deal needs a formal offer. Sometimes a conversation with a seller will give you the answer you need. Or sometimes a formal offer is exactly what you need. Besides, if we called this step *offer*, it wouldn't be the LAPS funnel. It would be the LAOS funnel, and that just doesn't seem as cool. But regardless of what it's called, you need to go after the deal, pursue it, and try to get to "mutual acceptance" on a price that works for both parties.

4. Success

How do you handle rejection? As a real estate investor, you need to get comfy with it because you'll be rejected over and over again. But as the great Wayne Gretzky once said, "You miss 100 percent of the shots you don't take." Therefore, of all the deals you might pursue, a percentage of them will go through to completion, and you'll find yourself with a Home Run Deal. Congrats!

Of course, we're not suggesting you go out and submit low-ball offers on every single property you find, but we are saying that you probably won't get all of your offers accepted. In real estate, regular rejection just means you are doing a good job hunting for the best. In the words of a good friend and real estate agent we know, "If I make an offer and it doesn't make me blush, I offered too much."

For this reason, learn to love rejection. Every *no* is just a step toward hearing a *yes*.

This is why the LAPS funnel is so powerful—once you understand it and learn to work with it. The LAPS funnel helps reduce or eliminate the emotion of deal hunting. If a lead doesn't pan out, no problem, there is always the next one. Furthermore, you can work the funnel to get as many successes as you want. After all,

If you want more success, you need to make more offers.

If you want to make more offers, you need to analyze more deals to determine their value.

If you want to analyze more deals, you need to get more leads to analyze.

That is how you find deals, even in a crowded market—by using this simple, powerful process known as the LAPS funnel. Rather than relying on hopes and wishes, you are relying on a system, a daily set of tasks needed to get you there. You don't need to worry about your goal when you focus instead on the process.

It's that simple. But it's never that easy, because the LAPS funnel requires the most heinous four-letter word to most people: *work*. But for those willing to work, deals will never again be impossible to find.

ERIC DRENCKHAHN

BiggerPockets Podcast ▪ Episode 251

Real estate investing was in Eric Drenckhahn's blood from birth. His father, an active real estate investor, had been collecting rental units for years. But after his father suffered a debilitating stroke, Eric stepped in to help manage the portfolio and discovered that he had a knack for managing these properties. Knowing the financial freedom that can come through rental properties, and knowing he could handle the management, Eric jumped in.

Eric started his journey by focusing on buying a small multifamily property. After some education, deal analysis, and making some failed offers, Eric finally landed his first deal: a fixer-upper fourplex for $318,000. While fixing up properties might not be in most investors' skill sets, Eric was excited about the challenge. He enjoyed doing the work, but even more, he enjoyed saving all of the money that he would have spent on someone else doing the rehab. The deal was so successful for Eric that he decided to repeat the process over and over again, each year finding better and better deals. Now Eric wants to make sure that others understand: The deals didn't get better, he got better. He worked the LAPS funnel again and again and again, sometimes analyzing 100 different properties before landing a deal. But with consistency and persistence, Eric's portfolio grew, eventually expanding into several house flips as well.

Although Eric had a solid job in information technology with a great 401(k) and excellent benefits, he soon realized that work had become optional and, in July 2016, he decided to leave that job to work on real estate full time. "Every weekend at 8 o'clock in the morning, I was there," Eric says. "Every day after work at 5:30, I was there. Sometimes even before work, I would run to the property to do a couple things that I could do. So I was pretty busy." In Eric's mind, any idle time is time an investor could be making money. "Every hour you sit on the couch, you're not making money. And any time you can get off your butt and turn it into something, even if you're only making $10 an hour, that's still $10 more than nothing."

So how did he get all these fancy rehab skills? He credits two sources: YouTube, and trial and error. "The first few times it may take you a little longer than a professional, but over time you get a little better. And changing a faucet isn't that hard. But once you change one, maybe you can change something else. Before you know it, you're pulling toilets and redoing shower valves or whatever."

Eric justifies the DIY work by how much money he saves doing it himself. "I hate to leave a dollar on the table. I probably increase my annual income by at least $50,000 a year doing property management and maintenance myself," he says.

While many investors outsource property management to free up more of their time and attention, Eric sees this as a waste. "Managing a property is a no brainer," he explains. "They [property managers] don't do anything. All they do is answer the phone. As long as you have phone access, you can be anywhere in the world and do it." If for some reason Eric is not able to work on the maintenance issue himself, he simply calls a contractor on his list or looks up a reputable company online. He admits that it will probably cost more, but it takes care of the problem immediately and effectively. Eric also coaches his tenants, sometimes over the phone, on how to fix minor problems in their units.

Despite loving to stay busy, Eric has been trying to take more and more time away from his investments to relax and enjoy life. He has been taking his girlfriend on trips around the country and is working on obtaining a fifth-wheel travel trailer, planning to visit national parks around the country.

27 Powerful Tactics for Finding Great Deals

The remainder of this chapter is going to focus on the tactics that will bring the leads into your funnel. But let us warn you, this chapter might feel a bit like you are drinking from a fire hose. There are many different ways to find real estate deals, and new tactics are being discovered and refined all the time. Some might work incredibly well in your market and for your niche, while others might be worthless. Therefore, we decided to unload a massive number of strategies on you, so you can get a high-level overview of each and find an acquisitions strategy that works for you. Don't worry about mastering each and every technique we're about to show you. Instead, find something that works, become an expert on that tactic, and stick with it.

Let's get to the tactics!

1. MLS/Real Estate Agent

Of course, let's start with the big one: the MLS. No, we're not talking about Major League Soccer. We're talking about the Multiple Listing Service. Back in the old days, when you wanted to sell your house with a real estate agent, your agent would write down all the information and then add it to their local list of available properties. Over time, these "lists" have become digitized and combined together to make what we commonly refer to as the MLS. In other words, it's all the properties that are currently for sale by real estate agents.

Of course, trying to search the MLS is not as easy as it might sound. Real estate agents hold on to this data like a cat clinging to the side of a bathtub while being bathed. It's not fun. You do have a few options, though.

First, you can try searching one of the third-party property portfolios, like Realtor.com, Zillow.com, Trulia.com, or Redfin.com. These websites have negotiated with the various MLS lists around the country to give you access to listings. The problem with using these sites is twofold:

- Their information might be dated.
- Their information is incomplete.

You see, many local real estate MLSs have decided to pull their listings from these sites to keep a tight rein on their monopolies. Some states or locations might be better than others, so these portals might be fantastic in your area, or they might be terrible. You won't know until you start searching. Additionally, some of the portals might be better or worse than others. In my area, Zillow.com has almost no listings, yet Realtor.com has hundreds. So, of course, I spend more time at Realtor.com. But your area might be the opposite.

The second option you have for searching the MLS is through a real estate agent *directly*. This means the agent will send you information you need to know about the properties that are for sale. Your agent should be able to set you up with an automated email that will send you properties when they meet your qualifications. You should definitely do this, because when it comes to getting deals on the MLS, speed is key. Once you find a deal on the MLS, you'll need a real estate agent to get the deal in your portfolio. A good agent will help you negotiate or help you find similar deals. But don't worry, that's the easy part, because the agent is typically paid by the *seller*. Start searching the MLS today and see what you can find in your area.

2. Driving for Dollars

Do you know how to drive? Okay, good. That means you can definitely do this powerful method for finding good real estate deals. Driving for dollars is the practice of getting into your car and ... wait for it ... driving. Driving for dollars isn't just about driving. It's about driving with a purpose. Your purpose? Looking for potential deals. We know what you are thinking: *What does a good deal look like?* For the purpose of driving for dollars, you are looking for any property that looks distressed, damaged, vacant, or has other signs that the owner might not want to own it anymore. This could include:

- long grass
- newspapers piling up
- legal notices on the doors/windows
- tarps on the roof
- old For Sale or For Rent signs that have been left behind
- or really anything else that makes you say, "Huh ... I bet they don't live there anymore."

Now, just finding the homes doesn't mean you are going to buy them. For that, you are going to need to do some extra work. Remember the funnel we talked about earlier? Find more deals, analyze more deals, offer on more deals, get more deals? We have another funnel here:

Find deals → Find address or phone numbers for the owners → Contact owners → Find out if they want to sell → Make an offer.

In other words, you need to do some work to find out who owns the property, and then you need to get in touch with them. This may not be the most scalable option on this list, but if you have more time than money to find deals, it can be a great strategy.

ERIK STARK

BiggerPockets Podcast ■ Episodes 93 and 218

Erik Stark co-owns and operates a real estate investing company with his business partner, Steve Mills. The two got their start in 2007 wholesaling deals in Michigan, and over time they transitioned into house flipping and finally into rental properties that include multifamily, commercial, and new developments. Erik handles the deal-flow side of the business, which includes the marketing, acquisition, deal structuring, and raising capital, while his business partner takes care of the big ideas and construction side of the business, including development, city planning, building, and zoning.

For anyone who is starting off trying to find deals, Erik gives the following advice: "You need to stop chasing opportunity and start working a strategy. Even if you are going to go out and do a driving-for-dollars campaign, pick one area that is relatively close, drive those streets, and create a campaign based on either highly distressed or highly desirable properties that you would like to mail over and over. To me, that's what we call working a strategy."

Erik still employs this strategy for his own company. He drives through A- and B-rated neighborhoods that are in demand and have a high concentration of sales. He takes yellow legal pads with him—one for single-family homes and one for multifamily properties. When he begins in a particular neighborhood, he writes the name of the street on the top of the page and then writes down each house number that he wants to target. When he reaches the next street, he flips the page and starts the process again. After he has compiled a list of a few hundred, he sends all of the addresses to his virtual assistant. She then enters them in a spreadsheet and researches the owners through their tax records. Erik sends the owners a very personalized letter and a free copy of a short book he created to stand out from all the other investors who send boring postcards and generic letters.

Erik sends out his mailers every Saturday morning, so people will typically get them by Tuesday or Wednesday. In his own research, he has found that he almost never gets a response if the person receives a mailer after Wednesday. He will then repeatedly send out more of his mailers. "The marketing statistics are clear," he says. "The response rate—the percentage of people who respond to the mailer—might only be 2 percent on the first mailing, but it can move up to maybe 4 percent on the next, then 7 percent, then 10 percent. Get that mail out as fast as you can." Erik jokes that you would not believe how often he gets a deal four years after he sent the homeowners their mailers.

After someone contacts him about the mailer, he attempts to set up a face-to-face meeting to start building a relationship with the potential seller. He asks them questions to learn about where they are and where they want to go so he can provide a solution. It is only then that they hammer out the specific details. It's this personalized process that gets him more deals than his competition in the end.

---

3. Walking for Dollars

Walking for dollars is almost identical to driving for dollars, except for one thing. Yep, you are walking. Walking for dollars will accomplish two things:

- It's a free method to find deals.
- You'll get in better shape.

While walking for dollars is almost identical to driving for dollars, walking has some distinct advantages over driving, besides the health benefits. By walking, you'll have more time to really look at the properties. I'd recommend setting aside one hour per day for this activity, and pick a new area each time. Within a few months, you'll become an expert on your local area *and* you'll be down a few pounds. Win-win, right?

Additionally, by walking, you'll be able to strike up more conversations with locals. Tell everyone you meet that you are looking to buy a property in the area and ask if they know anyone who would want to sell. Bring a stack of your business cards and hand them out to anyone you meet. You'll just need to follow the same steps that you learned under driving for dollars to track down the owners of any vacant properties. You can do this.

4. Civic or Religious Organizations

Religious gatherings are usually the largest networking events most people regularly attend. Maybe you don't go to church, but it's likely you attend some kind of similar club or organization, whether it's religion-based or not. The point is: Make sure people know what you do—wherever you go. People want to help you achieve your goals when they know what you want. Think about it: If someone were to tell you, "Hey, I'm looking to adopt a baby kitten," or, "I'm looking for a job in a lawyer's office," wouldn't you help that person out if you could?

The point is, when people know what you want, they will instinctively want to help you get it. So talk about yourself and what you want. Let people at your church know that you invest in real estate. It doesn't mean standing up in front of the congregation and shouting it. But don't hide the fact from those around you. When people ask what do you do, tell them.

This is how I (Brandon) found my first apartment complex. I had just finished reading *The ABCs of Real Estate Investing* by Ken McElroy. I was blown away! I knew that buying a fixer-upper apartment complex was going to be the path I would take to financial freedom. So I told everyone I knew about it, including a nice couple from my church. After I told them, they looked at me a little funny and said, "That's interesting, Brandon, because we actually have an apartment complex we are looking to sell." I would never have found that property without telling everyone I knew about what I wanted—even if it was at church.

5. Real Estate Clubs

In nearly every major city in the United States, you'll find real estate clubs and meet-ups. These are regular meetings held by regular people who all want to achieve their goals through real estate. Although many of the people at these clubs will be newbies, some will be advanced investors. Real estate clubs differ in size, quality, and purpose, depending on who's leading them. There are real estate clubs that exist only to make the organizer rich, and they often do that by partnering with traveling salesmen who pitch their products and pay the organizer a commission. Other clubs are simply made up of people who care about real estate getting together for a beer. Real estate clubs can be a great way to find deals because of the networking that happens. Think about it: dozens of people who all care about real estate in one room. Some might be wholesalers, which we'll talk about in a moment. Others might be lenders. Others might be tired landlords. You never know until you go and start talking. Check out www.BiggerPockets.com/events for a list of meet-ups in your area, and if you don't find one, consider starting your own.

6. Direct Mail

One of the most common and scalable ways to find real estate deals, direct mail marketing is the practice of sending out a large number of hard-copy letters or postcards that ask if the recipient is interested in selling their property. The goal with direct mail, of course, is to find deals from people who are motivated to sell but might not want to work with a real estate agent. Of course, most people will never call you back, but that's okay. It's all about having a funnel (as we've talked about numerous times already). Of course, direct mail marketing is not free. It costs money. You'll need to pay to get a list of people to send to, you'll need to pay to print the letters (though you can write them yourself), and you'll need to mail them. The goal with direct mail is to make more on the deals than you spend on the mailing.

Now direct mail might seem a bit confusing, so let me give you an example of how a direct mailing campaign might work:

- Bob sends out 2,000 letters, costing him $3,000 to do so.
- Of those 2,000 letters, 50 people call Bob to find out more information.
- Of those 50 phone calls, Bob is able to make ten appointments to look at their properties.
- Of those ten appointments (and ten offers), one person says yes and sells Bob the property.

You might be thinking, *Why would I spend $3,000 to get one deal?* Well, what if that deal gave you a $20,000 profit on a flip? What if it gave you $500 per month in passive income on a rental property? What if it gave you a quick $5,000 on a wholesale flip? Spending $3,000 doesn't seem so bad now, does it?

Of course, direct mail marketing is a good way to lose a lot of money *fast*. There are many moving parts, and you'll need to constantly monitor, test, and tweak your mailing campaign. You'll need to find the right people to send to, find the best material to send (postcard versus letter, handwritten versus typed, etc.), and you'll need to find the right system for handling all those calls. Plus, you'll need to know how to talk to people and negotiate a great price. This process is not easy, but it is effective for those who are willing to do the work needed to master direct mail marketing.

LANCE WAKEFIELD
BiggerPockets Podcast ■ Episode 236

Lance Wakefield knows what it's like to have everything, lose it all, and come back stronger. He started his entrepreneurial journey with a single rental property that he was able to house hack, not only living for free, but making $1,500 per month in profit as well. Even with the success of this deal, though, he hadn't yet realized the power of real estate investing. He instead focused his efforts on creating several used car dealerships and growing his family, marrying his girlfriend, and having a little girl. Everything was going great, but in 2013, his world came crashing down around him with one tragedy after another.

First, Lance's wife filed for divorce, moving his daughter across the country. Then his best friend died from sudden heart failure, followed immediately by the unexpected death of his brother. And the dark times weren't over yet. While Lance was attending his late brother's funeral, one of the managers from his Las Vegas dealership stole all of his files, sold all the cars for cash, and disappeared, devastating Lance's business overnight, leaving him with massive debt and no income. Lance was at rock bottom.

At this point, things began to improve. He met his current wife, who helped comfort him while he was grieving and recovering from these tragedies. With his parents' help, he was able to fix the mess with his business and get it straightened out, but Lance decided not to reenter the used car business. Instead, he decided to try his hand at real estate investing, focusing on flipping a house with a friend. Despite not making any money on that first flip, Lance learned a great deal and decided to press on anyway. His next flip made nothing as well, but Lance was determined to succeed. In order to make the kinds of profits he wanted, he knew he'd have to go about finding deals in another way. So Lance started a small direct mail campaign. The resulting flips gave him more lessons than money. But he realized that direct mail marketing would work and would be his ticket to financial freedom.

Around this time, Lance began to network with other investors on BiggerPockets and ended up partnering with a friend he met on the site. She had just wholesaled a deal that was down the street from a property he was looking into. She convinced him to wholesale that property to the same person that she had made a deal with, and together they each made $15,000—without needing to manage contractors or deal with the drama and risk of a rehab. He realized wholesaling might be a better fit for his business model, and after selling two other contracts at a local BiggerPockets meet-up, making $55,000 from that one event, he was convinced. "I never really made any money flipping homes," Lance remarks, "but with wholesaling it was like, boom! Here's $30,000. Boom! Here's another $25,000."

Lance took the money earned from those early deals and poured it back into his funnel, buying more and more direct mail marketing, and continually refining his system. "We're spending $50,000 a month in marketing," he says. "We have systems set up that create deals." Currently Lance and his team have 86 properties under contract; they send out 125,000 mailers a month. They have 13 employees, and his company's net profit is $400,000 per month ... and they continue to grow.

- - - - - - ━━━━━━━━━━━━━━━━━━━━━━━━━━━━━━━━ - - - - - -

7. Courthouse Steps

When a homeowner can no longer pay the mortgage on their property, the bank is forced to foreclose on the homeowner in order to get the property back. Entering into the middle of that foreclosure process can be a powerful way to find great deals, but it doesn't come without some risk. This tactic involves purchasing a property at a public auction on the courthouse steps. But before you get started with this strategy, here are a few important things you must know:

First, understand that you must pay cash—that's right, no bank financing available here. Typically you will need to bring multiple cashier's checks to the auction. You'll pay for the property the same day, so cash is required. However, you could also use a hard-money lender if your lender is willing to work with you to make it happen.

In addition, when buying on the courthouse steps, you are usually unable to get inside the property, which means that sometimes you don't really know what you are getting. Although you can get a decent idea by looking through windows, surprises are bound to pop up.

When you get to the courthouse for the auction, understand that you are bidding *against* the bank, even if a representative from the bank doesn't show up. So, sorry, that means you probably won't get a house for $1, even if no one shows up to bid, because, in most areas, the starting bid (and lowest bid) is whatever the debt is on a property. Therefore, if the bank that is foreclosing on the property is owed $150,000, you likely won't get the deal for any less than that. If no one bids on the deal (which is common), then the house automatically goes back to the bank that started the foreclosure process. It later will become a bank repo, probably listed on the MLS.

And when you buy on the courthouse steps, you are buying the house with all junk attached. I'm not just talking about physical junk (though you'll get that, too). I'm talking about the liens that have been placed on the house. For example, if the former owner was sued by a contractor, and that contractor placed a mechanic's lien on the house, that lien may be transferred to your responsibility. Therefore, it's important to do some title research before bidding on any courthouse-steps auction house. Make sure you know what you are bidding on.

After purchasing the property on the courthouse steps, the title will be transferred to your name. However, the former owners may still live on the property and will need to be formally evicted in order for you to get the house.

At this point, we've probably talked you out of ever buying a house on the courthouse steps, but that's not our intention. Many of the savviest investors we know today are successfully buying properties this way, and for some, it's their No. 1 avenue for finding incredible deals. If you plan to go this route, be sure to do your research and learn the best strategies to reduce the risk and snag a great deal.

8. Eviction Records

If you've ever had to do an eviction, you'll understand the frustrations involved. It's stressful, it's expensive, and it's depressing. Most landlords hate the process—so much so that they might be willing to sell. Therefore, if you want to find an amazing deal, why not call up local landlords while they are in the middle of an eviction? Let them know that you are looking to buy real estate, and ask if they have any problem properties they want to unload. Of course, not every landlord is going to say yes. But you don't need every one. You just need one. And, in the process, you'll likely gain a number of friends or colleagues who are in the same business you are in. Networking is a nice bonus to this strategy.

How do you go about contacting landlords who are going through an eviction? The eviction records from your local county are a matter of public record, which means you can get a list of all the current eviction filings. You can discover the name of the tenant being evicted and the address of the property, and probably the name of the owner as well (though it might be the name of the property management company). If you don't get the owner's name, a simple search at your county assessor's office will tell you the name and mailing address of the owner. Then get in touch and see what you can make happen.

9. Craigslist Ads

A lot of people don't have a pile of cash sitting around to start getting leads for their real estate business. That's why this tip is one of the first we recommend for people who are looking to get leads without spending any money. It takes just a couple of minutes per week and can even be completely outsourced: Craigslist ads.

Of course, you know Craigslist. The simple online classifieds page that completely destroyed the entire newspaper industry. You can use Craigslist for all sorts of things, like:

- getting a job
- selling your bike
- trading your Pokémon cards for Magic: The Gathering cards
- meeting a "nice lady"

You get the idea. With millions of people using Craigslist every single day, why not post a simple ad that says you are looking to buy a house?

There are several categories in your local Craigslist where you could place this ad, and you can test different places to find the best. But perhaps just start in the "Housing Wanted" section. The ad doesn't need to be complex, just something simple like this:

Feel free to copy this ad entirely, right now. Or come up with your own version. Be sure to renew the ad every week, so that it consistently pops up in the newest Craigslist listings.

10. Craigslist "For-Rent" Ads

Okay, so posting an ad on Craigslist is *easy*. But anyone can do that. And in some areas, many people do. We want to talk about another way to use Craigslist to find deals. It requires a bit more effort and can lead to tremendous results: Contacting landlords who post "For Rent" ads.

Not every landlord wants to sell, but would you imagine some of them would? Maybe 20 percent? Maybe 10 percent? Maybe 5 percent? Who cares! The point is, these landlords are giving you their phone number. And you already know they own rental properties, so why not give them a call and simply ask? By calling them, you'll get a lot of "no thanks" messages. And that's okay, because you now have a new landlord to network with. Maybe they'll become a mentor to you. Maybe you'll do deals together in the future. Maybe they'll sell you a property next year.

The point is, by calling the mom and pop landlords on Craigslist, you are accomplishing two major goals:

- Networking
- Deal Finding

And it's 100 percent free. So can you dedicate 20 minutes per day to call the landlords who are posting For Rent ads on Craigslist? How about 20 minutes per week? Give it a try for six months and see what happens.

11. Craigslist Automation

Let's talk about one more strategy for using Craigslist to find deals, and this one is especially cool because much of it can be automated. But before we get to the automation, let's talk about the strategy.

First, let's assume that some people want to sell their home for sale by owner (FSBO) and will use Craigslist to do it. Wouldn't you want to know about these people? Wouldn't you want to call them and inquire more? Of course! You could go on Craigslist every single day and look at the newest FSBO ads, but let's make it a little easier through automation. You can sign up to receive an automated email of ads that contain keywords you specify, such as:

- FSBO
- Fixer
- Needs work
- Handyman special
- Handyman
- Priced to sell
- Repairs
- Quick
- Cash only
- Cash offer only
- Reno
- Motivated
- Will not qualify
- Unpermitted
- Upside
- TLC
- Teardown
- Sold for land value
- As is
- Lots of potential
- Needs work
- Lot of work

It will take a few minutes to set this up, but then you'll be able to just wait for ads with those keywords to pop up. Or for those who are more computer savvy, you can use Ifttt.com to set this up as well, with its more advanced automation options.

12. The BiggerPockets Marketplace

The BiggerPockets Marketplace is where real estate investors go to buy and sell deals on BiggerPockets. Dozens of deals are posted every hour of the day, many that might fit your ideal investment.

Of course, the BiggerPockets Marketplace is a nationwide platform, so simply scanning the list might not be the most efficient use of your time if you are only buying in one area. Lucky for you, BiggerPockets has made it really easy to set up automated alerts for any term you'd like, so that you'll be notified instantly when a deal hits the market in your area. This is known as the BiggerPockets Keyword Alert System. While keywords can be used for anything on the BiggerPockets Forums (for instance, if you want to be notified about the words *flipping* or *wholesaling*), we'd highly recommend setting up keyword alerts for the names of cities near where you invest.

13. Signs

Okay, let's get out of the digital world and get to some tangible, real-world methods for attracting leads to your real estate business. The first method we want to talk about is also one of the oldest methods: signs. That's right, physical signs.

Signs come in a lot of shapes and sizes, and we'll talk about a number of them. Signs can be effective because of the mass quantity of eyeballs that read the message, even if only a small percentage ever respond.

One method taught by a lot of real estate gurus is the use of "bandit signs." Bandit signs are the small corrugated cardboard or plastic signs, sometimes handwritten, that have messages like "I will buy your house for ca$h! Call 555-555-5555." Investors, especially wholesalers, place dozens (or even hundreds) of these signs all around an area, usually on telephone poles or in lawns near popular intersections. The problem with bandit signs, though, is simple: They are often illegal (hence the name *bandit* signs).

Many jurisdictions in the U.S. have banned these signs, because, honestly, they look like crap, and they litter an area with garbage. No one likes to see an intersection with a bunch of handwritten bandit signs. Now we're not saying they don't work, but we don't ever recommend breaking the law to get deals. It's not sustainable, it gives investors a bad name, and it brings down the value of a community. If you want to use these kinds of signs, do it right. Talk to your local governing body and find out what is allowed. Some areas issue permits for signage; others have no problem with bandit signs. But be sure to check first. (And if you are rehabbing a property and you own the land, why not place a bandit sign in the front yard?)

If you've decided bandit signs are not for you, here are some of the most common other types used to attract leads.

14. Billboards

A billboard can be a great way to reach a large number of people, and depending on your area, a billboard might be cheaper than you think. Your billboard ad should be simple, big, and obvious. Why? Because people are driving by at 50 mph or faster. You have just a few seconds to grab their attention.

15. Car Signs

If you drive around a lot, you could consider placing an I Buy Houses sign on the side of your car, truck, or van. While you may think this is silly, consider: From 30,000 to 70,000 people might see your ad every month. Not so silly now, is it? A sign on your car can be as complex as a total car wrap, or as simple as a magnetic sign that you stick on both sides of the car. Just be careful—jerks tend to steal these magnetic signs just because they can.

16. TV and Radio

For those looking to really bring in a lot of leads for their real estate business, consider radio or TV ads. We know what you are thinking: *That's too expensive.* Maybe, but you might be surprised at how scalable and inexpensive mass media marketing can be. For example, how much do you think it would cost to hire a professional DJ to record a 30-second ad for you?

$5,000?
$1,000?
$500?

What if we told you that you could create a high-quality radio ad for just ... wait for it ... five bucks. Yes, that's $5. Impossible, you say? Not if you know Fiverr.com. Fiverr is an incredible website where you can hire people to do a variety of tasks for you, starting at just $5. For example, for five bucks, you could:

- Get a custom caricature of your face
- Get lyrics written for a song you wrote
- Get a video of a bunny rabbit playing drums with your company logo on it
- Hire a professional American radio DJ to record up to 100 words for you

Not bad, huh? You can also use Fiverr to create a TV ad spot, but that might take several "gigs" to get something you are proud of. Of course, you'll still need to pay to get the ad airtime on the radio or TV—and that's where the largest expense is. But we're not talking about taking out a Super Bowl ad here. We're talking about a 15- or 30-second spot on a local station. No, millions of people are not going to see/hear it, but you don't need millions. You need thousands.

And remember: It's all about the funnel. If you spend $5,000 but make $10,000, wouldn't you spend $5,000 every single day? Of course, you may not make a large return on investment with a radio or TV ad, but you won't know until you try. Call up your local radio or TV station today and see what they can tell you about ad rates. You might be pleasantly surprised.

17. For Sale by Owner Signs

As you likely know, most homes are sold with a real estate agent. The agent lists the home, other agents bring buyers in, and both agents get paid by the seller. But many people don't like this system and decide, instead, to sell the property themselves. This is known as for sale by owner or FSBO.

There are many reasons that someone might not want an agent to sell their home, but usually they want to save on the commission that an agent would make. When they go to sell their home, there are many things a homeowner might do to advertise their property, but typically you'll find they place a sign in the front yard.

Keep in mind that just because it is FSBO doesn't mean it's a good deal. In fact, we've found that most FSBO deals are actually priced way too high. People tend to be overly optimistic about what their home is worth and, as a result, they have incredible difficulty selling. This tip on finding deals connects closely to driving for dollars. You'll likely need to get in your car and drive around, looking for FSBO signs.

In addition, you can surf websites like:

- FBSO.com
- ForSaleByOwner.com
- Owner.com
- Craigslist.com
- Zillow.com

18. Expired Listings

Here's a secret for you: Many homes on the MLS never sell. Typically, when a homeowner signs an agreement with an agent to sell a property, a listing contract is signed that has a definite start and end date. After the end date passes, the home may become what agents often call an "expired listing."

Real estate agents love to get their leads from these expired listings. Many agents make it a regular practice to call all the expired listings in their area and try to get the homeowner to list the home again, this time with that agent. So why couldn't you, the investor, do the same?

If someone listed a house on the MLS for, let's say, six months, and then it didn't sell, what do you think might be going through that homeowner's mind?

- Distrust of real estate agents?
- Fear that the home may never sell?
- Fear that they might lose the house in foreclosure?

As we talk about often on BiggerPockets, real estate investors are problem solvers. So get out there and solve these homeowners' problems! Of course, there is not a website you can go to that has all these expired listings. For that, you'll likely either need:

a real estate license

OR

a real estate agent who will give you this list

Once you get the list, either mail letters, call, or simply knock on doors. Strike up a conversation and see if they'll be willing to sell the property to you. Emphasize that they will not need to pay a dime in real estate commissions, because you are buying the house directly. This can save them thousands, and you can close quickly. No need for showings, no need for them to clean their house, no need for them to struggle through a hard negotiation. Make it simple for them.

19. Family/Friends

How many friends do you have? How many family members do you have? How about acquaintances? If you are unsure, take a look at your Facebook friends list. According to Fool.com,[16] the average person has 350 Facebook friends. I know what you are thinking: *None of my 350 friends wants to sell their home to me.* Maybe, but let's do some quick math.

If you know 350 people, who also know 350 people, that means you have a second-degree connection with 122,500 people. Of course, assuming some of those are duplicates, let's halve that and safely guess 60,000 people are in your network.

Now think about it: If your Uncle Bob's neighbor is having a hard time selling his house, who's Uncle Bob going to tell them to call? If your best friend Adam's parents are looking to unload their rental properties, who is Adam going to tell them to call? If your sister's dog-sitter is losing her home to foreclosure, who will your sister tell them to call? Hopefully, you, but only if all your family and friends know what you do and what you want. How are they going to know unless you tell them? So tell them. Take a minute right now and go post this over on your Facebook wall:

"Hey, family and friends. I have some BIG news! Some of you know this already, but I'm going to become the biggest real estate investor in (insert your city or county name here)! However, I need YOUR help! If you know ANYONE who is thinking of selling their home, please give them my name and number. Maybe I can't buy their house, but it would benefit me AND them to have a conversation and brainstorm ideas. My goal is to help however I can. Thanks all for your support!"

---

[16] https://www.fool.com/investing/general/2015/03/28/the-average-american-has-this-many-facebook-friend.aspx

Your circle of influence is much larger than you probably thought because everyone you know also knows other people. And when you become the go-to person for solving real estate problems, you have the potential for a lot of leads.

20. Newspaper Ads

Although newspapers may feel like an endangered species, they can still be a powerful way to find sellers who are motivated to dump their properties. The cost of a newspaper ad will depend on the paper's distribution size, and it often offers steep discounts for those who take out ads for months rather than days.

There are several sections in which you might consider placing your ad. The most likely place would be in the classifieds section under "Real Estate Wanted" or "General." You will want to keep your ad short and direct, typically fewer than 120 characters.

SELL YOUR HOUSE FAST!
We buy any condition, fast closing, & pay CA$H.
Call Now: **555.555.5555** (24-hr REC MSG.)

You may also find reasonable rates for an ad directly in the newspaper. The cost of these ads will depend on the location and size of your ad. You could potentially get an ad as small as a business card or as large as a full-page spread.

21. Landlord Industry Magazines/Newspapers

Another type of newspaper you might want to place an advertisement in would be landlord- or real estate-focused industry magazines. For example, in Washington state, the Washington Landlord Association puts out a quarterly magazine to 43,000 landlords and property managers. Placing an ad in a magazine like this can be a great way to get in front of other investors who may be interested in offloading some of their properties. Ad rates can be surprisingly inexpensive.

22. Blogging/Content Marketing

Blogging ... now there's a word that wasn't around when you were a kid.

Blogging is the practice of writing articles online about a particular topic. For example, The BiggerPockets Blog focuses on articles about real estate investing. Blogs are relatively easy and cheap to start, and the content is often more casual in nature compared to newspaper or magazine articles. Great blog posts are often shared on social media and have the ability to "go viral," sending mass amounts of traffic to your site. This is known as "content marketing."

Content marketing is the practice of using information to draw people into your business. For example, you are most likely reading this book because of some form of content marketing, unless you happen to have found it sitting on the shelf of a brick-and mortar store or from browsing a bookstore's website. Maybe you read a blog post on BiggerPockets or asked Google a question that led you to the company, or you listened to an episode of the *BiggerPockets Podcast* and got hooked. That's proof that content marketing works.

So how can you use content marketing to get real estate leads? By following a three-step process:

1. Create amazing content (not "sales" content—actually provide value)
2. Promote that amazing content
3. Make sure visitors know that you buy houses

What kind of amazing content should you produce? Really, anything that you think local people are going to want to share. For example, blog posts about the following could be highly sharable in your area:

- The 10 Best Hiking Trails in [Your City]
- The 10 Healthiest Restaurants in [Your Town]
- 15 Things You Never Knew About [Your Town]
- 5 Tips for Getting a Job in [Your Town]

"But Brandon," you say, "these articles have nothing to do with buying or selling homes." Exactly. No one is going to share an article on Facebook page that says, "10 Reasons Why You Should Sell Your House to Me." Rather, content marketing is all about providing *real value* to your community, and in the process, building your brand and getting your message out.

23. Website and SEO

I (Brandon) made $50,000 in profit on a house flip last year because of a $100 website.

The seller was renting their home to family members and struggling to get them to pay any rent. Furthermore, the home was in horrible condition, and the seller feared having dozens of agents and potential buyers walk through it. Rather than listing with an agent, they searched the web for "house buyers in Grays Harbor" and ended up on my website. There, they learned a bit about what we do, how we do it, and how to contact us. A month later we purchased the house and, after a hefty rehab, my partner and I split that $50,000.

In today's tech-centered world, a website is a must. Having a well-designed website gives any business a "storefront" to the entire world, and real estate investors are no different. Potential sellers (or renters) may end up on your website from many possible sources for a variety of reasons, and they may choose to do business with you based on what they see. If nothing else, a website conveys professionalism and could be the difference between someone selling you their home or selling it to someone else.

In the past, having a website meant being a computer do-it-yourselfer, or hiring an expensive programmer to design and code a great website. Today, however, creating a website is significantly easier and faster than you could imagine. Sites like Squarespace.com and Wix.com can get your website up and running in less time than your last shower, and while it might look as if you paid someone thousands of dollars to build it, you can get it done for under $100 per year.

As this is the chapter on finding great deals, we want to share a few strategies for using your website to deliver just that. Let's get started by talking about the mostly free method, SEO.

SEO stands for search engine optimization. Essentially, it's the art and science of making your website "optimized" for search engines like Google or Bing. A search engine's job is to deliver the best answer to a searcher's inquiry, but being that search engines are not human, they must rely on certain rules to determine what a website is all about and ascertain the quality of that website. They deliver those results in order, depending on how well they answer the searcher's question. And in the SEO game, being at the top of the list matters. Nearly 50 percent of all traffic from a search term goes to the top three listings.[17] Which means you want your website to be in the top spots when a potential home seller is searching the internet for "sell my house," "how to sell my home," "home buyers in my area," or any other number of searches that motivated sellers might type.

How do you get your website to rank high?

Two primary rules:

- Provide great content that actually answers people's questions
- Get other websites to link to your website (known as "backlinks")

The first rule makes the search engines happy because they want to show valuable content. The second rule is how the search engine knows you are legit. After all, if others are talking about you, then you must have a good reputation.

Of course, there are many other technical ways to make your website more optimized for the search engines—more than we can discuss here—so be sure to do some extra research.

24. Paid Traffic

The second method used to drive traffic toward your website is through online paid marketing. You know, those little ads you see on the top and side of Google after making a search, or the ads you see in your Facebook newsfeed or in the sidebar. These ads are how Facebook and Google make most of their money. And as an investor, you can use them as sources to target potential sellers, buyers, or other business interactions.

While Facebook and Google ads may look fairly similar, they differ in several key ways:

- Facebook allows you to target who sees your ad based on their interests, location, demographics, and connections on Facebook.
- Google allows you to target who sees your ad based on their searches, web history, and location.

The benefit of these kinds of online ads is that you can arrange to pay only when the ad works. Imagine asking a local newspaper to charge you only when someone calls about your ad. There's no chance of that happening. But that's exactly what this kind of online advertising lets

---

17 www.ignitevisibility.com/ctr-google-2017/

you do. It's known as "pay-per-click" advertising, which means you only pay when someone clicks on an ad and goes to your site. With pay-per-click advertising (such as ads on Facebook, Google, or Bing), you only have to pay for the ad when it has accomplished the goal of placing people in your marketing funnel.

Most online pay-per-click advertisements allow you to be location-specific, which means you can choose to have your advertisement seen only by individuals within ten, 100, or any number of miles of your specified location. This is especially helpful for real estate investors trying to purchase a property in a particular location. For example, you can create a well-written advertisement offering to buy any house, any condition, for cash. Then you can target people within a certain age bracket or in certain income levels.

CHRIS CLOTHIER
BiggerPockets Podcast ▪ Episodes 26, 122, and 224

Chris Clothier knows a thing or two about marketing for real estate. You have to when you buy more than 20 houses per week. But in the beginning, he knew nothing about real estate, only stumbling into it after watching a TV program and learning that rental properties were a true way to build wealth. Chris, his father, and his brother created a turnkey investment company based in Memphis, Tennessee, in 2003. They started out working from the father's truck, buying one house at a time. But over the past 15 years, their company has grown exponentially, in both profits and regions of the United States.

To drive this deal machine, Chris has built a stable marketing funnel that brings in consistent leads to work the LAPS system from within. In previous years, Chris and his team would find deals on the MLS, but today, due to increased competition, they often have to rely on other methods to find deals, including buying properties that many other investors avoid (such as properties with mold or fire damage) and purchasing properties before they go on MLS. They employ direct mail marketing and advertisements on social media to drive interest from sellers (which is proving to be quite promising), but still, their most successful method for finding deals is through the solid relationships they've cultivated with agents, brokers, and sellers, using their reputation to beat out competition. Chris explains that they have built up a lot of trust because of their honesty and commitment to close on every deal they put under contract.

Once these leads enter their funnel, they immediately begin running the numbers to determine how much they can pay, and then they start making offers. Of course, many of their offers get rejected (hundreds per week), but because they focus on the process, in time, they get enough deals to continually grow their business. They've truly mastered all parts of the funnel.

Today, Chris's family's company, Memphis Invest, has more than 91 employees in six offices across the country (Memphis, Tennessee; Dallas and Houston, Texas; Little Rock, Arkansas; Oklahoma City, Oklahoma; and St. Louis, Missouri). They manage about 5,000 properties and have more than 2,000 clients, and their combined portfolios under management total more than $600 million. And it's all thanks to a strong marketing funnel.

For those who haven't done many deals and don't have an established reputation, Chris recommends that you start building relationships with people in your market. "You have to believe in yourself and sell yourself," he says. "You have to put yourself out there." He suggests that you find the three or four biggest real estate agents in your area, take them out to lunch, tell them who you are and what you want to do, and ask them to start making offers on your behalf. He says that if you are honest and up front, and show that you're serious and have a plan and funding in place, these agents are going to want to work with you because they're hungry and want to get to the number one spot. Chris also advises to partner up with a mentor who has experience, contacts, and an established reputation. "It's an absolute people business, and the more people you know, the more likely it is you're going to have success," he says.

- - - - - ———————————————————————————————— - - - - -

25. Wholesalers

Back in Chapter Five, we looked at the strategy known as wholesaling. If you'll recall, a wholesaler is someone who spends their time working the LAPS funnel to bring in great deals. Rather than purchasing those deals for themselves, they pass the deals on to another real estate investor for a fee. It would make sense, then, that if you are trying to buy real estate deals, you need to get to know some great wholesalers in your market, and have them looking for deals for you. After all, if you end up paying a wholesaler $5,000–$10,000 for a great deal that makes you ten times that, why not save the trouble and let them do what they do best?

If working with wholesalers sounds like the end-all-be-all strategy for finding deals, and you are ready to ignore every other tactic in this chapter, let us give you some bad news: Many, if not most, so-called wholesalers are actually terrible at what they do and will just waste your time. Because wholesaling is often touted as the "get rich the quickest" strategy by many real estate gurus, you'll find a number of wholesalers fresh out of a boot camp who have far less knowledge than you, but they're eager to make a buck. They'll send you leads that would never work out, and their inexperience often will lead them to present numbers that are completely unrealistic. Wholesalers are especially notorious for underestimating the cost of rehabbing a home, simply because they've never done it. However, when you find a great wholesaler—someone who understands marketing, understands rehabs, understands true value—hang on to them. They could become your No. 1 source for good deals.

To find a great wholesaler, just begin networking. Attend local real estate meet-ups in your area (check out BiggerPockets.com/events for a list of local meet-ups, and consider hosting your own event if you don't see any in your area). Connect with investors across BiggerPockets and ask around for referrals. Be sure to run your own numbers on whatever "deals" any wholesalers present to you. Show them how you analyze a deal and what makes it a Home Run to you. And finally, if you can't find a great wholesaler in your area, consider training your own. There are a lot of hungry hustlers out there who, with a little advice (and perhaps a copy of this book), might do an amazing job of finding you deals.

MIKE SIMMONS

BiggerPockets Podcast ■ Episode 50

Mike Simmons wanted something different than the 9-to-5 job he was working and began to look into becoming an investor ... in stocks. But after quickly discovering that trading nontangible assets bored him to death, he decided to look for other options. One day Mike stumbled across a website about real estate investing, and he was hooked. He immediately began to soak up any and all information he could on the subject.

As he learned more and more about REI (real estate investing), Mike began to switch from one real estate strategy to another. "Flipping houses, wholesaling, lease options. I started running toward every shiny object I saw and created this paralysis of analysis," he says. "I started learning a little about everything, but I didn't really know much about any one way of doing anything."

He began to attend real estate investor meet-ups. One week an investor would insist that one particular method was the best, and then the next week another investor would tell him that the first recommendation he received was wrong, and that this particular investor's method was truly the best. With so many different options and being uncertain about which way to go, Mike did what many do: nothing. "I sat on the sidelines for four to five years before I really took the first real step into real estate," he says. "I got caught up too much into reading and analyzing different methods and models."

Finally, after those long years stuck in analysis paralysis, Mike finally decided to take the plunge. "At some point, you have to just get out and do it," he explains. "You don't really learn anything until you do your first couple of deals."

Once Mike had made up his mind to finally commit to real estate investing, he put a house under contract and secured the loan through a small local bank. Unfortunately for Mike, the real estate crash of 2008 was happening, and his bank foreclosed overnight. Mike scrambled to get another loan but was unable to secure one before the deadline, and he ended up losing the deal and his $1,000 deposit with it. While many in that same circumstance would have thrown in the towel and walked away from real estate, Mike decided to persist and go for another deal.

His optimism and fortitude paid off; four months later he purchased a property in the same neighborhood as the one he had previously lost, for half of the listing price. Looking back, he recalls that he would have lost way more than $1,000 if that first deal had gone through, so he was grateful for his initial "failure." His second deal led to a successful flip and a healthy (and quick) profit.

After a promising period of house flipping, Mike decided to switch business models and focus on wholesaling. In the last two-and-a-half years, he and his company have wholesaled more than 200 deals. Mike, his business partner, and their six employees have consistently made a profit of $1,000,000-plus per year over the past two years. They're on track this year to make more than $2,000,000 in gross profits with upward of 150 wholesale deals.

---

26. Commercial Brokers

If you are looking to buy larger real estate deals, such as apartment complexes or strip malls, commercial brokers will be your new best friends. Like their residential counterparts, commercial agents generally get paid by the seller in a transaction, meaning it likely will not cost you anything to start getting leads. But unlike residential real estate, there is no centralized "list" of all the properties for sale (though some online platforms are gaining ground toward this end, which we'll talk about next). Instead, leads will generally come from the broker themselves. But getting a great commercial broker to begin sending you quality leads is harder than it might appear due to the nature of the commercial industry and the relationship aspect.

Commercial brokers tend to work closely with a few strong buyers within their "circle of trust" and only send out deals publicly after their clients have passed on a deal. No broker wants to waste weeks of time trying to put together a deal with a stranger only to have that stranger be unable to close. Therefore, you need to begin building that relationship now. Talk regularly with the broker, take action on what they present, let them know what you want (and what you don't), and do what you can to prove that you are a legitimate buyer.

How does one find a great commercial broker? While you could pull out and wipe the dust off your handy yellow pages, we'd recommend instead checking out the brokers who are actively listing properties on the online commercial marketplaces. What are those? Well, glad you asked.

27. Online Commercial Marketplaces

As mentioned above, there is no centralized list (like the MLS on the residential side) for commercial real estate. However, there are still ways to shop for real estate deals online through several commercial real estate marketplaces. While the exact platforms you search will differ, depending on the type of investment you are buying, there exist a few large notable players, including Loopnet.com and Crexi.com. Also worth noting, sometimes commercial deals are placed on the residential listing platforms such as Zillow.com, Redfin.com, or Realtor.com. And, of course, commercial deals are also presented on the BiggerPockets Marketplace.

JERED STURM

BiggerPockets Podcast ■ Episodes 124 and 205

Jered Sturm was exposed to real estate investing as a teenager when he was hired as a handyman for a local real estate investor. At the time, he had no idea the path that it would start him on. Upon graduating from high school, he purchased a house and house hacked by renting out the vacant rooms to friends. He then started a construction company with his brother and, with it, they were able to pay their way through college and save up enough money to start investing in real estate.

After graduating from college with construction experience and not much money, the brothers decided to find cheap properties that needed a lot of rehab, renovate the properties themselves, and then sell them. They purchased their first property for $125,000 and put $25,000 of materials into the rehab (not counting what they would have paid for labor). In about three weeks it was fixed up and they were able to sell it for $220,000, netting a huge profit that they reinvested back into their business. This act of self-discipline was a strategy that they would repeat over and over again. Soon Jered was able to quit doing construction jobs for other people and focus 100 percent of his time on his own projects.

Originally, Jered found deals on the MLS, but as he increased his business, he began to drive for dollars, send out direct marketing materials, and cold-call landlords. Almost immediately, he found a landlord who was looking to sell his fourplex. Jered purchased the property for $70,000 and, after he put $40,000 into rehab and converted it to a five-unit property, it was valued at $200,000. He was hooked on rental properties. Using the income from house flipping as a way to build capital ($3,000,000, in fact), Jered eventually added a new strategy to business: buying and holding large multifamily properties in Cincinnati, Ohio.

Jered and his team started their search for an apartment building with very specific criteria, making sure to communicate this to commercial brokers who, in turn, sent a consistent flow of leads into Jered's deal pipeline. After three months of searching, they were finally contacted by a broker who had a deal for them: a 42-unit building for $2,150,000. But Jered knew he could quickly increase the value closer to $3,000,000 with some minor improvements. Knowing he was young and financing might be an issue, Jered decided to use a portfolio lender from a local bank. He prepared a large booklet of information he had on every deal he had done up to that point and presented it to the bank. With the help of this booklet and his strong negotiation skills, Jered was able to secure the exact financing option that he had been hoping for.

Moving forward, Jered and his team plan to continue increasing their large multifamily portfolio as much as they can. But it's not about the money, he says. It's about "being the best they can possibly be while helping others in the process."

Wrapping It Up

Overwhelmed yet? As mentioned earlier, you don't need to use *all* of these strategies. Instead, seek to become the best at using one or two of them. If you are looking to scale your business, then add new marketing strategies as you master old ones. Soon you might have a dozen different strategies all working simultaneously to drive consistent leads into your pipeline.

But then comes the next big hurdle: What do you do with the leads when they start coming down the pipeline? How could you possibly afford to *pay* for all the properties that you'll soon have the ability to buy? Well, if only someone would write a chapter about financing their real estate deals ...

CHAPTER SEVEN

12 Ways to Finance Your Real Estate Deals

James Bond is overrated. Sure, he gets the girl, beats the bad guy, and saves the world. But almost anyone could do what 007 does if they had his secret weapon: Q. For those unfamiliar with the films, Q is an essential character who creates and equips the hero with all the latest technological innovations that make it possible for Bond to get the girl, beat the bad guy, and save the world. When Bond found himself trapped aboard an exploding train in *GoldenEye*, his handy Omega wristwatch with built-in laser cut an escape hole in the floor. When evil henchmen and a deadly helicopter pursue Bond in a high-speed chase in *The Spy Who Loved Me*, his Q-supplied car drives off a pier into the water and transforms into a submarine. And after Bond fights and defeats an enemy agent at a French château in *Thunderball*, our hero escapes the clutches of the enemy with his portable jetpack.

You see, in each of these scenarios, Bond would be dead without Q and his gadgets. Although Bond doesn't know the extent of the danger he's about to be caught up in, he's always prepared with a plethora of fancy gizmos supplied by Q. The more gizmos he has, the greater chance he has of saving the day, no matter what situation he finds himself in.

Although it's unlikely you'll encounter henchmen, helicopters, and exploding trains in your real estate business, like Bond, you will encounter challenges, and perhaps no challenge is greater than the need for money. Luckily, there are many different methods an investor can use to finance a deal. The more methods you are familiar with, the greater chance you have of winning the deal.

The purpose of this chapter is to be your Q and hand over a dozen gadgets that you can use to finance your next deal. Just as we said about your acquisition phase, you don't need to use all the strategies we're about to list. But the more financing tactics you are aware of, the greater chance you'll have of putting together a deal, so let's get you a summary of many financing options. The list contained in this chapter is by no means comprehensive but will give you a good idea of some of the more popular financing methods.

1. All Cash

Many investors choose to pay all cash for a property. According to a joint study by BiggerPockets and Memphis Invest, 24 percent of U.S. investors use no loan at all—just their own cash—to finance their real estate investments.[18] To be clear: Even when investors use terms like *all cash,* the truth is, no "cash" is actually traded. In most cases, the buyer brings a check, usually certified funds, such as a bank cashier's check, to the title company, and the title company will write a check to the seller. Other times, the money is sent via a wire transfer from the bank. This is the easiest form of financing, as there are typically no complications. But for most investors, and probably the vast majority of new investors, all cash is not an option.

Additionally, the return given from an all cash deal will not be the same as a deal that's leveraged. Let's explore this further via an example:

John has $100,000 to invest. He can choose to use that $100,000 to buy a house that will produce $1,000 per month in income, or $12,000 per year. This equates to a 12 percent return on investment.

John could instead use that $100,000 as a 20 percent down payment on five similar homes, each listed at $100,000. With an $80,000 mortgage on each, the cash flow would be approximately $300 each month per house, which is $1,500 per month each, or $18,000 per year. This equates to an 18 percent return on investment—50 percent better than buying just one home. But adding loans adds risk, so deciding how much you should leverage comes down to your personal feelings on risk.

---

18 https://www.biggerpockets.com/rei/residential-real-estate-investor-survey-biggerpockets-memphisinvest/

2. Conventional Mortgage

As you can see from the example above, financing your investment property can produce significantly better returns than paying all cash. Most investors, then, choose to finance their investments with a cash down payment and a traditional conventional mortgage. Most traditional conventional mortgages require a minimum of 20 percent down, but may extend higher—up to 25–30 percent—for investment properties, depending on the lender. Conventional mortgages are the most common type of mortgage used by homebuyers and generally provide the lowest interest rates.

3. Portfolio Lenders

Conventional mortgage loans can originate from a variety of sources, such as banks, mortgage brokers, and credit unions. In most cases, these lending sources are not actually using their own capital to fund the loan, but are acquiring or borrowing the funds from another party or reselling the loan to government-backed institutions, like Fannie Mae and Freddie Mac, in order to replenish their own funds. As a result, most lending institutions must adhere to a very strict set of rules and guidelines when it comes time to finance an investment. These strict rules can make conventional financing difficult to obtain for many, especially for real estate investors and other self-employed borrowers.

Some banks and credit unions, however, have the ability to lend from their own funds entirely, which makes them a portfolio lender. Because the money is their own, they are able to provide more flexible loan terms and qualifying standards. Oftentimes a portfolio lender will have funds available with less-restrictive qualifications than a conventional lender.

Most banks or lending institutions don't advertise that they are portfolio lenders, but you can find them through referrals and networking with other investors. You can also simply Google institutions in your area, call each one, and ask if they offer portfolio lending.

4. FHA Loans

The Federal Housing Administration (FHA) is a United States government program that insures mortgages for banks. If you have health insurance or car insurance, you already understand the concept: pooling money to spread the risk for everyone. FHA loans are designed only for homeowners who are going to live in the property, so you cannot use an FHA-backed loan to buy a pure investment property. But you can take advantage of the exception to the rule that allows the FHA-financed home to have up to four separate units. In other words, if you plan to live in one of the units, you could buy a duplex, triplex, or fourplex.

The benefit of the FHA loan is the low down-payment requirement: currently just 3.5 percent. This can help get you started much sooner because you don't need to save up 20 percent. However, every blessing comes with a curse. While the lower down payments the FHA offers are great, the FHA does require an additional payment, called private mortgage insurance. PMI protects the lender and is required when the down payment on an FHA loan is less than 20 percent. The extra PMI payment can make your monthly outlay slightly higher, thus reducing your cash flow.

CRAIG CURELOP
BiggerPockets Podcast ▪ Episode 35 and 252

Craig Curelop was living in Silicon Valley, working at a job that he didn't really love. On the last night that he would be seeing his girlfriend for a while, his boss called and informed him that he was required to complete a project that night. This was the final straw and Craig started looking for a way out of his job. As he researched books on real estate investing, he found one that seemed to make a lot of sense called *The Book on Rental Property Investing* by Brandon Turner. After reading it and realizing that it was possible to make a living through real estate investing, even without having a lot of money to invest, he was hooked. Seeing the book was published by BiggerPockets, he became a member of the community and soon moved to Denver to work with the BiggerPockets team.

Once in Denver, he set a goal to quickly buy an investment property. He talked with five or six agents and five or six lenders until he found the right ones. "When you are looking to start REI, your first step is to find a lender and an agent. You don't need a team. Once you get those guys involved, they're going to start looking for deals, and they're going to hold you accountable," Craig says. He vetted these agents by taking the time to sit down with them and ask them questions like this:

- How long have they been in business?
- How many properties have they sold?
- Have they worked with investors before?
- Are they real estate investors themselves?

He used the same strategy with the lenders as well. "Don't just go with the first lender. Even though these loans get sold off to Fannie and Freddie, you'd be surprised at what different lenders can do for you. So make sure to do your research and due diligence," he says. "And don't be afraid to ask dumb questions. These guys are pros at first-time home-buyer situations. So ask the questions. They will answer the questions and won't make you feel stupid."

Because of the obvious financial benefits, especially in an expensive city, Craig decided he would house hack his first deal with a small multifamily property. His due diligence paid off because he ended up finding a great deal on a duplex that was less than two miles from his office at BiggerPockets. He put in a modest offer and, surprisingly, it was accepted, and he was able to purchase the house for $385,000. He financed the house with a 3.5 percent FHA loan and thus only had to put $13,475 down. The house had been newly renovated and was ready for him and a tenant to move in. Craig wasted no time in finding a tenant for his vacant unit and, in fact, had them sign the lease the same day he closed on the house. He had made sure to search for and vet potential tenants while he was waiting for the deal to close, and he recommends other new landlords to do the same, cutting down on the time the unit sits empty.

After all is said and done, today the PITI (principal, interest, taxes, and insurance) for his property totals $2,300 per month. He rents out one of the units for $1,750. This leaves him to pay the remaining $550 per month to cover the difference. But Craig is truly committed to having as few expenses as possible (to save up for his next deal) so he rents out his own room through Airbnb many nights and sleeps in his living room. Renting his room out has brought him an average of $1,100 per month, giving him the ability to live for free and make an additional $550 each month in cash flow.

---

5. 203K Loans

A subset of the FHA loan program, the 203K lets a homeowner borrow money for the house purchase and home improvement with one loan. Like the normal FHA loan, the 203K loan still allows for a low down payment, currently 3.5 percent. This loan type is also applicable for duplexes, triplexes, and fourplexes, but, like the FHA loan, it's only for owner occupants.

Because we want to make sure you fully understand the power of the 203K loan, let's walk through a quick example. John found a small duplex for $100,000 that he wants to move into, with plans to live in one half and rent the other half out. The property is in need of about $12,000 in new paint and carpet. John is able to include that $12,000 into the cost of the loan and pay just a 3.5 percent down payment of the $112,000 needed. In other words, John is able to purchase the property for a total of $3,920 down, plus closing costs. He can now get the new paint and carpet (paid for by the loan), move into his renovated home, rent out the other half, and begin making cash flow and building wealth. John is a happy camper.

6. Owner Financing

Banks or other giant lending institutions are not the only entities that can finance a property for you. In some cases, the owner of the property you want to buy can actually fund the property, and you will simply make your monthly payment to them rather than a bank. Typically, the only time property owners will do this is if they already own the home free and clear, meaning the seller cannot have an existing mortgage on the property. Seller financing can be a great option for both the buyer *and* the seller. A buyer can potentially purchase a property without the hassle and requirements of a traditional loan, and a seller can get regular fixed income for many years.

RYAN MURDOCK

BiggerPockets Podcast ▪ Episode 234

After working in the field of electronics manufacturing in Southeast Asia for several years, Ryan Murdock decided he wanted to return to the United States and start investing in real estate. Moving to Bangor, Maine, in 2007, he and his wife purchased a duplex, deciding to live in one unit and rent the other out. At the time, Ryan didn't know much about being a landlord, so he thought that since the tenants paid rent on time and didn't trash the place, they were fine. It did not take long for him and his wife to realize that there is more to having a good tenant than on-time rent payments. They struggled sharing the duplex with these tenants and eventually ended up having to evict them. While this was a difficult and daunting task initially, Ryan learned the rules for evicting tenants and he became more comfortable with the process.

After a few months, they purchased another duplex followed by additional small multifamily properties. Since managing his own properties began to take up his time, Ryan decided to start his own property management company and begin managing other people's properties as well. Within a few years, he was managing 200 units, 28 of them his own.

Ryan soon stumbled onto a deal where the seller was offering 20 units spread out over a few different buildings and willing to cover 90 percent of the financing. He crunched the numbers and it seemed like it would be a great deal, so he jumped on it. He knew that the buildings needed a lot of work and that several of the units would need to be vacated, fixed up, and rented out, but what he didn't expect was the total cost to do these tasks—especially when several evicted tenants completely destroyed the units in the process. As the costs mounted and his cash reserve vanished, Ryan was forced to go back to the seller and work out a special payment plan. It took five years of stress and headache, but eventually he was able to turn the units around, fill them with great tenants, refinance the properties, and pay back the seller the full amount. This lesson taught Ryan that, although low-money-down deals work, investors need to prepare for the unknown and worst-case scenarios.

Today, Ryan is more careful when analyzing deals. He currently owns nearly 100 units of his own, ranging from single-family homes to a 46-unit mobile home park. He funds many of his deals through owner financing (including the purchase of a ten-unit property and the 46-unit mobile home park) from an investor he met on BiggerPockets. The seller required a small down payment but was happy to provide the financing for the rest, as it ensures completely passive income for the owner for the rest of his life.

In addition to owner financing, Ryan also uses small local banks for financing, advising others to consider the same. "I think it's very important to build a relationship with a local lender," he says. "There are a lot of deals that I don't think I would have been able to do if I didn't have a personal relationship with that loan officer. He knows me and knows what I'm doing. I would not have been able to do that with a big national bank."

7. Hard Money

"Hard money" is financing that is obtained from a private business or individual for the purpose of investing in real estate. While terms and styles change often, hard money has several defining characteristics:

- Loan is primarily based on the value of the property
- Shorter term lengths (due in six to 36 months)
- Higher than normal interest (8–15 percent)
- High loan "points" (fees to get the loan)
- Many hard-money lenders do not require income verification
- Many hard-money lenders don't require credit references
- Does not show on your personal credit report
- Hard money can often fund a deal in just days
- Hard-money lenders understand when the property needs rehab work

Hard money can be beneficial for short-term loans and situations, but many investors who have used hard-money lenders have been placed in tough situations when the short-term loan ran out. Use hard money with caution, making sure you have multiple exit strategies in place before taking out this type of loan.

To help on your search to find a hard-money lender, BiggerPockets created the world's largest Hard Money Lender Directory, which you can access for free at www.BiggerPockets.com /HardMoneyLenders.

8. Private Money

Private money is similar to hard money in many respects, but is usually distinguishable because of the relationship between the lender and the borrower. Typically, with private money, the lender is not a professional like a hard-money lender, but rather an individual looking to achieve higher returns on their cash. Often there is a close relationship between a private money lender and an investor. Private money usually has fewer fees and points, and the term length can be negotiated more easily to serve the best interests of both parties.

Private lenders will lend you cash to buy property in exchange for a specific interest rate. Their investment is secured by a promissory note or mortgage on the property, which means if you don't pay, they can foreclose and take the house (just like a bank, hard money, or most other loan types). The interest rate given to a private lender is usually established up front, and the money is lent for a specified period of time, anywhere from six months to 30 years.

A private lender typically does not receive any equity stake in cash flow outside of their predetermined interest rate, but there are no hard-and-fast rules when it comes to private capital. Generally, private money is financed by one investor. These loans are also commonly used when you believe you can raise the value of the property over a short period of time, so you can take on the debt from that private money, refinance the property after adding value, and pay back the private lender. Just as with hard money, private money should only be used when you have multiple, clearly defined exit strategies.

If you are trying to build relationships for private capital, developing credibility is a must. Whether it's through blogging online about your real estate endeavors, posting your real estate updates on Facebook, talking about real estate investing in casual conversation, or attending your local real estate investment club, you need to be visible. Are you maximizing your visibility? Are you creating opportunities to highlight your investing experience to others? You don't need to be a braggart, but next time someone asks what's new in your life, share a few details of your real estate endeavors. You never know what might transpire.

9. Home Equity Loans and Lines of Credit

Many investors choose to tap into the equity in their own primary home to help finance the purchase of their investment properties. Banks and other lending institutions have many different products, such as a home equity installment loan (HEIL) or a home equity line of credit (HELOC), which allow you to tap into the equity you already have. For example, an investor may purchase a property, but instead of going through the normal hassle of trying to finance the investment property itself, they can instead take out a HELOC on their own home to pay for the property.

In order to obtain a home equity loan or line of credit, you must first have equity in your home. Banks will typically only lend up to a certain percentage of your home's value in total. This percentage differs among lenders, but it is not uncommon to find a lending institution that will offer to lend up to 90 percent of the value of your home. Let's make this even more clear with an example.

John's current home is worth $100,000. John visits with his local bank and learns that they will allow up to 90 percent debt on that home. John, therefore, can borrow a total of $90,000 on the house. If he already owes $50,000 on a first mortgage, the home equity line or loan would be capped at $40,000 to ensure the total loans didn't exceed 90 percent.

Using home equity loans and lines of credit have multiple benefits over traditional loans. First, the lien placed by the lender on the property is placed on your primary residence, not the newly purchased property. This means that the bank providing the loan won't typically even look at the new property. They don't generally concern themselves with what your intent is with the money, only your ability to pay it back. As such, the new property can be in terrible condition, and the bank likely won't care. Furthermore, because you can obtain the HELOC or HEIL before you ever buy the investment property, you can be ready with the cash in hand to put an offer on a property, giving you the ability to buy without a lender. As we briefly covered earlier when talking about buying "with cash," this can often help your deal get accepted before others.

Home equity lines and loans may also have certain tax benefits, such as the ability to deduct the interest paid on the loan if it's used for a real estate deal, as allowed by the IRS. See a qualified CPA or attorney for more information on this. And because the loan is secured by your primary residence, the interest rate on home equity loans and lines is typically very low compared to hard money or private money.

Finally, even if you don't have enough equity in your primary residence to fund 100 percent of the new deal you want to purchase, you could utilize your HELOC or HEIL to fund the down payment on the new property and obtain a regular loan for the rest. For example, let's say Sarah, an investor, wants to buy an investment property for $100,000, but doesn't have any additional funds for a down payment. She does, however, have a lot of available equity in her own primary house (she owes $50,000, but the home is worth $100,000). Sarah opens up a $20,000 home equity loan on her personal home to fund the down payment, and then gets a conventional mortgage from a bank for the remaining $80,000 on the investment property.

10. Partnerships

Back in Chapter Three we spent a good deal of time talking about real estate partnerships, so we don't need to dive too deep here. However, finding a good partner to help fund a deal is one of the best ways to finance a piece of real estate, and one that many investors without a lot of cash will love.

Partnerships work great because of something we call the Deal Delta. To put together a real estate deal, three things are required:

THE DEAL DELTA

- Knowledge
- Hustle
- Money

While all three are required to put together a good real estate investment, understand that all three don't need to be provided by you. Instead, partners can make up the difference. For example, you might bring the hustle and the knowledge, but a partner can bring the money (or some of the cash, which can be combined with another type of loan). Now you have all the parts needed for a deal to happen.

Back in 2012, a triplex came on the market in my (Brandon's) area for the incredibly low price of just $60,000. I immediately jumped at the opportunity. The deal needed about $20,000 of rehab work, in addition to the $15,000 down payment and closing costs, for a total investment of $35,000. But then I remembered: I didn't have any money, and I didn't have a W-2 job. In other words, I had no ability to fund the deal. But where most people would simply give up, I asked myself the all-important question: *How do I get this deal done?*

The answer I stumbled upon: Bring in a partner.

I spoke with Gary and Judy, friends from church I had known for many years and whom I knew shared an interest in real estate. Gary and Judy both worked stable government jobs, had good income, excellent credit—and no time. They wanted to get into real estate, but lacked the time (hustle) needed to complete the Deal Delta. So I proposed a solution: They could come up with the $35,000 needed, and I would take care of the rest. I would bring the knowledge and the hustle; they would bring the cash. We've owned this deal now for almost six years, and each year we save up our cash flow until the end of the year, then split everything evenly, 50-50. On average, we've each earned around $5,000 a year (that's more than $400 per month—each) in profit from this deal. In addition, we now have about $100,000 in equity in the property that someday we'll split and likely turn into future (larger) deals. That is the power of a partnership when funding deals.

When I tell this story, I get two completely opposite responses:

1. Why would Gary and Judy agree to lose 50 percent when they were bringing all the money? Why wouldn't they just do it themselves and get 100 percent?

2. Why would you be so generous to give someone 50 percent just for bringing the money? You found the deal, negotiated it, managed the rehab, and now manage the property on a continual basis to make sure it produces a profit. They don't have to do anything!

Funny how those two responses are the complete opposites, and each response is based on predefined opinions of what "value" is being brought. After all, I could not do the deal without their cash. They could not do the deal without my hustle/knowledge. To me, that's a perfect partnership, so we split it 50-50. But it doesn't have to be 50-50. Your partnership can be whatever you've defined it to be, based on how you and your partner view the value each party is bringing.

Finally, a partnership is like a marriage. When it's good, it's really good. But when it's bad, it's really bad. Be sure to take the time needed to find and vet your potential partner. Don't jump into bed with the first person who wants to work with you. Find someone who fits within your style, your goals, and your ambitions.

11. Commercial Loans

If you are shopping for a commercial property, such as an apartment complex, retail shop, office building, or something similar, you'll likely use a commercial lender to fund the deal. But commercial loans can also be used for residential real estate. You might go directly to a bank or credit union and speak to its commercial loan department, or you might work through a commercial loan broker, who shops several different lenders to get you competitive rates and terms.

Commercial real estate loans tend to have higher rates and fees, while also offering shorter terms. Rather than a fixed-rate loan amortized (spread out) over a 30-year period, you are more likely to get a loan that is amortized over 25 years, but only fixed for three to seven years, and then turned into a variable after five to ten years, at which time the bank will require you to pay back the loan or refinance (this is known as a "balloon payment"). While the terms might not be as friendly as a residential loan, a commercial loan can be significantly simpler to obtain than a residential loan, as the strength of the property is the primary decision-maker. Commercial lenders understand the weird nature of a real estate investor's tax return, while also understanding the desire for creative financing. Because commercial lending is far less regulated than residential lending, commercial lenders also have much more leeway in how they structure the loan, including down payments, rates, fees, and more. Decisions made by a commercial lender are made on a case-by-case basis.

When you apply for a commercial loan, the lender will typically look at three things:

1. The profitability of the deal
2. Your cash reserves
3. Your track record/financial position

Let's look at each of these separately.

The Profitability of the Deal

A commercial lender giving out multimillion-dollar loans knows that you, personally, will probably not be able to make the payments if something goes wrong. It's just too expensive. Therefore, they will look heavily at the deal itself to make sure it can support the payment. The primary metric they use to determine this is the debt service coverage ratio, or DSCR for short. This formula looks at how much cash flow, as a percentage, the property should produce.

The formula for DSCR is as follows:

DSCR = Net Operating Income / Total Mortgage Expense

Net operating income is the money left over in your bank account after all the bills have been paid (except the loan payment). So if a property makes $10,000 in rental income, and the non-mortgage expenses come to $6,000, the net operating income is $4,000 ($10,000 - $6,000 = $4,000). Let's just assume the mortgage payment (principle + interest) is equal to $3,000 per month. As you know, that means your cash flow prediction should be $1,000 per month (because you had $4,000 each month left over to pay the mortgage, and the mortgage is $3,000). Now, back to DSCR:

Net Operating Income / Total Mortgage Expense = DSCR

$4,000 / $3,000 = DSCR

$4,000 / $3,000 = 1.33

The DSCR on the above example would be 1.33. In other words, anything above one should provide positive cash flow (because there is more net operating income than expenses), but anything below one will provide negative cash flow (because there is less net operating income than expenses).

Each bank has defined what it believes is an acceptable DSCR, but usually that number hovers between 1.2 and 1.3. Below 1.2, and you'll have a lot of trouble getting a lender to fund your deal.

Your Cash Reserves

Although the bank knows you probably can't personally make the loan payment on this deal, they do want to see that you can weather any unpredictable storms. What if the economy goes into a recession and your rents drop 15 percent? What if your property manager is horrible and doubles the vacancy rate? What if asbestos is discovered in the property and an expensive removal is required? These are possible scenarios, and the lender wants to ensure that situations like this won't bankrupt you and force them to take back the property in foreclosure. The amount required in reserves will differ by lender, but a general rule of thumb is to assume 3–6 percent of your total loan balances. If you have $1,000,000 in loans on your real estate, your lender will likely require between $30,000 and $60,000 in cash reserves.

Your Track Record and Financial Position

A commercial lender knows that commercial real estate deals can be complicated. Therefore, they will look at your track record to make sure you have the skills and knowledge necessary to manage such a large amount of money. Have you done any real estate deals before? Have you invested with others? Do you pay your bills on time? How's your credit and your income? The lender knows that no matter how good a deal is, they are still investing in you, and even an incredible deal can blow up in your face if mismanaged. And as usual, each lender will have their own requirements for your track record and financial position. Some banks might only lend to you if you've been a real estate investor in the past. Others might take a risk on you if your finances are strong enough. But you won't know until you start building relationships with commercial lenders. So if your goal is to start your real estate journey with some commercial investments, start having those conversations now.

SERGE SHUKHAT

BiggerPockets Podcast ▪ Episodes 60 and 131

Serge Shukhat was a corporate controller for a tech start-up in the Bay Area when he was sent to Mesa, Arizona, for a work project in 2008. He decided that it would be best to stay in Mesa while he worked on this project, so he moved there and rented out his California home, realizing how powerful rental real estate could be for building wealth. In January 2009, he began to look for potential investments in the Arizona market. He soon found a single-family, four-bedroom home with a pool. He ran the numbers and felt he could rent it out for $1,000. He bought it for $52,000, hired a contractor, spent $4,000 fixing it up, and had it rented out in a week. Serge didn't know much about landlording at the time and did not screen his tenant very well. Within 30 days, the house began to fall apart. But with improved systems, the property stabilized and soon rent checks were coming in. Serge was hooked.

He knew that the rock-bottom foreclosure prices would not last long, so his plan was to buy up as much as he could, while he could. He was only interested in properties that most other investors were not looking into. For example, he chose properties that had unique characteristics such as at least four bedrooms, in-law suites, pools, RV parking, etc.— anything that would make his properties stand out from his competition. His original goal was to buy as cheap as possible and maximize his return on investment (ROI), but as properties began to fall apart, he realized he needed to change his strategy and buy newer/better properties.

Serge originally started looking for deals on the MLS, but over time he built a relationship with a group of guys from Texas who were buying $1 million worth of foreclosed houses at a time and would let him cherry-pick three or four of them. From the beginning, he had specific criteria when selecting potential properties. "I look for cash flow, equity, and value-add. Some say you can't get all three, but I seem to find them," he says.

As the market began to rebound, the cheap single-family homes window looked like it was closing, so he switched gears and started focusing on multifamily homes. He soon came across a property that was one of ten communal foreclosed fiveplexes. He was able to buy the first for $42,000, but there was a lot of risk due to the remaining nine vacant fore-closed properties. He quickly set up his own HOA and over time ended up purchasing, fixing, and selling all 10 of the fiveplexes. He then rolled the money from selling those fiveplexes into a 56-unit condo complex.

In the same way that Serge has adapted to the changing market, he has adapted his method for obtaining financing as well. For his first four purchases, he used conventional bank loans. After that, he found a regional bank and explained what he was doing. They said he could purchase as many properties as he wanted as long as they cash-flowed well. After he got to 12 properties, the regional bank cut him off, stating that their rules had changed. Luckily, around that time the company that he worked for was being sold, and he received a severance check that he used to buy more properties. He then began to acquire funding through syndication and commercial loans. "Commercial lending is, right now, the easiest," he says. "I once got a loan on a commercial property over the phone without them even looking at my tax returns."

Today Serge owns more than 100 units, mostly in Arizona, and manag-es them all through his own property management company. As the mar-ket continues to change, Serge continues to adapt to meet those changes.

- - - - - - - —— - - - - - -

12. Retirement Accounts (Yours — Or Someone Else's!)

Retirement accounts can be a way to fund real estate deals in two ways: Your own retirement account can fund deals, or someone else's retire-ment account can fund your deals. The two most common types of retirement accounts are:

- 401(k)
- Individual Retirement Account (IRA)

However, not just any IRA or 401(k) will work, because most em-ployment retirement accounts dictate where you can invest that mon-ey—and it's usually not in real estate. Therefore, to use these plans for your real estate investing funding source, the IRA or 401(k) must be self-directed, which means the plan holder can invest in whatever they want (but still must follow the rules).

Let's dive into more detail on each of the two primary types.

Self-Directed 401(k) Accounts

In the 1980s, employers started to move away from pension plans and offer 401(k)s to their employees. Most W-2 employees are familiar with this type of retirement plan, sponsored by their employers. Some plans offer the incentive to participate by matching employees' contributions; the average contribution is 2.7 percent[19] of an employee's salary to the 401(k). The advantage is that employees can put money aside before taxes, although taxes are taken when distributions are made from the account starting at retirement age (59.5 years old). As of 2018, an employee can contribute only up to $18,500, or $24,500 annually. These retirement accounts are composed of stocks, bonds, mutual funds, and money market investments selected by your employer's plan sponsor. Real estate, in most plans, is not an investment option within a 401(k), hence the need to turn one's 401(k) into a self-directed 401(k).

Solo 401(k) Accounts

Another option that can work even better for real estate investors is the solo 401(k). This retirement account is made for those who run some kind of business and have no full-time employees in that business. To qualify for a solo 401(k), you must have self-employed income from a business, such as a sole proprietorship, limited liability company, partnership, C corporation, S corporation, or other business entity. Similar to a typical 401(k), the solo 401(k) plan can consist of mutual funds, index funds, exchange traded funds, and individual stocks and bonds. But when that solo 401(k) is self-directed, the fun begins because you can use this money to invest in real estate. Even more enticing, rather than the $18,500 annual limit on normal 401(k) contributions, you can—as both the employee and the employer—make an *additional contribution* (profit sharing) of up to $36,500, based on the type of corporation you filed as and your revenue. This means you can potentially contribute up to $55,000 each year toward your investments—way more than most other retirement accounts.

Self-Directed IRA Investing

In addition to the self-directed 401(k) and solo 401(k), there is also the option of the self-directed IRA, which allows an individual to place up

---

19 www.401khelpcenter.com/benchmarking.html#.WpioXPCnGHs

to $5,500 per year ($6,500 if you're age 50 or older) into a retirement account that can be used, when self-directed, to buy real estate or real estate notes. If you have an IRA and your current custodian doesn't allow for a self-directed option, you should be able to change providers to a company that does. Then that money can be used to invest in real estate, as long as certain rules are followed, which we'll discuss in a moment. But first, let's turn this "theory" into a couple of examples to make sure you understand the concepts.

Two Examples of Retirement Account Investing

1. An investor has $170,000 in his self-directed retirement account. He buys a rental for $150,000, keeping the other $20,000 as reserves. He holds it for ten years and, at retirement, all cash flow goes into the account. After ten years, he sells the property for $300,000. That cash flow and profit from the sale may be tax-free, because the money used to purchase it was from his self-directed Roth IRA.

2. John has a self-directed Roth IRA. He lends you money to do a flip. You pay him 10 percent interest on that money, and when the property sells, you pay him back directly into his retirement account. He just made a 10 percent return, and you got funding for your deal. This is a great option for newbies to get involved in real estate investing if you don't have your own self-directed IRA or large cash reserves.

Important Rules to Follow When Investing With Your Own Retirement Account

- The property usually cannot be mortgaged; therefore, you must have a decent-sized retirement account to begin investing with this method.
- Retirement account funds must be used for the deposit, purchase price, all expenses, repairs, taxes, etc. In other words, you can't mix personal or business money with the retirement money.
- You aren't allowed to participate in the rehab or management of the property if it is held within your account; nor may anyone considered a "disqualified person," such as a family member, fiduciary, or plan sponsor who is connected with the retirement plan.
- All income associated with the property must be deposited into

the IRA. No touchy until retirement age.

- The property cannot be used for your personal benefit. (Sorry to crush your dreams of having your vacation home be a part of your IRA, or having a family member as your tenant—not going to happen, according to the IRS).
- As always, maintain good records of income and expenses for the property owned by the retirement account.
- And always check with a tax professional if you have specific questions.

Using retirement funds to invest in real estate may be a more advanced strategy, but understanding the basics will help you when the time comes. You don't need to master it now, but when someone approaches you and says, "I have a few hundred thousand bucks in an old IRA. Can I use that to invest with you?" you can now say, "Yes, yes, you can. Let's go."

MATT AND LIZ FAIRCLOTH
BiggerPockets Podcast ■ Episodes 88 and 203

Matt and Liz Faircloth became interested in real estate investing after playing Robert Kiyosaki's Cashflow board game while they were dating in 2002. Matt purchased a home for himself and house hacked by renting out the spare bedrooms, introducing the couple to the power of passive income. While engaged to be married, they partnered together and purchased a duplex in Philadelphia using a private loan from Liz's father. After they rented out both units for a few years, they sold the property and utilized a 1031 exchange (more on this in Chapter Nine!) quadrupling their investment and purchasing two fourplexes in the same area.

The power couple decided to focus their efforts on building a well-rounded investment company that focused on both fix-and-flips and buy-and-holds in New Jersey. As their portfolio grew, so did their need for more capital to fund their deals. To accomplish this, they turned to private lenders.

Today Matt and Liz raise capital from investors through both private lending and private equity. With private lending, they are getting short-term loans of six to 12 months. These loans fund their fix-and-flips and also help them complete the BRRRR strategy—buy, rehab, rent, refinance, and repeat. Most of these private loans are from various investors' self-directed IRAs. Matt loves using these retirement vehicles because they provide a win-win: The owner of the IRA can invest their capital back into the next deal without tax consequences, and the real estate investor can use the capital again and again.

For private equity investments, the investor becomes a partner by purchasing a stake in that property, which they hold for the long term, and receives a quarterly dividend check. Their passive investors get the tax benefits of owning real estate without having to handle the day-to-day operations, while Matt and Liz get to do larger deals with their passive investor partners. They currently own small rentals and apartment buildings in North Carolina, New Jersey, and Pennsylvania.

Wrapping It Up

There are so many ways to fund real estate deals, and this list is nowhere near exhaustive. You can bring a lot of money to the table, or you can bring very little. You can bring in others, or do it yourself. You can work with bankers in business suits or partners in swimming suits. Our goal in this chapter was to help you realize that when you have the right deal, and the right approach, you can fund your next real estate deal. So don't let your lack of riches stop you from investing. The more you work on your creative finance skills, the stronger your skills will become. Soon no good deal will go unfunded.

At this point, you have a solid financial foundation, you know how to build a plan, you know how to find deals, and you know how to fund them. Now it's time to jump to an entirely different part of the real estate investor's journey—the one that could make you the richest: unloading your deals. Whether you plan to sell a property this year or in 30 years, the next chapter is going to show you exactly how to get it done.

CHAPTER EIGHT
Real Estate Exit Strategies

Buying real estate is great, but no one gets into real estate because it's a fun hobby. Investing in real estate is a means to an end: wealth-building. Over time, your property should gain serious equity and provide you with substantial income from cash flow and, hopefully, appreciation. Some investors choose to hold on to their investments indefinitely. Some will simply hold on to cash flowing properties until the day they die, with no intention of getting rid of them. However, in your investing career, you will most likely choose to get rid of one or more of your properties for various reasons. Choosing the best strategy for exiting your real estate investment is just as important as deciding which one to buy. This chapter will give you a broad overview of the various exit strategies you can use in your investment career.

Traditional Selling with a Real Estate Agent

When listing your property with an agent, be sure to interview several agents to find one you are comfortable with and who you know will get the house sold. In the world of real estate agents, the 80/20 Principle often seems to hold true—20 percent of the agents sell 80 percent of the listings. It's important to find that 20 percent and allow them to work their magic. A real estate agent will generally:

- List the home on the MLS, which is accessed by all real estate agents across the country.
- Put the sign in the yard to advertise the home.
- Show your property to prospective buyers.

- Market to the best of their ability through networking, Craigslist, and other online or offline media.
- Manage negotiations with potential purchasers.
- Handle all the paperwork.
- Hold your hand, emotionally, through the entire process.

When you choose the agent you want to list your property, you will typically sign a "listing agreement" with that agent, giving them the right to earn the commission if they sell the home. The agent will discuss with you all the important features of the property and enter them into the MLS. At this point, you will decide the price the property should be listed for. Pricing is very important, as you do not want to list too high (adding months to your holding time) or too low (leaving money on the table). A good agent should be able to look at other similar properties and determine the best price to list at.

The listing agreement also spells out the commission to be earned by the agent. The typical commission for a real estate agent is 6 percent (though that can change slightly, depending on price, property type, and location). This fee is usually split 50-50 with the agent who brought the buyer. In the case where your selling agent is representing both you and the buyer, the whole commission is given to the agent.

Many individuals feel that this is the end of their duty in selling the property, and the agent will take it from here. However, this is not the case. There are many tricks and techniques that you, as the seller, can do to ensure the property sells for the highest amount, the quickest. Start with making sure the appearance of the property is desirable, including both the interior and exterior. Look around at competing properties and aim to look better than the rest. If selling a single-family home, consider staging it with furniture, artwork, plants, flowers, and other accessories to help the buyer imagine a home rather than simply an empty house. If selling a multifamily or commercial property, be sure all units are filled and operating at peak efficiency.

Once an offer is received, negotiations begin, and, hopefully, both parties can agree on a price and terms for the sale. Just as when you purchased the property, the paperwork for the sale will be handled by either a local "title and escrow" company or an attorney, depending on the common practices in your area. Both parties will sign the documents, the money will be funneled through the title and escrow company or attorney, and the deal will close, leaving you with a large check to invest in more real estate and grow your empire.

Selling FSBO (For Sale By Owner)

While the majority of homes are sold with a real estate agent, there is no legal reason that you have to do so. For some, the cost of a real estate agent is too high, so they choose instead to sell for sale by owner, or FSBO. A major deterrent in selling FSBO is not getting your property listed on the MLS. This document (or documents) is all the homes listed by all the real estate agents, known as Realtors, across the country. When you look for homes online through sites like Realtor.com, you are looking at the MLS listings. Without being on the MLS, you'll lose the ability to reach the vast majority of individuals looking for a property.

One recent tool used by some to sell is known as a flat fee MLS listing service, in which a seller will pay a "flat fee" to a real estate broker to list the house. This fee generally ranges between $150 and $400 and includes very limited help from that broker. The broker will simply place the home on the MLS and may even offer to put a sign in the yard, but will do very little beyond that. This leaves negotiation, setting up title and escrow, and managing the closing in the hands of the seller. Additionally, since a real estate transaction includes both the buyer's agent and the seller's agent, a commission is still paid to whatever agent brings a buyer to the deal. Instead of 6 percent, it usually will end up being around 3 percent out of pocket.

Selling Using Seller Financing

Seller financing (also known as "carrying the contract") takes place when an owner sells a property to a buyer but carries the mortgage rather than requiring the buyer to get their own mortgage. This is done by many investors all over the world for a variety of reasons and across different investment types. In a normal sale, the buyer will go to a bank to get financing for the house, and the seller will receive the total sale price (less selling closing costs) in one lump sum. With seller financing, the seller is the bank, so the buyer will provide a down payment directly to the seller and make monthly mortgage payments to the seller for the life of the loan, or until the buyer decides to sell someday.

Why Consider Selling with Seller Financing?

There are a number of reasons to consider seller financing, but typically it is used for buyers who don't typically qualify for a normal mortgage. Depending on the market, it can be tough for many buyers to obtain traditional financing. They may not be able to document all of their income, they may be self-employed, or they may have some blemishes on their credit reports.

Keep in mind that seller financing isn't only for the benefit of buyers who normally don't qualify for a mortgage. Many investors choose to sell off their properties using seller financing because they want to receive monthly income that doesn't involve maintenance, tenants, or rentals. When a property is sold via seller financing, the property is 100 percent the new buyer's responsibility, including all the rights and expenses that come with ownership (including taxes, insurance, and maintenance).

A seller may also choose to use seller financing in order to offset the taxes due at the end of their investment career, as the IRS classifies this as an "installment sale" and allows the seller to spread out any capital gains taxes that may be due. (See your tax adviser for more information on the tax benefits of seller financing.)

When offering seller financing, the seller should require a large nonrefundable down payment up front to protect their interests and to prevent the likelihood that the buyer will stop making their monthly payments. The higher the down payment, the lower the risk to the seller. For example, if a seller requires a $1,000 down payment, there is not a lot of incentive for the buyer to uphold their obligations. However, if the down payment required is $30,000, there is a lot more incentive to perform. In addition, it is important that the seller goes through the same process as they would during a normal sale, using a title company, attorneys, and other legal paperwork to ensure that the sale is done correctly.

Who Can Sell with Seller Financing?

Seller financing is generally only applicable if the home is currently owned without a mortgage. If you have a mortgage through a bank or other lending institution and decide to sell the property to another party using seller financing, you will break the "due on sale clause" in the fine print of that mortgage, and the bank may foreclose on you. Therefore, seller financing is really viable only for a free-and-clear house.

After a property has been sold with seller financing, the seller may choose to sell the mortgage, or note, to another investor. This opens up the world of "note buying," which is beyond the scope of this guide, but which is a very common strategy among experienced investors. For more on notes, pick up a copy of *Real Estate Note Investing* by Dave Van Horn.

What Are the Risks with Using Seller Financing?

The largest risk in using seller financing is having your buyer stop making payments at some point, and then you, the seller, will have to foreclose. In this case, you are subject to the same laws and foreclosure process as any other lending institution, which takes time and money. Each state is different, but you will probably need to hire an attorney to get through the process. After the foreclosure is complete, you will get the house back and be able to sell it all over again, but you may have to deal with repairs and other issues before the home is ready to go back on the market.

While the risks of having to foreclose can't be completely avoided, they can be minimized if the note is managed properly. You do that by screening the buyer carefully, so that you are fully aware of any issues that might arise. Furthermore, as mentioned earlier, the best way to reduce your risk is to get the highest down payment possible. The more money you receive up front, the less likely you are to have problems.

The 1031 Exchange

Recently, I (Brandon) sold a 24-unit apartment complex in which I was going to owe more than $100,000—almost half of my profit—to the government in taxes. Ouch. However, I paid them nothing from that sale, and instead used the money to buy 70 more units. And I did it all legally using an IRS rule known as a "1031 exchange."

As with any business venture, when you are successful, Uncle Sam is there to collect his share. When it comes time to sell a property that you own, chances are you will have significant taxes due, especially if you followed the advice in this guide and bought a great deal. Thankfully, if you are paying taxes in the United States, the government provides the 1031 exchange as a way to defer those taxes to a later date—possibly forever. (For rental investments only ... sorry flippers!)

A fun way to look at the 1031 exchange is to think of Uncle Sam as a real uncle. For some reason, you owe your uncle money when you sell a property, but he puts his big arm around you and says, "Listen, bud, you did such an awesome job with that real estate deal. I'm proud of you. And I know you owe me a bunch of money now, but listen—because you did such a great job, I want you to keep the money you owe me and put it into another deal to buy. Essentially, I'll invest with you on it! You'll have more money to use for the next one, so you can buy a bigger deal. Then I'll grow my wealth, and you'll grow yours. We'll settle up later in life. We'll be kinda like partners. Whaddya say?"

Nice uncle, huh?

But then, as soon as you agree, he fires a gun in the air and says, "Go! You have 45 days to find that perfect property, and then 180 days to close on it, or the deal is off the table."

And *that* is a 1031 exchange.

Of course, there are a number of rules that need to be followed, but if done correctly, you can reuse the money you would have paid toward capital gains tax, and use it as funds for your next property. The cool thing is you can do this over, and over, and over again. Yes, someday you'll need to settle up with that uncle, and the tax bill might be huge at that point, but so will your wealth. In the meantime, you get to enjoy the cash flow from those properties.

Oh, and if you simply hold these properties until you die, your uncle forgives the entire debt, and your kids won't pay a dime of that tax. Whoever said the government isn't your friend?

But it isn't all daisies and sunshine. As mentioned above, the government gives you just 45 days to find (identify) a replacement property to buy. If you've been involved in real estate investing for any length of time, you'll realize that 45 days is not a ton of time to find a great deal—especially in a competitive market. Clearly, the law was written by someone who didn't invest in real estate. This can make the 45 days incredibly stressful, and even cause investors to buy bad deals because of the tax alternative. For this reason, many investors choose not to use the 1031 exchange and simply pay the tax to the government and move on.

The 1031 exchange can be a powerful tool for building wealth, but it isn't for everyone. But getting a firm understanding of how it works—and how it might fit into your business plan—is important for every real estate investor.

16 Tips and Tricks For Selling Your Properties

Selling your home can be quite the daunting experience. Not only is there a ton of money at stake, there can be a ton of hoops to jump through as well. When one mistake can cost you thousands of dollars or a missed opportunity, you want to make sure you are doing things right. But have no fear. Mindy Jensen, author of the book *How to Sell Your Home* provides 16 tips and tricks to help you sell your home like a pro.

1. Have Your Property Inspected Before You List

While it is commonly recommended to have a home inspected prior to purchasing it, Mindy recommends having your home inspected yourself before you list it. This will reveal problems that you can fix before you list. Mindy states that professional inspectors will nearly always identify problems and can often make minor issues seem huge, so it's better to have them identified and fixed before your potential buyer has it inspected. If you come to them with your inspection report and the list of things that have already been taken care of, it can put the potential buyer at ease and make them much more likely to close on your house.

2. Clean Up Your Home and Keep It Clean When It's on the Market

You may have the most gorgeous house, but if it is dirty or cluttered, many potential buyers will pass on it. Mindy states that she is shocked with how many houses she has shown to potential buyers that are dirty and/or cluttered. "You want it to look like nobody lives there," she writes. If you don't have the time to clean, spending money on professional cleaners is worth the cost if it helps sell your home.

3. Make Sure You Pass the Sniff Test

Along with making sure your home looks clean, you also need to make sure that it smells clean as well. If your home smells like cigarettes or cat pee, potential buyers will just move on to the next house. Since most of us are noseblind to our own house, Mindy recommends asking your agent what it smells like. "If they don't smell anything, you pass the test," she states. If it does smell, she says, you can leave out dishes of white vinegar and/or charcoal briquettes to remove odors. She does not recommend using air fresheners, because they can just mask the smell and even become a repelling odor. Another tip to make your house smell great is to bake cookies or an apple pie, or even warm up a few caps of vanilla at 350 degrees prior to showings and open houses to make it smell inviting.

4. Take Great but Honest Pictures of Your House

Your photos should represent your house accurately. Mindy advises against taking weird shots that make it seem like a room is much bigger than it really is, or editing the photos to hide certain blemishes. "If it has warts on it, show them, because people will see them when they visit your house anyway," she writes. When taking photos for your listing, make sure they are great photos. You want well-lit, clear, and descriptive shots. If you are not a great photographer, consider hiring someone who is.

5. Be Available for Showings

When your house is on the market, you want to keep it in "show condition" nearly all the time. You don't want to miss out on a potential buyer because your house is not ready to be shown that day. If you have a tenant in the unit that you are selling, create an incentive for them to keep it show-ready or just wait until they move out to show the unit.

6. Be Informative

When selling your home to potential buyers, make sure they are aware of all the updated information for the property. Let them know what you've done to the property to make it better. If you put on a new roof, make sure they know about it. People buy off emotion but justify with logic, so telling them what you have done to improve the property can help encourage them to close on the deal. And don't be afraid to share what still needs work. If you try to hide something, it will most likely come out during the inspection anyway, so build up trust by being honest and open from the start.

7. Know Your Competition

Unless you live in the middle of the Alaskan wilderness, chances are good that your house is not the only one on the market in your area. Comparing your house to others in the area can inform your price. Mindy recommends physically visiting comparable houses that are for sale in your market to get a good grasp on what they're offering. If all the similar houses have new carpet and appliances and yours does not, you may want to update your place a little or drop your price below theirs.

8. Use an Agent

You may think that For Sale by Owner is cheaper, but Mindy states that agents can sell homes quicker and often for more money, so despite their fee, it's a better option than trying to sell your place on your own. When you use an agent, you have someone who knows your market, and knows how to price and quickly sell your home in that market. It's important to find a good agent, though, so ask your friends or acquaintances for recommendations. Don't settle on the first one that you meet or hear about, and don't be afraid to ask them questions. If they are not working out, fire them and hire a new one.

9. Ask Your Agent for Selling Advice

As mentioned above, a good agent knows their market well, so don't be afraid to pick their brain. Ask them for any and all advice that will help you sell your home. If you are wondering whether you should invest thousands of dollars in new appliances to boost your home's appeal, your agent can tell you if that would be worth it in your market. Your agent is your ally, so don't be afraid to use them.

10. Price Your House Right

There is almost an art form to pricing your house when selling. If your house is priced too high, potential buyers will pass it up, and then the longer it sits on the market, people will think there is something wrong with it and won't look at it. If it's too low, potential buyers may think there's something wrong with it and pass it up, or they may buy it at that low price and you could be getting a lot less than what it is worth. When your agent gives you the price that you should list at, ask them to justify that price point.

11. List in Peak Market Time

The housing market has peaks and valleys. There are great times for buyers and great times for sellers. When selling your home, make sure you are selling during a peak time. For example, more people are looking to buy during the spring than during the winter. List your house accordingly.

12. After the Property Has Been Listed, Double-Check the Listing to Make Sure All the Information Is Correct

Listing mistakes happen all the time, so it's important to look over your house's listing right away and notify the agent of any mistakes that you find. "You don't want people coming to see your house to find out that your 'three-bedroom' is actually only a two," Mindy states. It's easy to fix listing mistakes, but your agent probably won't notice it unless you point it out to them.

13. Stage Those Weird Spaces That Don't Have an Obvious Use

If you have weird spaces that are vacant, stage them so people have an idea of what they could do with those areas. For example, Mindy mentions that one house she was showing had a very small, weird-shaped space. The owners put a chair and a lamp there and called it a "book nook." Creatively staging rooms and spaces can help potential buyers imagine living there, and thus help you close the deal with them.

14. Leave During Showings and Take Your Pets with You

Make sure you and your pets are not around when potential buyers are coming to see your home. People who are checking out your house do not want to see you there, because it's awkward. It's a good idea to leave at least several minutes before the showing is supposed to start and come back at least a few minutes after it has ended. If you have tenants, make sure they are not there. You do not want your tenants talking to potential buyers.

15. Be Prepared to Walk Away from an Offer

It's okay to turn down and walk away from offers. For example, if the potential buyer is "nickel-and-diming" everything, they may not follow through with the deal and could be wasting your time. Another example is if someone makes an offer that's significantly higher than other offers. They may tie up your house and then lower their price after it has been appraised. Mindy states that it's better to turn down the deal, unless they are willing to match the difference between their offer and the appraisal.

16. Tell Everyone You Know That Your Property Is for Sale

Even with an agent, it doesn't hurt to tell everyone you know that your house is for sale. Post it on social media, tell your family and friends, and talk about it at social gatherings. Mindy mentions how one of her clients sold her house to a friend who outbid others because she had always wanted her friend's house. You just never know where that buyer is going to come from.

If you want many more tips, tricks, and strategies for selling, let me remind you to get Mindy's book, *How to Sell Your Home*, for sale anywhere books are sold and on BiggerPockets.com

Wrapping It Up

Selling a property is a natural part of the investor's life. While it's possible you'll buy real estate and hold on to it forever, chances are you'll need to unload a property someday, so we hope the lessons in this chapter have prepared you for that day.

And now, as we turn to the last chapter, it's time to figure out how to make all this work together—in the limited amount of time you have. After all, you don't have dozens of hours each week to devote to your investing. So in the next chapter, we want to lay out some simple ways that you can get way more done in all areas of your life in far less time. You are about to learn how top performers *get stuff done.*

CHAPTER NINE
How to Work (FAR) Less and Get (WAY) More Done

So you want to achieve wealth and financial independence through real estate investing, but one little problem is getting in the way:

Your life.

Your spouse, your kids, school, work, commuting, PTA nights, swimming lessons, dinner with friends, sleeping in, camping trips, that two-week vacation to Greece. We get it. Life is *full*. Fuller today than, perhaps, at any point in human history. Every minute of the day is filled with some sort of activity that keeps you from having the time to work on your real estate business.

But let's fix that, right now. I want to share with you four powerful techniques that we use to work way less than most, while still getting way more accomplished.

1. Be the General

Let me (Josh) tell you two stories of my life.

Story #1: Years ago, I was locked in my basement, typing for 14 hours a day. Working hard, head down, trying to build BiggerPockets to become *the* resource for real estate investors. My rental properties, which were thousands of miles away, were suffering drastically. I was losing money and making next to nothing. So I worked harder—16 hours a day, 18 hours a day. My wife and kids wondered who the stranger in the basement was that emerged to eat the occasional meal but quickly had to disappear again. I was "the guy who gets stuff done." And I did. For years. To the detriment of my family.

Story #2: Several months ago, my daughter got sick due to complications from a routine surgery. In a second, I dropped everything work-related. No more podcasts, no more meetings, no more commuting, no more real estate deal-hunting—no more anything. I spent 24 hours a day next to my little girl, taking care of her. I never went to the office. But during this time, BiggerPockets exploded (in a good way). So much stuff got done while I stayed at home to work on the one thing that really matters: my family.

Both these stories are completely true, but showcase two very different times of my life. Today I get 100 times more done with 100 times less effort. What's my secret?

I learned to stop being a cadet and start being a general.

You see, to win a battle, a general doesn't typically pick up his rifle and walk out to the frontlines. The general is needed to run the operation, to make the big decisions after seeing the big picture. The general spends his time finding the right people, processes, and procedures that will ensure victory.

If you are tired of being the cadet and you are ready to become the general, let me give you three tips for transitioning roles.

Being the General Is a Mind-set

Change in the physical world begins with change in your mind, which costs nothing. Nothing changed for me and my business until I made a change mentally. I came to a strong realization of what I was doing and where I wanted to get to. I had to see that I was holding my rifle on the frontline before I could even think about stepping back. I also had to understand that my insistence upon doing everything myself stemmed more from ego than from truth. "If you want something done right, do it yourself" was the mantra that I lived by. I had to learn that I was not the all-powerful doer of all things in my life, and that others could do some things better. In fact, for every single activity in your life that you are not good at, or that you simply hate doing, someone puts food on their kitchen table by doing it. But again, it begins with a mind-set shift.

Start Small

Once your mind-set has been changed, and you are no longer the cadet, it's time to start ordering your troops. I know what you are thinking: *That's great for you, Josh, but I don't have the money to start hiring people. I'm living your story #1 above!* But don't think that you need to hire a full-time team right away. Today I command a company of about 30 people, but it didn't start that way. It started with a single person, part-time, as an independent contractor. As I outsourced some small tasks, I was able to focus more of my efforts on the few tasks that brought the most impact (that is, dollars) to the business. Which allowed me to hire more tasks to get done. Your real estate empire won't be built in a day. You might need to still do 95 percent of the tasks on your plate. But maybe next month, it'll be just 90 percent.

You Have to Control Your Troops

Many people feel that by becoming the general in their life, they can sit back and let others run the show. But there is nothing further from the truth. Imagine if the night before D-Day, General Patton had said, "Well, looks like you guys have this all covered. I'm going to take a quick beach vacation." We'd likely all be speaking a different language right now. Being the general doesn't mean no work, it just means different work (and, in time, less work). When I first hired a property manager to deal with my rental properties, I made the mistake of letting them just "do what they do" with very little accountability or oversight. *Huge* mistake. Your troops need to be evaluated, corrected, and often disciplined. And you, the general, need to make sure it happens.

How to Be the General in Your Real Estate Business

Okay, let's take this from the theoretical to the real world. How can you use the concept of being the general in your efforts to build a real estate business? First, remember that being the general is a mind-set, and once you have it, every single thing you do will be filtered through that lens. But to lead off your brainstorming, here's a list of just a few tangible ways you can become the general in your real estate business.

- Hire a property manager to look after your rentals
- Find a partner who is analytical to analyze deals
- Get a family member or friend to answer your real estate-related phone calls

- Hire a project manager to manage your flips
- Get a graphic designer to make your business cards
- Pay a college kid to design your Wix.com website
- Hire out many of the non-real estate tasks in your life; if you are mowing your lawn or changing your oil, you are not actively looking for your next deal
- Hire a virtual assistant to scan Craigslist each week, looking for "mom and pop" rental property listings that you can call to ask whether they'd consider selling
- Hire someone to make all those phone calls listed above
- Hire someone to do market research on a possible city to make investments in
- Get someone else to do your bookkeeping
- Hire a handyman to do repairs on your properties

Again, this is just a brief list of tasks that you can begin implementing, but the real power comes from changing your mind-set. You'll find many things to outsource in your life when you are proactive in getting them done.

And finally, does the general occasionally need to pick up his weapon and fight in the trenches? Definitely. But in those times, you'll be fully engaged, fully prepared, and incredibly dangerous to oppose. So become the general in your life starting today, and learn how to get way more done while working way less. Because, like me, someday you might find yourself unable to work on your business, and you need to know it's going to continue to provide you a lifetime of financial independence.

2. Being Effective Vs. Being Efficient — The Difference Is Vital

Are you efficient or effective?

If you are like most people, the first thought that popped into your mind when reading that line was, *What's the difference?*

- The difference is getting stuff done right vs. getting the right stuff done.
- The difference is watching your business vs. watching your business grow.
- The difference is managing your life vs. changing your life.

- The difference is looking cool on the football field vs. scoring touch-downs and winning games.

You see, many people focus on being efficient. They can get a lot of stuff done. They have systems and processes for answering emails and filing papers. They maximize their schedule to get more done in less time. They know the fastest route to work each morning. They multitask like a boss. They are incredibly productive. But at the end of the day, nothing changes. In *The 4-Hour Workweek*, Tim Ferriss quips, "In fact, if you want to move up the ladder in most of corporate America, and assuming they don't really check what you are doing (let's be honest), just run around the office holding a cell phone to your head and carrying papers. Now, that is one busy employee! Give them a raise."

Being effective, on the other hand, is the practice of continually making the right moves and accomplishing important tasks. You can be incredibly efficient, crossing off hundreds of items on your to-do list. But if those tasks aren't getting you closer to your end result, toward the goal, you are not being effective with your time.

Therefore, to work less and get more done, it's vital that you continually zone in on being effective in all that you do. Is the task you are working on really going to get you the end result? Or is the task designed just to make you feel like you are accomplishing things?

Here's an example many newbie real estate investors find themselves doing: designing business cards, car magnets, or their website. Things that make them feel as if they are accomplishing something important but are likely just a substitution for action. It's fun to design stuff. It's not fun to pick up the phone and cold-call a possible motivated seller. Designing business cards or forming an LLC or reading book after book might make one feel like they are doing good work. But many times, it's simply efficiency vs. effectiveness.

Of course, this isn't to say business cards, websites, or books don't have a place in an investor's life. At certain times, they might be the result of your taking the right action. But they shouldn't be used as a substitute for real, hard work.

So how do you know what the most effective tasks are? You don't, always. But by simply asking the question, continually, you'll be able to evaluate your actions to make sure you aren't simply killing time to avoid doing the most important thing. Take a photo of the following message and make it the wallpaper on your smartphone, so that every time you use your phone, you are reminded to ask:

3. The True Enemy of Progress: Dead Space

How long does it take you to read a novel?

A few days if it's really good? A few weeks perhaps? Maybe that book will sit on your nightstand for a month? I know there are some novels I've (Brandon) read bits and pieces of for several years but have not yet finished. The funny thing is: A book is likely 80,000 words, and most people can read around 300 words per minute. Doing the quick math, the average book should take no longer than 266 minutes to read—

fewer than five hours.

So the true answer for "how long does it take you to read a novel" is more accurately "five hours."

"But," you object, "I never sit down for five hours straight to read a book!"

And that's exactly the point. For any big task we do in life—from reading a book to buying a house to starting a business—the actual amount of time it takes to do all the steps is far less than most think. We do a little bit here and then a little more the next week and then a little more the week after. Over time, we accomplish those projects, but most of the time is spent actually not working on the project itself.

Most of the time is spent in between a few moments of doing the task—something I call "dead space." If you want to accomplish more in your life at a rate faster than you've ever imagined, you can. You have to kill the dead space. Here's how.

Dead Space: The Silent Killer

Most tasks in life are significantly easier than we'd like to believe. In fact, nearly every goal you have is really just made up of a series of small decisions followed by short actions. However, it's the in-between that consumes the most time: the dead space.

For example, when it took six months to find your first rental property to buy, did it really take six months? Or was it four hours of work spread out over a six-month period?

When it took two weeks to fix the leaky dishwasher in your house, did it really take two weeks? Or was it an hour of work after a two-week delay waiting to get the parts from the hardware store?

When it took three years to learn how to play the guitar, did it really take three years to learn the guitar? Or was it 50 hours of practicing, spread out over the 26,280 hours found in those three years?

As you can see, most of the time spent in life is not spent in action; it's spent in dead space. It's time we spend not working toward our goals. It's the waiting that exists between moments of action or decision.

Dead space could manifest itself in numerous ways. Fear, uncertainty, lack of focus, distractions, limiting beliefs, waiting on other people, or even physical restraints are all part of dead space. It doesn't matter what form this dead space takes, nor does it matter who caused it. Maybe the dead space is your fault, maybe it's not. It's still dead space.

Furthermore, understand that dead space is not inherently evil. Most tasks cannot be simply worked on 24/7 until completion because life exists outside our projects and our work. We don't expect you to spend 50 hours straight learning how to play the guitar. It's okay to spread tasks out over time. The problem is, we give the dead space far too much room in our lives, pushing our goals further and further away all the time.

Supercharging Productivity by Identifying Your MINS

Dead space is the real reason you aren't accomplishing your goals. It's the real reason you haven't lost that belly fat, the reason you haven't finished that house flip, the reason you haven't found your next investment.

Therefore, our argument is simple: If you want to accomplish significantly more in your life, faster, you need to minimize the dead space.

How do we reduce this dead space? It's easier than you think. Below, we've identified three incredibly simple steps. Just follow these three steps, and you'll immediately begin to reap the rewards.

Step 1. Identify Your MINS

Most dead space is caused by one essential thing: You don't know what the next task really is. Therefore, the first step in minimizing dead space is to identify what your Most Important Next Step (MINS) is on your journey. What is the smallest action you can do next to move your goal forward just a bit? Be specific. You'll likely find that, surprisingly, it's usually something quite quick and easy to do.

Maybe it's something as simple as "read Chapter Four" or "send an email to my real estate agent." Or maybe it's something a bit more complex, like "get in the car and drive to the apartment complex" or "fire my assistant." Right now, for us, our MINS is to finish this chapter and get 1,000 words written. What's yours?

If you can't accurately identify your next task, don't feel bad; sometimes this can be tricky. We'd recommend asking a friend, mentor, business coach, or mastermind group to help. Sometimes outsiders have a vantage point to see the path more clearly than the wanderer trudging through the weeds.

Let's use an example in the real estate investing space. Chris's goal is to buy a duplex near Boston within the next three months so that he can house hack. Chris might spend weeks or even months not doing anything to accomplish his goal unless he has identified the next step, his MINS. In this case, his MINS might be "talk to a mortgage broker and find out if I qualify for a mortgage." That's a simple 30-minute phone call and, once completed, Chris is now significantly closer to accomplishing his goal.

Once that has been finished, he will identify another MINS—perhaps, "post on Facebook, asking my family and friends for recommendations for a real estate agent in the Boston area." Now that's a simple five-minute task that could have huge implications—but only if it actually gets done. Notice how these steps in Chris's life really are fairly basic tasks that are quick and easy to knock out.

You'll likely find the same is true for your goals. Most big goals are really just a series of small, easy-to-accomplish tasks. And it all begins with identifying what they are. However, just identifying your MINS is not enough. It's time for action.

Step 2. Do That Task Now (or Time-Block It)
Now that you've identified what your MINS is, you must actually do it as soon as possible. Remember, most of your next steps are just quick tasks, so there is a good chance you can do it now. But if you cannot do it immediately, time-block the task into your calendar and hold yourself to it like you would a meeting with the president.

Time-blocking is the practice of scheduling appointments with yourself to accomplish your most important tasks. After all, we schedule meetings with other people, so why not schedule meetings with ourselves to accomplish those things that really matter? To use Chris's example above, maybe he can't call a mortgage broker right now because it's after hours. Instead, Chris will go to his calendar and schedule 30 minutes for the following morning at 9 to call a local mortgage broker.

Step 3. Repeat Steps 1 and 2 Until Success Is Achieved
Repeat steps one and two again and again until the goal has been met. The faster you can identify your MINS and the faster you can do the task, the faster you can get to your next MINS, followed by the next, and the next, until completion. Before you know it, the goal has been met and you are living the life you've always dreamed of. The apartment complex has been purchased, the debt has been paid off, the job has been quit, the weight has been lost.

To give you an idea of how powerful setting a MINS can be, take a look at the following two timelines in Chris's goal of buying a duplex in Boston. On the left, we see the typical timeline for accomplishing a goal. On the right, we see what could happen if Chris were continually (daily) identifying his MINS and working to accomplish them:

Day 1 Set a goal to buy a duplex	Day 1 Set a goal to buy a duplex
Day 7 Read part of a book on buying rental properties	Day 1 Read part of a book on buying rental properties
Day 11 Read more of the book	Day 2 Read more of the book
Day 19 Finish the book on buying rental properties	Day 3 Finish the book on buying rental properties
Day 30 Call a mortgage broker to get qualified	Day 4 Call a mortgage broker to get qualified
Day 40 Get paperwork to the mortgage broker	Day 4 Get paperwork to the mortgage broker
Day 50 Get more paperwork to the mortgage broker	Day 4 Get more paperwork to the mortgage broker
Day 51 Get approved for a mortgage	Day 4 Get approved for a mortgage
Day 80 Post on Facebook looking for a real estate agent	Day 5 Post on Facebook looking for a real estate agent
Day 85 Decide on one agent to work with	Day 5 Decide on one agent to work with
Day 90 Go look at a duplex with the agent	Day 6 Go look at a duplex with the agent
Day 107 Go look at another duplex with the agent	Day 8 Go look at another duplex with the agent
Day 120 Go look at another duplex with an agent	Day 8 Go look at another duplex with an agent
Day 122 Decide to make an offer on the latest duplex	Day 8 Decide to make an offer on the latest duplex
Day 123 Offer is accepted	Day 9 Offer is accepted
Day 125 Inspection is scheduled	Day 9 Inspection is scheduled
Day 130 Inspection happens	Day 11 Inspection happens
Day 155 The duplex is purchased	Day 30 The duplex is purchased

Notice the difference between the two timelines. The steps are exactly the same. However, as the second timeline demonstrates, when Chris started living proactively rather than reactively, and began identifying his MINS on a daily basis, the timeline condensed considerably—from

155 days down to just 30. And most of the dead space in the second timeline was waiting for the title company to actually close the deal, between days 11 and 30. (Yes, sometimes dead space is unavoidable. Sometimes you truly do have to wait. The key, however, is to make sure you are doing everything in your power to eliminate dead space.)

Sometimes it's out of your control, but usually it's something you can directly act to minimize if you truly take the time to intentionally destroy it. You'll find that when you seek to minimize the potency of dead space, you will increase your own productivity and accomplish amazing things in less time than you could imagine. People will whisper about you behind your back, saying, "I just don't know how he/she gets so much done!" You'll appear to be superhuman to everyone around you but will find yourself with more free time, less stress, and a clear sense of direction.

So get into the habit of always asking what your Most Important Next Step is. And then *do it*.

JAY PAPASAN
BiggerPockets Podcast ■ Episode 113

Jay Papasan started in real estate after moving to Austin, Texas, with his wife. He started working for Keller Williams Realty, Inc., and one day discovered that the founder, Gary Keller, was writing a book on real estate. Since Jay had a background in publishing, he offered to help Gary with the book. After three-and-a-half months of working together, they finished the book, *The Millionaire Real Estate Agent*, which became one of the top-selling real estate sales books in the world. After the success of the first book, Jay and Gary went on to write several more together, including *The Millionaire Real Estate Investor* and *The One Thing*.

Jay is more than just an author, he's a real estate investor as well. But it wasn't an easy road getting there. "When I was starting down this journey, the first thing I did was start analyzing deals. Before we pulled the trigger on our first deal, I bet we had done the numbers on 100 homes," he states. In addition to analyzing deals, Jay worked extra part-time jobs for two years to save up enough for a down payment on his house, living on just 60 percent of the family's income and saving the rest. His first rental was a primary residence for him and his wife to live in, but they later turned that home into a rental that they still own. They began to acquire more rentals, and soon his wife was able to quit her job to spend time with the kids, manage their growing portfolio, become a real estate agent, and eventually create their own sales team, Papasan Properties Group. "We wanted to be millionaires. We thought it would take us ten years. It took us six," Jay says. In 2017, they sold 244 homes, more than $74 million in sales volume, in Austin, Texas, and St. Louis, Missouri.

He and his wife realized that action is how you make progress in life, and creating great habits is the best way to have consistent action. According to Jay, "The most successful thing you can do is learn to make habits in your life. If I want something to happen, I have to think, 'What's the habit that will drive that thing?' My wife and I get up at 5:10 a.m. three days a week to work out. Because we understand if we want to get stuff done, we need to do it before everyone is awake."

As the couple began to build their own rental portfolio, they made the decision to narrow their criteria to renting mid- to high-class properties to professionals—the type of people they would have over for dinner. While these properties did not cash-flow a lot, they seemed to have a lot fewer problems, headaches, and stressors as opposed to more run-down properties in less affluent neighborhoods. As their portfolio grew, so did the types of properties that they obtained. "If I could go back, we would have bought a duplex every 18 month as fast as we could, and after four or five years, we would have nine streams of income behind us," Jay says. Later, through a partnership, they invested in a warehouse, making a $1.7 million profit on the sale. Today, in addition to writing books, Jay continues to "move up the property ladder." The goal, according to Jay, is to have fewer roofs but more net worth and more cash flow over time.

- - - - - - ──────────────────────────────────── - - - - - -

The Final Key to Long-Lasting Success: Giving Back

"Wait ... how can I give back when I haven't 'gotten' yet?"

You might be wondering why you, a real estate newbie, should be concerned with giving back already. You haven't yet achieved huge success. But don't underestimate the power of giving back to others in helping you achieve greater levels of success—even at the beginning of your journey. Giving back, studies have shown, can have a profound impact on your life in three major areas: your happiness, your health, and your wealth. Let's dig into all three.

Giving Can Make You Happier

According to a study published in *Nature Communications*,[20] neuroscientists from the University of Zurich conducted an experiment to see if generosity correlated with happiness on a neural level. For the study, one group (the experimental group) was informed that they were going to receive $100 per week if they publicly pledged to spend it on someone else, and the other group (the control group) was informed that they were going to receive $100 per week if they publicly pledged to spend it on themselves. Participants in each group were then given functional MRIs while they performed independent decision-making tasks involving being generous or not. After comparing the brain scans of participants in the two groups, the scientists discovered that participants in the experimental group made more generous choices and had stronger increases in self-reported happiness. This study reveals that not only does generosity beget more generosity, but that it also increases happiness.

A similar study published by professor Michael Norton from the Harvard Business School in 2008 came to the same conclusion.[21] For this study, participants were given between $5 and $20. Half of the participants in the group were told to spend it on others, and the other half were told to spend it on themselves. Both groups were surveyed to measure their level of happiness before and after the experiment. Participants who spent the money on others reported higher levels of happiness at the end of the day than participants who spent the money on themselves. The study also revealed that the amount of money spent did not have a significant impact on the levels of happiness, despite the participants' common belief that more money spent would equal a greater amount of happiness.

Giving Can Make You Healthier

Numerous studies have come out over the past 60 years linking altru-

---

20 https://www.nature.com/articles/ncomms15964

21 https://news.harvard.edu/gazette/story/2008/04/money-spent-on-others-can-buy-happiness/

ism/generosity and improved physical health and longevity of life. Dr. Stephen Post, a professor of preventive medicine at Stony Brook University, has written several books on the subject, including *Altruism and Health: Perspectives from Empirical Research*, in which he cites more than 23 studies revealing the positive impact that generosity has on a person's physical, emotional, spiritual, and mental health. One long-term study conducted by sociologist Michele Dillon, PhD, concluded that children who were more generous in adolescence tended to grow up to be more successful and in better health, especially better mental health, than children who were not.[22]

Giving Can Make You Wealthier

It would probably not surprise too many people to hear that the more wealth people accrue, the more generous they tend to become. What is more surprising, though, is that the more generous people are, in some cases, the wealthier they become. A survey completed in 2000 called the Social Capital Community Benchmark Survey (SCCBS)[23] revealed that people who gave generously made significantly more money than people who did not. The SCCBS surveyed about 30,000 people across the U.S. taking into account differences in education, age, race, religion, and other personal characteristics. Using what is called an instrumental variable, researchers in the study were able to predict how much people would donate financially, based on the time they spent volunteering. When the predicted amount donated correlated to the amount of income, the researchers were able to positively confirm that giving was increasing income—not just the other way around. Based on their analysis, they were able to predict that out of two nearly identical families, if one family donated an average of $100 more than the other, they would earn an average of $375 more than the family that donated less.[24]

So, as you build your real estate empire, don't get lost in greed and ambition. Give back to others in the same way others have given to you. Whether through your money, your time, your knowledge, or something else: give back.

---

22 scholars.unh.edu/cgi/viewcontent.cgi?referer=https://scholar.google.com/&httpsredir=1&article=1047&context=discovery_ud

23 https://www.entrepreneur.com/article/185662

24 sites.hks.harvard.edu/saguaro/communitysurvey/docs/exec_summ.pdf

Wrapping It Up

As we've described several times throughout this book, real estate investing is a journey. You are on the same path that we are on, and we're all walking toward the same end: financial independence. As such, just as we wrote this book as a way to help you on your journey, you can look back and help those who are just starting—even now. By sharing what you've learned, maybe even giving this book away, you are taking someone by the hand and saying, "Let's do this together. Here's what I've done so far."

And *that* is the spirit of BiggerPockets.

Now it's time to put it into practice. BiggerPockets is a community of more than 1,000,000 real estate entrepreneurs who are here to help build each other up with knowledge and support. They are also using the site to network and to find partners and clients. We want you to be a part of our community. Ask (or answer) questions on the forums, read the recent blog posts, create a company profile for your business, or just hang out with other investors. If you are not currently associating with successful real estate investors, let BiggerPockets help you with that.

Now, because it's easy to put down a book, no matter how good, and make no positive changes in your life, we want to leave you with some action steps that will help launch your real estate journey. We've covered hundreds of different points throughout this book, so we want to give you a simple checklist of four activities you can do today on your move toward becoming a real estate investor.

1. Fill Out Your Financial Forms

In Chapter Two we dug deep into the world of personal finance and explained how knowing where you stand financially is foundational in building a real estate empire. Therefore, if you haven't yet filled out your Personal Financial Statement as well as your Financial Spending Plan, do so now.

2. Meet Local Investors

If you decided to become an expert skier, would you rather hit the slopes with your drunk buddy from high school who's never seen snow, or the buddy who's been skiing since he was 3 years old and has won local ski events? While the drunk buddy might be fun, something tells us you'll learn significantly faster—and enjoy the sport significantly more—by skiing with the expert. The same is true for your real estate investing. You need to surround yourself with experts who are further along the journey than you are. Therefore, set a goal to meet with at least one local investor from your area in the next two weeks. Even better, attend a local networking event. To search the 1,000,000-plus members on BiggerPockets to find someone in your area to take out to coffee, head to www.BiggerPockets.com/events. Or, to find local real estate events, check out Meetup.com.

3. Find Some Deals and Analyze Them

It doesn't matter too much where you get your leads from. Keep it simple and pull up the available listings on Realtor.com or Zillow.com, and practice doing the math on the deal. Remember, every property has a number that could make it a good deal. Analyze the deal until you know what the number is and continue to practice this daily. Before you know it, you'll be able to analyze any deal in just minutes, and you'll feel 100 times more confident to start making offers. If you haven't yet checked out the BiggerPockets Real Estate Investment Calculators, you can find them at www.BiggerPockets.com/analysis.

4. Get Active on BiggerPockets

Finally, be sure to sign up for a free account on the site. It's the largest real estate community on the planet, so getting active on the site can be incredibly beneficial to your long-term success. You'll learn new things, meet new people, get inspired, and inspire others. It doesn't hurt that it's free, either! Leave a New Member Introduction post in the forums, read some blog posts, send some private messages, and/or attend a live online webinar (there's one taking place, live, at least once every week).

Our goal at BiggerPockets is simple: to help you achieve your goals through real estate investing. But no one can do your push-ups for you. Which is why we want to conclude this book with a warning and some encouragement:

You *can* do this. You have every piece of knowledge needed to begin moving forward. But you need to take the steps. Every time you read a book like this one, you have a choice—to act, or not to act. Act. Do. Go.

And while many do fail, many do give up, and many more never get started, those who want it bad enough, get it. And they find an incredible life on the other side.

As the great philosopher Jim Rohn said, "If you really want to do something, you'll find a way. If you don't, you'll find an excuse."

So go out and get it. We're here for you, every step of the way.

Your friends,
Josh Dorkin and **Brandon Turner**

Acknowledgments

This book wouldn't be possible without all the mistakes and failures we've made; without the trials and tribulations we've faced; without the challenges we overcame. Many have told us that we would never succeed in real estate and other ventures—we owe those doubters a great deal of thanks for all the motivation they provided us so we could prove them wrong.

This book is meant for everyone who dreams of a different kind of life.

Thank you to the BiggerPockets family and community for encouraging us all these years. This book has been a work in progress for half a decade and to the millions who have read its precursor, *The Ultimate Beginner's Guide to Real Estate Investing*—thanks! This book is for all of you. May you all find boundless success!

We wanted to directly thank the team at BiggerPockets who made this book happen: Katie Askew, Taylor Hugo, Janice K. Bryant, Katie Golownia, Wendy Dunning, and Jarrod Jemison—awesome job all of you!

In addition to the book team, we have assembled one of the greatest teams in business at BiggerPockets. The lives of real estate investors will only get better thanks to their efforts.

Finally, this book couldn't have happened without all the amazing women in our lives who drive us to do better and be better every day. We love all of you.

About the Authors

Joshua Dorkin is a serial entrepreneur, investor, podcaster, publisher, and former actor. Once he started investing in real estate, he realized that he needed help with his investments but had nowhere to turn for answers. Joshua started BiggerPockets as a simple internet forum to help solve his own real estate problems, but the uplifting, community-based platform immediately began to spread like wildfire, growing into a community that he could never have imagined. Today, BiggerPockets is the premier real estate investing website, reaching tens of millions of people with the message of financial freedom through real estate investing. Joshua, along with his wife and three daughters, make their home in Denver, Colorado.

Brandon Turner is an active real estate investor, entrepreneur, and writer. With nearly 100 rental units and dozens of rehabs under his belt, he continues to invest in real estate while also showing others the power, and impact, of financial freedom. His writings have been featured on Forbes.com, Entrepreneur.com, FoxNews.com, *Money Magazine*, and numerous other publications across the web and in print media. He is the author of *The Book on Rental Property Investing* and *The Book on Investing in Real Estate with No (and Low) Money Down*, and coauthor of *The Book on Managing Rental Properties*, which he wrote alongside his wife, Heather. A lifelong adventurer, Brandon (along with Heather and their daughter, Rosie) splits his time between his home in Washington state and various destinations around the globe.

More from
BiggerPockets Publishing

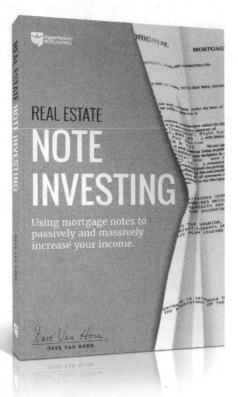

Real Estate Note Investing

Are you a wholesaler, a rehabber, a landlord, or even a turnkey investor? *Real Estate Note Investing* will help you turn your focus to the "other side" of real estate investing, allowing you to make money without tenants, toilets, and termites! Investing in notes is the easiest strategy to make passive income. Learn the ins-and-outs of notes as investor Dave Van Horn shows you how to get started—and find huge success—in the powerful world of real estate notes!

If you enjoyed this book, we hope you'll take a moment to check out some of the other great material BiggerPockets offers. BiggerPockets is the real estate investing social network, marketplace, and information hub, designed to help make you a smarter real estate investor through podcasts, books, blog posts, videos, forums, and more. Sign up today—it's free! **Visit www.BiggerPockets.com.**

The Book on Rental Property Investing

The Book on Rental Property Investing, written by Brandon Turner, a real estate investor and cohost of the *BiggerPockets Podcast*, contains nearly 400 pages of in-depth advice and strategies for building wealth through rental properties. You'll learn how to build an achievable plan, find incredible deals, pay for your rentals, and much more! If you've ever thought of using rental properties to build wealth or obtain financial freedom, this book is for you.

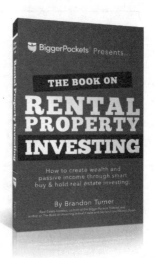

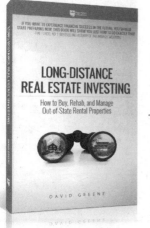

Long-Distance Real Estate Investing

Don't let your location dictate your financial freedom: Live where you want, and invest anywhere it makes sense! The rules, technology, and markets have changed: No longer are you forced to invest only in your backyard. In *Long-Distance Real Estate Investing*, learn an in-depth strategy to build profitable rental portfolios through buying, managing, and flipping out-of-state properties from real estate investor and agent David Greene.

More from
BiggerPockets Publishing

The Book on Investing in Real Estate with No (and Low) Money Down

Lack of money holding you back from real estate success? It doesn't have to! In this groundbreaking book from Brandon Turner, author of *The Book on Rental Property Investing*, you'll discover numerous strategies investors can use to buy real estate using other people's money. You'll learn the top strategies that savvy investors are using to buy, rent, flip, or wholesale properties at scale!

The Book on Tax Strategies for the Savvy Real Estate Investor

Taxes! Boring and irritating, right? Perhaps. But if you want to succeed in real estate, your tax strategy will play a huge role in how fast you grow. A great tax strategy can save you thousands of dollars a year. A bad strategy could land you in legal trouble. That's why BiggerPockets is excited to offer *The Book on Tax Strategies for the Savvy Real Estate Investor*! You'll find ways to deduct more, invest smarter, and pay far less to the IRS!

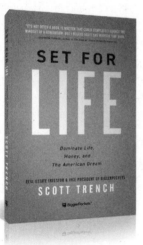

Set for Life: Dominate Life, Money, and the American Dream

Looking for a plan to achieve financial freedom in just five to ten years? *Set for Life* is a detailed fiscal plan targeted at the median-income earner starting with few or no assets. It will walk you through three stages of finance, guiding you to your first $25,000 in tangible net worth, then to your first $100,000, and then to financial freedom. *Set for Life* will teach you how to build a lifestyle, career, and investment portfolio capable of supporting financial freedom to let you live the life of your dreams.

Raising Private Capital

Are you ready to help other investors build their wealth while you build your real estate empire? The road map outlined in *Raising Private Capital* helps investors looking to inject more private capital into their business—the most effective strategy for growth! Author and investor Matt Faircloth helps you learn how to develop long-term wealth from his valuable lessons and experiences in real estate: Get the truth behind the wins and losses from someone who has experienced it all.

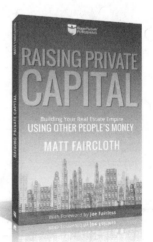

Connect with BiggerPockets

and Become Successful in Your Real Estate Business Today!

Facebook
/BiggerPockets

Instagram
@BiggerPockets

Twitter
@BiggerPockets

LinkedIn
/company/Bigger
Pockets

Website
BiggerPockets.com